AN INTRODUCTION TO LAW, LAW STUDY, AND THE LAWYER'S ROLE

AN INTRODUCTION TO LAW, LAW STUDY, AND THE LAWYER'S ROLE

James E. Moliterno
Fredric I. Lederer

CAROLINA ACADEMIC PRESS
DURHAM, NORTH CAROLINA

Dedications

To Professor Moliterno's family

and

To Caryn and Alyssa Lederer, who may choose this path; and to
Gregory Davis, student, attorney and counselor at law,
colleague, and friend.

LCC Number: 91-70489
ISBN: 0-89089-452-3 paper
ISBN: 0-89089-453-1 cloth

Manufactured in the United States of America
Carolina Academic Press
700 Kent Street
Durham, NC 27701
(919) 489-7486

Contents

Preface

Viewed from a variety of perspectives, lawyers perform and fill many roles in our society; some of those are regarded as socially valuable and others are not. Even among those favorable roles there is wide variety. Lawyers are business people; learned, intellectual professionals; helping professionals; professional writers; people of moral influence; producers of justice; advocates; and counsellors. The lives of many lawyers are often a complex mesh of all these roles; while others have chosen to emphasize one or several of these roles to the point of nearly extinguishing the others. In part, this book is meant to introduce you to some of these roles and their interrelationships, and to help you begin, should you so desire, the difficult process of weaving your own unique cloth.

This book is intended primarily for those who are interested in learning what law is and how law students become lawyers. However they see themselves or are seen by others, nearly all lawyers do have one thing in common: they were all once beginning law students. For those who plan to attend law school this book is meant to make that potentially horrifying time much less so. In doing so, we will introduce you to a number of skills that are critical to law students, such as opinion reading and briefing, classroom participation, writing, and interpersonal relations. If there is any efficacy to legal education as a preparation for the practice of law, as we think there is, you would expect that these same skills would be as useful to lawyers as to law students. Happily that is the case. As a result, what you learn today as a student of the law will be valuable to you as a lawyer as well.

Our fundamental goal is to provide you with some early insight into what law is. Thinking early about the nature of law itself should help those of you who are or will be law students better understand your law school course work and enrich your life as a lawyer.

Although changing, legal education remains primarily a study of appellate court opinions. Those opinions, rendered by judges who have never seen the parties to the disputes being resolved, are distant from the facts that underlie the dispute, the parties' original interests, and the early lawyering functions that began the process of dispute resolution. Because the study of appellate opinions all too often occurs in academic isolation, students may fail to see or appreciate the legal and pragmatic consequences that flow from the lawyer's representation of the client. We hope that this book will aid your study and understanding of the law and those appellate court opinions by providing you with a perspective on the beginnings of the process that is not apparent from reading opinions alone.

Finally, though not unimportantly, this book may provide special insights into the law school world that are valuable for anyone considering entry into the field. We hope that an undergraduate student, knowing what to expect from the law school experience, will be better positioned to make informed career choices.

We believe that any given piece of writing must be written with both its intent and its audience in mind. As a result, in writing this introductory book we have, quite consciously, attempted to make it easy reading. To accomplish this goal, we have chosen an informal prose style without the multitude of citations and footnotes customary to formal legal writing. We hope that you will not be disappointed with their absence.

This book is an outgrowth of the Introductory Week of the Marshall-Wythe Legal Skills Program which the authors helped develop. As such, it is impossible to individually thank all the people who have contributed directly and indirectly to this text. At the risk of omission, we would like to particularly note John Levy, Allen Black, Laura Dahl, Lizbeth Jackson, Paula Sinozich and Jane Taylor.

We would also like to thank and acknowledge: the members of the Marshall-Wythe Class of 1991; the partners and associates of **Moliterno, Wooledge & Grove** and its successor firms; the partners and associates of **Lederer, Posey, Kelley, Barker, Tompkins, Brisbay, Stone, Weber & DeVan**; and all of our partners in the Marshall-Wythe Legal Skills Program.

AN INTRODUCTION TO LAW, LAW STUDY, AND THE LAWYER'S ROLE

1

The Beginnings

Welcome to the world of law students and lawyers. We assume that you are either a law student or are interested in law and legal education. It is our task to introduce you to law study and its relationship to law practice.

Nearly all law schools suffer from a form of institutional "schizophrenia." They have as their primary goals both the traditional educational and research functions of the university and the need to prepare law students in three short years to actually perform as functioning lawyers. This is the dichotomy between education and training.[1] In all candor, we confess that these goals can be contradictory. Despite their importance in practice, some forms of professional preparation can be so devoid of intellectual content that it would be inappropriate to include them in university education.[2] This is not true, we believe, however, of most of the skills necessary for the competent practice of law. Legal research and writing and appellate practice have long been recognized as valid and necessary topics of academic study as well as fundamental skills needed by practicing lawyers. We believe that other skills, including interviewing, negotiating, counseling, alternative dispute resolution, and trial practice are of similar importance. This belief is reflected throughout the pages that follow along with our deep conviction that every component of practice must be ethical and that every component of law study requires consideration of relevant ethical issues. To the degree that law study takes account of the realities of actual law practice, we believe that it is enriched just as preparation for law practice ought not to take place without careful consideration of not just legal rules but also their history and academic rationale. Although our perspective is not shared by all law faculty, as some prefer to leave most "skills" education for post law school activities, our view shapes the materials that follow and should be kept in mind while perusing them.

---

1. *See, e.g.*, Bergin, *The Law Teacher: A Man Divided Against Himself*, 54 VA. L. REV. 637 (1968).

2. Knowing where to file various legal documents is essential, for example, but normally inappropriate for law school instruction.

With only a few exceptions[3] lawyers begin as law students and are shaped
by the content and nature of legal education. Based on the introductory week
of the Legal Skills Program of William and Mary's Marshall-Wythe School of
Law, this book has been written to mirror to the degree possible a thorough
one week introduction to the study of law. It should supply you with the same
information and assist you in developing the same skills that law students
should learn and master in such a program.

Let us then suppose that this is your first day in law school. You are seated
in a large lecture room or auditorium with the rest of your new colleagues.
You are understandably somewhat anxious. The movies you have seen and the
books that you have read have made you uneasy. Law school must be a cut-
throat demanding environment. At the same time, you may feel unsure of your
motivation in becoming a lawyer. Like others, you no doubt have many reasons for your decision to come to school. Your idealistic reasons may, however,
seem foolish as you look around and eavesdrop on some of the remarks made
by your peers.

The President of the university and the Dean have both welcomed you. You
have laughed at the obligatory jokes, and wondered what the rest of the day
will bring. Next is the keynote speaker. Justice John Charles Thomas of the
Virginia Supreme Court rises to address you. With a strong, forceful voice that
carries with it absolute conviction, he begins:[4]

> Our nation is built on the rule of law. Long ago as a people, we rejected
> the authority of kings, the whims of Princes, the iron grip of dictators,
> and concluded that the best way to provide for the development of full
> human potential was to make law supreme. Thus, law is the lifeblood of
> America. You are taking the first steps to becoming servants of the law. It
> will not be easy. Yet it is of utmost importance.
>
> When our Constitution was written no one had any idea that courts
> and lawyers would become so much involved in running the nation. Ar-
> ticle I of the Constitution, which concerns the legislative branch, is very
> long and involved setting forth the ages of office holders and a great many
> other details about that branch of government. Article II, which concerns

3. Some states like Virginia permit individuals to "read law," to effectively apprentice
themselves to practicing lawyers in lieu of law school. Like law students, these individuals must also take the bar examination.

4. The remarks that follow are an edited version of the keynote address given by the
Honorable John Charles Thomas at the Marshall-Wythe School of Law, College of William & Mary in Virginia on August 14, 1989, © 1989 by John Charles Thomas. All rights
reserved. This material is reproduced with the permission of the author. No further re-
production may be made of it, in whole or in part, except by permission of the author.
The youngest person ever to be appointed to the Virginia Supreme Court, Justice Thomas
is now a partner in the firm of Hunton and Williams.

the executive branch, is a little less detailed but explicit enough. Article III, which concerns the judiciary, brings up the rear; it appears to have been but an afterthought. It is written as if the drafters were almost finished writing about the branches of government when someone said, "oh by the way" the judicial power of the United States shall be vested in a Supreme Court and such other inferior courts as the Congress may from time to time establish. Article III of the Constitution contains no age requirement, no geographical requirement, no educational requirement, no citizenship requirement, it contains no detail at all. Nothing.

From the structure of the Constitution and the key role of lack of representative government as a catalyst to the revolution, it is plain that the preeminent branch of government was supposed to be the Congress. There the people were to bring their problems; Congress was to debate the great issues; then Congress was supposed to pass legislation which remedied the problems. But things did not evolve that way.

The Supreme Court ruled that it had the power to say whether a law complied with the Constitution and from that day forward — first slowly, now at a rapid pace — courts and lawyers became ever more involved in resolving the problems of the nation. If you listen closely, you will find that our citizens even talk in the language of law and of the courtroom. They forever say that they have a "right" to do something or have something:

> women's rights
> civil rights
> fetal rights
> environment rights
> minority rights
> seniority rights
> victims rights

To talk of rights is to talk courtroom talk because courts have told the citizens that if the citizens possess a right then the courts are duty-bound to fashion a remedy because the violation of a right for which there is no remedy means that the right is meaningless.

Our citizens found out, probably in the late 40's and early 50's, that the place to go for the resolution of difficult issues was court. They found out that they got no "run around" in court; no tabling the matter, no study commissions, no committee deadlocks that resulted in complete inaction. The citizens found that at court, when you pay your money[5] and say the right things, you will get an answer.

---

5. The financial implications of our current system for the delivery of legal services is

That's where you come in, learning how you say the right thing, learning to make the legal system respond to the legitimate needs of clients. You will learn many things while you are here. You will learn the intricacies of the basic legal subjects and others which are esoteric. But the most important thing you must bring to the law is something we cannot teach you: that is a sense of honor, of justice, of the right. These are things which we hope you have developed at the knees of your parents and grandparents, in the company of members of your faith, as you faced the challenges of life. If you have no moral compass, if you have come to this place in an effort to find ways to twist the law to improper purposes, we do not want you among us.

A lawyer is to our society as a doctor is to your physical body. Lawyers hold the lifeblood of America in their hands, molding and shaping things that can affect the whole nation. Even a little case, in a little town, in an out-of-the-way court can go on to establish great legal precedent. We want the very best among us to be servants of the law. To engage in this kind of work you must have a moral compass set on finding the right and rejecting the wrong. You must know where the line is and you must not cross it.

If you are here to make money, that goal will not sustain you. What you are about to undertake is too challenging to be supported by such a slender reed. You must have come to learn; you must take studying seriously. You must not seek to advance yourself by denigrating others. You must seek excellence for yourself and demand it in others.

Learning the law is an all consuming process; it is not for the faint hearted. The language of the law will be new; the teaching approach will be new; the volume of work will exceed your wildest projections. Learning the law is meant to be tough because it is meant to be a weeding out process. You are being evaluated to determine whether you will be allowed to participate in the critical cases of a problem plagued society.

Though it will be tough, I have a secret for you, I know that if you truly learn how to swim you will not care whether the water is 10 feet deep or 10,000 feet deep. You will not care because you will be swimming on the top. I know that if you truly learn the law you will not fear competition nor complex problems.

I fully expect that when I see you later as lawyers you will be practicing in a way which adds lustre to this institution; you will be at the forefront; you will rise to the top. Good Luck.

---

a matter of crucial importance and merits your ongoing consideration. As Justice Thomas recognizes, even court appearances entail expense. Legal rights are of little importance to those who cannot afford to claim them. Society may choose to make aspects of legal appearance or representation free for individuals in some or all cases. Cost to someone, however, is unavoidable, and who must pay the bill and when is a difficult policy decision.

After Justice Thomas finishes, you are dismissed for lunch and thoughtful reflection. Do lawyers really care about ethics? Are they serious about public service? Is there any connection between academic study and the real world of the practicing lawyer? All this, and more, will be answered in the days and pages that follow.

2

The Profession

In the following scenario,[1] George Beach represents the plaintiffs, Mr. and Mrs. Valdez, who have filed suit against defendant Alloway's Garage alleging that its mechanic negligently failed to tighten the lug nuts on the wheel of their car. They claim that as a result of that negligence, the wheel collapsed causing the death of their only son. Alloway's insurance company is represented by Sam Kepler.[2]

* * *

Valdez v. Alloway's Garage

Scene 1: The office of an attorney who is representing a couple whose son was killed in an automobile accident. The office is cluttered and untidy; papers are strewn about the desk. The attorney appears to be in his late 20s; he is unkempt and seems somewhat pressured. Ed Eads, the attorney's investigator, enters the office to discuss the case:

Eads:	Hey, George. You busy as usual?
Beach:	Yup. Be with ya in a minute, Ed.
Eads:	Hey, I got time.

---

1. The scenario is the transcript of an ABA Consortium on Legal Education videotape titled, *Dilemmas in Legal Ethics: Negotiation* which was jointly produced and written by Gary Bellow, Joel Henning and Phil T. Nicholson. Bracketed material has been added for descriptive purposes.

2. There is of course a distinction between the garage and insurance company. For purposes of this chapter, and to avoid unnecessary complexity, let us assume that the insurance company and garage have identical interests and that Mr. Kepler is representing both with their knowledge and consent.

Beach: Alice? Alice? [Calling a much older woman into the office with impatience and mild anger.] Take care of these right away, will you please? . . . And, uh, get on this, I need this typed right away, And, uh, when the Valdezes come, show 'em in right away, all right? And Alice, where's the Valdez file?

Alice: Right there on your desk.

Beach: Oh, yeah, yeah, yeah. Uh, thanks.

Eads: Hey, George. You need anything else on Valdez? Ah, how about the mechanic, you know, uh, Rossini, the guy who missed the lug nuts: Maybe I oughta go see 'im again . . . you know . . . just for safety's sake?

Beach: Naw . . . forget it. We already got his deposition. I mean, I don't want you to put any more time into this. I can't afford to put any research into this either. I mean, I feel sorry for the couple, but the case is a dead loser. I mean, there's no use even researching it. At best the case is not worth more than . . . ah . . . five thou at best.

Eads: I just thought I'd check by. Nothin's up, I . . . got things to do. Who you up against on this one anyway?

Beach: A guy named Kepler from downtown. You know him?

Eads: Sure! Hey, he's a biggie. He doesn't miss nothin'. Ah . . . ya know . . . I know his investigator . . . He's pretty tough, too, I hear.

Beach: Damn, just what we don't need . . . Now I know we're gonna hafta settle . . . All right, what the hell . . . I'll see ya tomorrow, Ed, all right? [Phone rings. Beach answers.]

Beach: Yeah? Yeah, Beach here, right Tom?

Alice: Mr. and Mrs. Valdez are here.

Beach: Yeah, yeah, yeah, yeah, right, yeah. Right, okay. Listen, can I get back to ya a little bit later? Okay, fine. All right, Alice, send them in. [The following lines are heard over still photos of the Valdez' deceased son.]

Mrs. Valdez: It was a month ago he died. To me . . . it is still yesterday.

Mr. Valdez: He was our only son, Mr. Beach. That's all that matters to us. Not the car.

Mrs. Valdez: I tell him, "take off your seat belt. That way you sleep better . . ."

Mr. Valdez:	They say ... with a seat belt, maybe he survive. But who knows?
Mrs. Valdez:	He's gone ... our only child ... our little ... our little boy ... our future ... all gone. [Picture reverts back to Beach's office.]
Mr. Valdez:	You see how she is, Mr. Beach ... We do not want to live this thing again. If there is any other way ... we do not want the court ...
Beach:	Maybe they'll settle ...
Mr. Valdez:	Yes, that would be best.
Beach:	But ... we're gonna be lucky to get one or two thousand ... I mean, maybe enough to cover the medical bills ... uh ... maybe a little bit more. But, like I told ya, it's the seat belt issue. Uh, we can't get around that.
Mr. Valdez:	Get whatever you can, Mr. Beach. For me, I must consider what is best for my wife ... for both of us. We do not want the court.
Beach:	Look, I see what'cha mean. Um ... I'm gonna do my very best for ya, Mr. Valdez. I can shave my fee a bit to, uh, help stretch things.
Mr. Valdez:	Thank you, Mr. Beach. Oh ... Mr. Beach ... there is one more thing.
Beach:	Yes?
Mr. Valdez:	The other attorney ... the lawyer in the big office downtown ... he talk with us? After we came to see you, I think?
Beach:	You mean Kepler?
Mr. Valdez:	Si ... He knows about us ... he say in the talk that we have.
Beach:	You mean about your illegal immigration?
Mrs. Valdez:	We're afraid ... he can send us back.
Mr. Valdez:	We don't want to go back, Mr. Beach.
Beach:	Look, don't worry. I'll handle it. I see Kepler this afternoon.
Mr. Valdez:	Thank you.

Scene 2: The office of the attorney who is representing the defendant insurance company. The office is large and impressive. Kepler, well attired in a suit and looking calm and professional, is dictating.

Kepler: This is a pre-negotiation memo ... date it March 10 ... the case is Valdez v. Alloway's Garage. I spoke this morning with Mrs. Green, chief adjuster for Mutual Insurance Company. I informed her that plaintiff's failure to use a seat belt would not bar recovery in this particular instance since the accident occurred immediately after the effective date of the new comparative negligence statutes. However, plaintiff's attorney may not realize that contributory negligence no longer bars his client's claim.[3] While this is bound to come out in trial, I think we should attempt to settle this quickly before it comes to their attention. Mrs. Green reported that Mutual is worried about setting a precedent in this case, and they wish to settle out of court. They've authorized me to offer up to $20,000 for that purpose. Have you got all that, Miss Riley?

Secretary: Yes, Mr. Kepler.

Kepler: In my opinion, we can settle for less. The plaintiffs are here illegally ... On the other hand, the case is loaded with problems that make its outcome at trial uncertain from our point of view. Hold, uh, hold up a second ... do you have the Valdez file with you?

Secretary: Yes, Mr. Kepler.

Kepler: In particular, I'd like to see Investigator Clark's report ... [She hands it to him.] We'll continue now ... Investigator Clark's memo of February 2nd indicates a key witness for our client, a mechanic by the name of Rossini, has changed his story from an earlier deposition. His most recent version directly undercuts our client's position in this case. He now says the Valdezes definitely asked for full inspection and that there was none done. I do not know if the plaintiff's counsel is aware of this change ... but Rossini is quite frightened about his part in this action. [Phone intercom buzzes.] That'll be all, Miss Riley ... at least for now. Yes?

**Receptionist's
Voice:**   Mr. Beach is here.

---

3. When a person is injured by another due to that person's negligence, the injured person may sue to recover damages. Until comparatively recently, many states had a rule, the "contributory negligence rule," which provided that the injured party could not recover damages if he or she had been in any way also legally responsible, no matter how slight that responsibility. That rule has been replaced by the "comparative negligence rule" which allocates damages by degree of fault.

Kepler:	Oh, thank you. Would you direct him to my office, please? [Beach knocks on door.]
Beach:	Sam.
Kepler	George. How are you? Have a seat.
Beach:	Fine.
Kepler:	Have a seat, George.
Beach:	Thanks.
Kepler	How long is this going to take, George? I have another appointment...
Beach:	Oh, no, it won't take long. Ah, we can get right to the point; ah, my client would like to know whether or not you were thinking of, like, settling the case.
Kepler:	Ah yes. Of course settlement is always best whenever feasible. But to be perfectly frank with you, I don't know whether we can reach an agreement in this matter. Now, I'm, speaking from the perspective of my client, you understand, not for myself.
Beach:	What's the problem?
Kepler:	They're under pressure. They don't want to get a reputation for settling this type of case out of court for a very high figure ... which is what you're asking them to do in this case. It's their policy to try the case where the facts appear to relieve them of liability, as in this instance.
Beach:	Oh, sure, but the, ah, jury is going to be very sympathetic to the Valdezes ... you know that. Look, even so, uh, would your client consider, uh, any offer?
Kepler:	I doubt it very seriously. Of course, if you could give me some reasonable ball-park figure. For example, medical expenses. I could ask them for that.
Beach:	Uh, what figure are we talking about, exactly?
Kepler:	Oh, say ... two thousand dollars.
Beach:	Two thousand dollars? ... You can't be serious! I can't accept that! This is a wrongful death case, maybe ya forgot that. My clients lost their only son. You gotta go a little above that!

Kepler: [somewhat patronizing] Now you see why I don't think we'll reach a settlement in this matter. I've laid all my cards on the table. I hope you'll be equally frank with me.

Beach: Look, I know we've got a problem. The seat belt issue would legally bar any recovery before a judge, but I can't go back to these poor people who've lost their only son with nothing but medical expenses. And you never know before a jury. They may ignore any contributory negligence claim.

Kepler: We're prepared for that.

Beach: And let me tell ya something else. Your case isn't as strong as you think. You got a witness that no one's gonna believe.

Kepler: Who's that?

Beach: Rossini...the mechanic...the guy who missed the lug nuts?

Kepler: Rossini? I don't know what you hope to find there. His deposition is solidly on our side.

Beach: Yeah, but the deposition just doesn't ring true. I'm gonna give 'em a lot of trouble on cross-exam. I mean, we're not gonna give up everything just to avoid a showdown in court! I can tell ya that right now!

Kepler: Now wait a minute. Don't get hot with me! I told you I'd see what I could do. I'm in a difficult position myself. I know your clients are here illegally...and I don't want to hurt them or anyone else, but I have a duty to my client...to keep them informed of every facet in this case. Now you can't expect me not to raise that fact with them. And once they have that information...well, neither one of us is in any position to control how they're going to use it. I don't think we want that to happen...do we? Now, look, George, I don't want to be hard-nosed about this. I wanna settle this matter. I'm prepared to call my clients and ask them for medical expenses and enough for you to make a nice fee. Now tell me, George, what authority do you have to settle this case?

Beach: Well, I could, ah, settle because of the...ah...special circumstances here...I could...ah...settle for...three thousand dollars?

Kepler: Let's see what I can do.

Beach: I, ah, hope this won't take too long.

Kepler:	No, it shouldn't take too long. Oh . . . ah, I assume the three thousand dollars is a firm offer?
Beach:	Yeah, that's right.
Kepler:	Okay. [He leaves office, and returns shortly.]
Kepler:	Good news. I'm authorized to settle this case for $3,000.
Beach:	Say, that is good news. This is gonna make the Valdez family very happy, and it's gonna save your client a lot of time and trouble.
Kepler:	I'm surprised. I didn't think we'd be able to reach an agreement on this one.
Beach:	Will you draw up the papers and, ah, drop 'em by my office tomorrow?
Kepler:	Oh, by the way, remember I'll have to deduct expenses in this case. I've had over $500 in deposition costs.
Beach:	I thought we had an agreement! $3,000! That's what you said, Sam.
Kepler:	I'm not changing anything I said. I assumed you knew that my client's legal expenses would be deducted. You know, I'm surprised you're not aware of that practice.
Beach:	[leaving office with a sigh] Just send me the papers.
Kepler:	Miss Riley, would you come in please? I'd like to dictate a follow-up memo on the Valdez case.

Introduction

There you have it: a dispute, two clients, and two lawyers, each lawyer representing one of the clients. The lawyers have each represented their clients, have negotiated their dispute, and reached a settlement. Justice has resulted, hasn't it? No? Well, let's leave "justice" for awhile. How about the individual lawyers: was Beach or Kepler the better lawyer? Which lawyer would you want to represent you?

The odds are that you prefer Kepler. Clearly, he was the more prepared of the two lawyers. He not only was on top of the facts, he also knew the law. Further, his client came out far ahead. His client would have been willing to pay up to $20,000.00 and yet had to pay only $2,500.00. Had Beach been prepared and competent, Mr. and Mrs. Valdez would have done far better. From our vantage point as a "fly on the wall," Beach doesn't seem to have had any real interest in helping the Valdez family. He just wanted out of this case as rapidly as possible.

So, will you agree that Kepler was the better lawyer? Is Kepler a role model for new attorneys? Should we invite him to be guest of honor at the next bar association dinner?

It may be that the scenario depicts reality as you believe it to be or, indeed, have personally experienced it. But, is Kepler—or Beach—the type of lawyer you want to be? Beach was unprepared, lazy, and incompetent. Kepler, on the other hand, was highly competent. He, however, took grievous advantage of Beach's mistaken view of both the facts and the law and remained silent when Beach mistakenly asserted that contributory negligence applied. Further, arguably he lied, and "not in a small way," either. Having initially suggested that a settlement was impossible and that the case would have to go to court, Kepler said that the mechanic Rossini's "deposition is solidly on our side." He then stated that he was authorized to settle for "$3,000.00," and then surprised Beach with deducting $500.00 in defense deposition costs despite his "firm offer." In the midst of all this, he warned Beach that he had a "duty" to advise his client that the Valdezes were in the country illegally, and that he wouldn't be in a "position to control how they're going to use" that information.

Some, or all, of Kepler's actions may strike you as acceptable if not ideal, but do Kepler and his activities sit well with you? He "won." Is that all there is to the law and law practice?

A Profession

Did Beach and Kepler listen to Justice Thomas?[4] Did they lose the sense of "honor, justice and the right" somewhere along the way? Have they crossed some of the lines? Perhaps lawyering is not such an honorable profession after all. Certainly neither Beach nor Kepler seem to be "swimming at the top" as Justice Thomas encourages.

What sort of profession is it that you are about to enter that would allow the Valdezes to be so taken advantage of? Perhaps our problem is in the definition of "profession." As with so many terms, the word "profession" means different things to many people. And to complicate matters, different people see the legal profession in many different ways. At the least, a profession is an occupational calling characterized by specialized knowledge, monopoly, status, and a duty of self-regulation.[5] There is more, however, to the definition.

---

4. *See* chapter 1 *supra*.

5. Every jurisdiction in the United States has a formal ethical code for lawyers, a code which is usually based upon the American Bar Association's Model Code of Professional Responsibility, or its more recent Model Rules of Professional Conduct. *See* note 13 *infra*. We concede that adoption of rules of conduct, even if adequate, is not the same as compliance with them. As we discuss below, there is often little agreement on how lawyers should behave in some specific situation because lawyers do not necessarily agree on the definition of their professional duties.

To some, a profession is a calling that has interests that come before profit-making. Healing the sick for doctors, helping others learn for teachers, and producing justice for lawyers come to mind as interests of professionals that overshadow profit-making in their respective fields. In this sense of the word, professionals are motivated primarily by these higher interests and garner wealth only to the extent that our social order rewards them by making their activities valuable to those willing to pay for them. Ethics are a primary concern of such people. Given this definition, we might call "unprofessional" a lawyer who was motivated primarily by profit-making.[6]

To some though, the word "professional" has another, less attractive connotation: that of defining an elite that has its own care and survival as its primary motivation. Under this connotation, lawyers are primarily motivated to take care of other lawyers. Other interests, client, public, community, and justice, come second. Lawyers who regard the profession in this way would regard ethics as primarily an internal etiquette, concerned primarily with the way in which lawyers treat each other.

For many observers of the legal profession, a better perspective than that of professionalism is service: service to client in the form of representation and service to community, society, and the justice system. This perspective has the appeal of being oriented toward those outside the profession itself. It describes the lawyer's work in terms of what the lawyer does for others, rather than focusing on the profession as an entity. Even within this perspective there are differences seen in the source of the obligation to serve and in the lawyer's primary duty. Some would regard the lawyer's service as a result of noblesse oblige, others as a result of a simple desire to serve one's fellows, and still others as the result of the lawyer's role or place in the adversary system of dispute resolution. Some would regard the lawyer's duty to client as primary while others would assert that the lawyer's first duty is to justice, or the legal system.[7] These different perspectives have their own implications upon the balance of duties that lawyers owe.

Lawyers' Duties

All would acknowledge that lawyers owe duties to clients, the justice system, the public and community, opponents or third parties involved in their clients' affairs, the profession itself, and themselves. The differences lie in the lawyer's

---

6. Such as the lawyer who chases ambulances to coerce accident victims into hiring his services or the corporate lawyer who adopts the business ethic that would allow for measuring the worth of human life by the likelihood and cost of litigation that might result from the death claims.

7. This suggests a dichotomy. Many would argue that given the nature and structure of our legal system, a lawyer's duty to the system and society is best performed through service to the individual client.

day-to-day resolution of the conflicting duties that pervade practice. Legal ethics is not a set of clear rules that govern some finite set of problems that lawyers from time to time face; rather, it is a way of living a life in the law that itself expresses the lawyer's resolution of conflicting duties.

When Kepler makes his deal with Beach, he arguably serves his client's interests well.[8] He provides what lawyers are charged with providing their clients: zealous representation.[9] At the same time, he took advantage of Beach's unpreparedness to deprive the Valdezes of a "just"[10] result. Presumably, Kepler has resolved conflicts between duties to client and duties to third parties in favor of serving client interests. Quite clearly, as a general matter, we would have a very different system of dispute resolution than we now have if the duty lawyers owed to their client's adversary was equal to the one they owe to their own client. In that world, we would need only one lawyer per dispute, and the lawyer's role would probably more resemble that of claims processor or judge rather than advocate.[11] But conceding that the system would not accommodate an equally valued duty to client and adversary, mustn't there be some limit to how far a lawyer may go in the service of client when that service unduly harms the interests of others? Should the decision on whether the service "unduly" harms the interests of others be measured by an ideal sense of what a just result would be in the matter?[12] Or should it hinge upon attributes of the lawyer's dealings with the others that we think are likely to produce less than just results when employed? For example, Kepler may have misled (some would say "lied to") Beach during the negotiation. Might lying to others be an attribute of the lawyer's dealings with others that would so regularly produce unjust results that the practice itself should be prohibited? And wouldn't this approach (prohibiting certain practices) allow us to govern members of the profession and make justice more often attained without engaging in the likely futile endeavor of measuring results against the abstract notion of the just resolution of any particular dispute? Did Kepler mislead Beach at a level that ought to be prohibited?

---

8. We say "arguably" because of reasons that will become apparent; clients may have interests other than maximizing wealth.

9. Model Code Canon 7; Model Rule 1.1 through 1.3; *see* note 13 *supra*.

10. Defining what "justice" means is beyond the scope of this book. Consider, though, whether justice is an abstract term designating an ideal or whether, once we have "bought into" our adversarial system of dispute resolution, justice should be regarded as being no more than the *result* of a *system* that is itself regarded only as the "most just" one available. Our current adversarial system itself has often been attacked for being wasteful, unjust, and inconsiderate of human needs.

11. Some soundly argue that this might be a better world. Others would argue that given human fallibility this would deprive individuals of their opportunity to be properly heard.

12. Some would maintain that the result is irrelevant, and that "right" conduct is always called for. Such a position might well condemn a lawyer's misrepresentation or falsehood without consideration of its possible systemic or specific results.

Governing Ethical Rules and "Obedience to the Unenforceable"

Before determining whether Kepler's actions were improper, we must have some idea of the source of the rules that might prohibit this or any other lawyer conduct. There are, as you might expect, published rules of conduct for lawyers. Although these rules differ from state to state, with few exceptions every state's rules are based on one or the other set of rules that have been promulgated by the American Bar Association.[13] When most lawyers talk of ethical or professional conduct, they mean conduct that complies with the minimum standards of the particular state's published rules of ethics.[14] A lawyer who violates these rules may be subjected to bar discipline including censure, suspension from practice, or disbarment.

But it should be remembered that the published rules are merely the minimum enforceable rules of conduct: they are incomplete, they do not aspire, and many would argue strenuously that they are meant more as a protection *of* the profession than as a protection of the public *from* the profession. Beyond the minimum represented by the published rules is what some call "professionalism" and others call "real" or "general" or "capital 'E' " ethics. This something more, whatever it may be called, is what makes a lawyer more than a business person. We agree that "[t]rue civilization is measured by the extent of Obedience to the Unenforceable."[15] The hardest questions are those seeking

---

13. These two sets are the American Bar Association (ABA) Model Code of Professional Responsibility (1981) and the ABA Model Rules of Professional Conduct (1983). For a brief history of the adoption process, see KAUFMAN, CASES AND MATERIALS ON THE LEGAL PROFESSION 15–20 (3rd ed., 1989). As you study legal ethics, you will undoubtedly study both sets of rules. Having two sets of rules to study is good. On the surface, it may seem easier to have a single rule as a guide, but in reality no single accepted rule exists (nor did it in the days preceding the Model Rules' adoption). If they did nothing else, the Model Rules debates demonstrated this lack of consensus on important issues. Therefore, having two sets is good because it allows us to frame, at least in the context of the two choices offered on key points by Rules & Code, the real questions about, for example, what approach to client confidentiality is the best? We say "best" rather than "better" because there are sensible rule choices represented by neither the Code's nor the Rules' resolution of some questions.

These sets of ethical rules are far from the only source of legal ethics law. These sets of ethics rules are constrained by Constitutional concerns (*e.g.*, advertising rules are constrained by the 1st Amendment), are interpreted and applied in case law and bar association ethics opinions, and are expounded upon by writers in books and law review articles.

The ABA is not the governing body for the legal profession; rather it is a voluntary membership organization that often takes the lead in making proposals for the governance of the profession as well as any number of other legal issues. The governance of the legal profession is a state by state affair, rather than a national one.

14. Professor Lederer often suggests to his classes that "professional" ethics is at best a potential subset of "real" ethics, however they are to be defined.

15. Lord Moulton, quoted in H. DRINKER, LEGAL ETHICS 2 (1953).

to determine when the lawyer, perhaps *you*, should resolve a conflict among duties by resort to that something more and when the lawyer should follow the minimum standards set forth in the published rules. Because, make no mistake, when the lawyer pursues one duty beyond the minimum requisites of the published rules, some other duty is likely to go unfulfilled.

Even the published rules may be interpreted in differing ways to comport with the interpreter's sense of what the profession is. One example comes from the application of a rule of longstanding that the Beach-Kepler scenario raises: the prohibition against contacting an opposing party who is represented by counsel without the permission of that party's counsel. Remember that the Valdezes told Beach that Kepler had contacted them after they had retained Beach?[16] Both the Model Code and the Model Rules have provisions that pro-hibit lawyers from communicating with a represented opposing party about the subject matter of the case unless the party's lawyer consents.[17] These rules might be seen as primarily designed to protect the party from being taken ad-vantage of by the opposing lawyer. Professor Wolfram, for example, says in his excellent treatise on legal ethics that this rule "is founded upon the possibility of treachery that might result if lawyers were free to exploit the presumably vulnerable position of a represented but unadvised party."[18] But it is also pos-sible, if you have the perspective on the profession that dictates the mainte-nance of primary protection of the profession and its members, to see this rule as one designed for the protection of the *lawyer* of the contacted party. Henry Drinker, longtime Chairman of the ABA Standing Committee on Professional Ethics and Grievances, wrote that among the "primary characteristics which distinguish the legal profession from business [is] . . . a relation to colleagues at the bar characterized by candor, fairness, and unwillingness to resort to cur-rent business methods of advertising[19] and encroachment on their practice, *or dealing directly with their clients*.[20] In either event the rule probably prohib-ited Kepler's contact with the Valdezes.[21] The point here, however, is that long-standing rules[22] may lend support to differing views of what the profession is.

---

16. Indeed, it appears that the reason for the contact was to threaten to expose the Valdezes' illegal immigration status. The content of this communication itself raises a possible ethical violation on Kepler's part. *See, e.g.,* Model Code DR 7-105.

17. Model Rule 4.2; Model Code DR 7-104(A)(1).

18. C. WOLFRAM, MODERN LEGAL ETHICS 611 (1986).

19. The advertising reference is obviously dated, but disputes continue over the kinds of advertising that should be permitted and the use of in-person solicitation of clients.

20. H. DRINKER, LEGAL ETHICS 5 (1953) (emphasis added).

21. As you will see later in chapters 3 through 6, the reason supporting a rule's exis-tence is the central element in our chosen system of legal analysis and interpretation. As such, a judge might view the application of this particular rule quite differently depend-ing upon the judge's view of its underlying rationale.

22. This particular rule seems to have been first expressed in the United States in num-ber 33 of David Hoffman's 50 "Resolutions in regard to Professional Deportment", first

As to Kepler's deception of Beach, there seem to be two distinct areas that were the subject of possible deception or dissimulation, the law and the facts. Should they be treated differently? Is it different to deceive a lawyer on the law than on the facts?

An expectation that all lawyers will deliver competent service to their clients pushes toward a conclusion that the lawyers should worry only about their own understanding of the law and should have little or no duty to either state their own objective views of the law or enlighten an opposing counsel about the true state of the law. After all, that is why we require lawyers to go to law school and be licensed to practice: we expect that they have learned some law and its workings. Forcing a lawyer to give his or her legal work to the other side would radically change the process of dispute resolution itself: lazy or incompetent lawyers would have nothing to fear because the other lawyer would be under a duty to provide the law that the lazy lawyer has missed. Clients might not be taken advantage of or disserved, but the incentive to study the law and construct arguments that the law needs for its own internal development (from which the society presumably benefits) would be lost. The expectation that all lawyers will deliver competent service, which unfortunately does not always conform with reality, is itself the underpinning of the adversarial system of dispute resolution that dominates in the United States. Should Kepler have been required to tell Beach about the change in the law? The published rules say not. In general, *until* the matter is before a court, a lawyer is under no duty to disclose law that is adverse to the lawyer's position.[23] The directness of the dissimulation would also matter, of course. Kepler never said anything like, "You are smart enough to know, Mr. Beach, that the current contributory negligence standard in our state will mean that any negligence on the Valdezes' part will totally bar their recovery." While this is a reasonably accurate statement of contributory negligence law, the law, as we remember from the scenario, had been changed to another standard, comparative negligence, that is more favorable to injured plaintiffs. Had Kepler made this sort of direct statement with the intent to deceive Beach, the standards would treat

---

published in 1834. Hoffman's Resolutions, while not a published, binding code were the basis (along with Judge George Sharswood's Professional Ethics, published in 1854) for the first of the binding, published codes of lawyer ethics, that of the Alabama Bar Association published in 1887. Hoffman's Resolutions contain many of the rules that survive today, but also include a few that would surprise modern lawyers. For example, numbers 12 and 13 would prohibit a lawyer from pleading on a client's behalf certain technical defenses to contract liability that no modern lawyer would give a second thought to pleading. Indeed, today's understanding of the duty of zealous advocacy probably requires the lawyer to plead those defenses.

23. *See* Model Code DR 7-106(B)(1); Model Rule 3.3(a)(3). In contrast, Hoffman, in another surprise from his time, says in Resolution 5, "[N]o man's ignorance or folly shall induce me to take advantage of him...."

his conduct differently, without regard to whether it related to a legal or factual deception.[24]

As to factual deception, some of Kepler's statements come closer to this sort of directness, but even these leave some doubt as to whether they would be interpreted as "false" within the meaning of the published rules. For example, regarding Rossini's story, Kepler said, "I don't know what you hope to find there." Kepler knew very well what Beach *would* find there if he went back to Rossini, and the statement seems clearly to have been calculated to inhibit Beach from going back to Rossini and to allow the negotiation to proceed on the assumption that Rossini's story had not changed since the deposition. Kepler also said, "[From the perspective of my client,] . . . I don't know whether we can reach an agreement in this matter. . . . It's their policy to try the case where the facts appear to relieve them of liability, as in this instance." Kepler knew quite well that the facts were not all on his side, and that his client *did* want to settle the case. But here we run into the nature of negotiation itself as a limitation on what should be regarded as a false statement. Every negotiation involves some measure of intentional deception. It is the rare negotiator who begins a negotiation by announcing his or her "bottom line," what it would take to make the deal. We doubt that any of you who may have purchased a car began the price negotiation by saying, "I am willing to pay up to $3000 for the '88 Isuzu on your lot with the window sticker that asks $3100."[25] In fact, even if you were desperate for transportation and thought Isuzus were the best made vehicles on earth, much of the negotiation dance in this example might well be designed to convince the seller that you weren't in any great need for a new car and that you were not altogether sure about the assertions of quality and value made by the Isuzu television ad spokesman. Whether negotiation is an efficient and justice producing method of dispute resolution may be subject to debate, but in its current form, it cannot help but contain elements of dissimulation. The published rules themselves acknowledge that some level of dissimulation attends negotiation by stating that

---

24. Model Rule 4.1 (a) says, "[While representing a client, a] lawyer shall not knowingly make a false statement of material fact or law to a third person. . . . " Model Code DR 7-102(A)(5) is to similar effect.

25. *See, e.g.*, White, *Machiavelli and the Bar: Ethical Limitations on Lying in Negotiation*, Am. B. Found. Res. J. 926–30 (1980). For a contrasting view, see Rubin, *A Causerie on Lawyers' Ethics in Negotiation*, 35 La. L. Rev. 577, 589 (1975). Judge Rubin argues that appropriate, and effective, negotiation requires early and firm disclosure of the negotiator's limits. A great controversy was created in the early fifties with the publication of an article exclaiming that a lawyer's duty often required the lawyer to make the most explicit sorts of false statements to further the client's interests. Curtis, *The Ethics of Advocacy*, 4 Stan. L.Rev. 3 (1951). The reaction was quick and heated. *See, e.g.*, Drinker, *Some Remarks on Mr. Curtis' "The Ethics of Advocacy"*, 4 Stan. L. Rev. 349 (1952).

"[u]nder generally acceptable conventions in negotiation, certain types of statements ordinarily are not taken as statements of material fact. Estimates of price or value placed on the subject of a transaction and a party's intentions as to an acceptable settlement of a claim are in this category . . . ."[26] Reasonable people might differ in their categorization of Kepler's statements, but we suspect they would not be regarded as "false statements of material fact." Should this be an occasion when Kepler should be "obedient to the unenforceable" and disclose what he knows, or does that ask Kepler's client to give up too much?[27]

Ultimately, should this be an occasion for Kepler to raise with his client the prospect of offering *more* in settlement than the opposing lawyer seems willing to accept? Before you answer, project what the Beach-Valdez response to such an unusual offer might be. Might Beach, now armed with the knowledge he should have acquired earlier on his own, advise the Valdezes that their claim may really be worth $100,000, or a million? Is this a result that fits with the adversarial system of dispute resolution? If their claim really is worth a million dollars, does the adversarial system of dispute resolution that produced a $2500 settlement in the scenario have even the remotest relationship to an ideal concept of justice?

We have referred to the relationship between the assumption that clients will be served by competent, zealous counsel and the adversarial system of dispute resolution. Was Beach's representation of the Valdezes incompetent? Had Beach been better prepared, would Kepler's sharp negotiating practice have been effective? As you would expect, one important attribute of a profession is a requirement of competent performance; the published rules governing the law profession require it,[28] as certainly does any broader concept of ethics or professionalism.

Two different areas of Beach's representation present a contrast that may illuminate the nature of the competence requirement. Beach did not know the facts in that he had not gone back to interview Rossini. We might expect that

---

26. Model Rule 4.1, Comment.

27. We assume for simplicity's sake that the insurance company is operating consistently with the accepted character of any corporate entity: its purpose is to maximize profit. We should not be misunderstood, however. Clients, sometimes without their lawyers ever realizing it, often have goals other than winning the maximum amount of money possible. Clients often have goals that relate to maintaining relationships, maintaining a reputation for fairness, or even *being* fair. Lawyers too often allow their own egos and drive to "beat" an opponent to overcome any interests their clients may have that are more complex than "winning." It would not have been improper for Kepler to have called his client and recommended a larger settlement in the interests of justice. Given Kepler's duty to zealously represent his client, it would have been improper for him to have himself increased the settlement offer unnecessarily.

28. Model Code DR 6-101; Model Rule 1.1.

a lawyer's grasp of the facts is an essential element of competence, and as a general matter that would be true. But the focus should be on lawyer activities rather than the final level of actual knowledge of the facts those activities produce. Here, Beach had taken Rossini's deposition.[29] Although it would have benefitted Beach to re-interview Rossini in this particular case and on these facts such an interview should have been conducted, it could be argued that it would be unusually burdensome and wasteful to require each lawyer to maintain a kind of continual updating of every witness's story. How would a lawyer know at any given moment whether the witness has changed his story in the moment immediately preceding? Still, one might argue more forcefully that Beach should have re-interviewed at least a key witness before an important settlement conference. Such a failure is more likely to be regarded as a mistake that would support a malpractice claim by the Valdezes than as indicia of ethical incompetence. A more convincing argument can be made that Beach has been incompetent in his failure to know about an important change in the law. After all, what could be closer to the core of a lawyer's competence than knowledge of the law applicable to a client's case? You should realize that the law is far too broad in scope and too complex in nature for any lawyer, or judge for that matter, to be the master of it all. Failure to know the most central legal principles that govern a client's case at the time of the matter's resolution is inexcusable, however. Whether Beach knew the negligence rules when the Valdezes arrived at his office for the first time is not the issue; that he was unaware of such a central principle at the time of compromising their claim is the crucial fact.[30] Such a failure clearly constitutes a malpractice and likely ethical incompetence as well.

Although there may be more important ethical requirements, it is at least arguable that a broadly defined duty of competence is the most important from a functional perspective as it is most likely to avoid many of the problems discussed above. If Beach had truly been competent, what effect would Kepler's behavior have had?

Self Governance

No less central an attribute of a profession than the competence requirement is the notion of self-governance. The legal profession primarily governs

---

29. A deposition is a formal, recorded questioning of a person having knowledge of the matter under litigation that all parties' lawyers are entitled to attend.

30. One might also argue that Beach's general office management and procedures are also a measure of his incompetence. Some of the difference between Beach's operation and Kepler's is no more than a difference in resources, but Beach's careless attitude about his work, if not incompetent itself, is likely to lead Beach routinely into the sort of blunder that hurt the Valdezes. Operating an office in a manner that lends itself to these blunders pushes Beach's conduct closer to ethical incompetence than that of simple negligence. That the Valdezes likely have a claim against Beach for malpractice is also a separate matter.

its own members. The published ethics codes in the states are largely based on ABA models and were thus drafted, in essence, by the largest professional association of lawyers to govern the conduct of lawyers. Further, the bar association of each state takes initial responsibility for policing compliance with that particular state's published code of ethics. Disciplinary procedures within the state bar associations are followed to determine the facts of alleged violations and mete out punishments from private reprimands to disbarment. In addition, lawyers are charged by every state's code to report certain kinds of misconduct of their fellow lawyers to the policing authority.[31] Under these rules, should Beach be required to report Kepler's unauthorized contact with the Valdezes? Should Kepler be required to report Beach's failure of competence?[32] Although the obligation to report a fellow's misconduct is pointed to with pride by the profession, the degree of enthusiasm among lawyers for turning in their fellows has been very low. In Illinois recently, a lawyer was disciplined for failing to report a fellow lawyer's misconduct.[33] Although the full ramifications are not yet clear, the immediate result was a marked increase in the number of Illinois lawyers reporting misconduct of their colleagues.[34] Time will show the benefits or harms that result from Illinois' experience.

The Profession at Present: Service vs. Profit

Although it may be customary for one generation to always decry the alleged faults of the next, it is apparent that at least the *normative* standard of the legal profession is changing. Until fairly recently, lawyers appear to have accepted the notion that they belonged to a "higher calling" which had service to the public and the individual at its core. Today, many lawyers appear to have supplanted the service motive with the profit motive. In the process, much of the "heart" may have gone out of the profession for some. Large United States law firms are larger than lawyers a generation or two ago could have imagined. Firms merge and break up at a dizzying rate, and lawyers seem to have everdecreasing loyalty to their firms. The rapid pace of today's high technology world creates unprecedented time demands while in some quarters, legal salaries are so high as to price many lawyers out of the reach of low- and middle-

31. Model Code 1-103; Model Rule 8.4.

32. Other ethics issues could be raised from the scenario, but this chapter is meant to be an introduction to the profession rather than a full explication of any, let alone all of the many lawyer ethics issues. Among the other conduct issues that could be raised for examination is the conflicts of interest issue raised by Beach's consideration of Kepler's intimation that Beach would have enough settlement to "earn a nice fee." Do not, however, focus on particular ethics "problems" to the exclusion of consideration of the pervasive lawyer ethics question, "Who do I want to be as a lawyer?" Do you aspire to Beach-hood, Kepler-hood, or something else?

33. In Re Himmel, 125 Ill. 2d 531, 533 N.E.2d 790 (1989).

34. *The Duty to Inform*, A.B.A. J., May 1989, at 17.

income citizens while requiring a form of junior lawyer exploitation that is hard to endure.

Recently, lawyers have reported unprecedented levels of dissatisfaction with their work, especially those working for large firms. Some of this dissatisfaction seems to be the result of a shift in the nature of the practice, at least as it exists in large firm settings. Although not as many new lawyers go to work for large institutional law firms as the popular culture would have us believe, those who do go to large firms may need to change their expectations or clamor for institutional change. Large firms, with some important exceptions, operate more in line with the business perspective on the profession than with the service perspective. New lawyers in large firms make a great deal of money;[35] they should expect that large firms, operating from a business perspective, will ask much of them in exchange. Hours will be long and the opportunities to do the public service work that brings some students to law school may be quite limited. Again, because of the business perspective, many new lawyers with large firms will be asked to specialize in very narrow aspects of the law; those who do will not be likely to develop into well-rounded lawyers who have the good judgment that comes only with exposure to and responsibility for treating many kinds of problems faced by many kinds of people and entities. It may also be that this diminution of opportunity for development of good judgment by lawyers will reduce the influence that lawyers have long had in public service and government.

This bleak picture is not being painted to discourage you; on the contrary, we hope that you will be moved to reflect now and often on what a legal career should be and on what it can do for others. Lawyers hold critically important positions in our society. The practice of law, however, is not immune from outside influence or, indeed, regulation. Non-lawyers must be aware of the direction toward which the legal profession is moving and be prepared to call it to task if necessary. As to future and new law students, in our view, the profession is about you, its newest members, because you have the opportunity to make of it what you will by your conduct and daily way of living. In the final analysis, that is what lawyer ethics really is: the way that lawyers choose to conduct their daily lives.

The material that follows will assist you in learning about the law, lawyers, and law school. The most central question, however, is quite simply: what should a lawyer be, and if you are to join the profession, what type of lawyer will *you* be?

---

35. Although as some would say, if you are really after money, don't be a lawyer in a large firm, be successful in a business and have the large firm work for you.

3

The Nature of Law[†]

It is all well and good to become a lawyer and seek to do what lawyers do. More fundamental however, is the need to determine what *law* is. One can hardly interpret and apply the law without first at least defining it. Unfortunately, law defies simplistic definition. Accordingly, let us for the moment defer formal definition in favor of a more pragmatic approach. Let us create our own legal system. In the process, we will seek to introduce:

> The contemporary concept of law;
> The general structure of the American legal system;
> The concept of legal analysis and reasoning.

To accomplish these goals we will emphasize the law of homicide. First, a word of caution. Although the law that we will develop will be generally accurate, at least so far as the United States is concerned, our development will be artificially limited and will not necessarily supply a rule of law usable in any specific jurisdiction. In the scenario that follows, please take the facts given as true and assume that at trial the factfinder is adequately convinced of their truth.

The Scenario

It is the year 2291. Interstellar commerce is commonplace but still somewhat risky. Most civilian traffic travels via huge vessels that carry both passengers and cargo. Seventeen days after its departure from Earth, the *Blackstone* has a major engine room explosion which destroys its faster than light drive. As luck would have it, the ship is near an unknown but fully habitable world. The ship makes a successful crashlanding.

---

†. This chapter is adapted from copyrighted materials of the same name written by Professor Lederer and published in ASPECTS OF AMERICAN LAW (Virginia Law Foundation 1988; 1989).

Two thousand people survive. The passengers take stock of their situation. Because of the location of the control and engine rooms, all of the ship's officers were killed as were a number of the technical staff. All faster than light communications equipment was destroyed, and the survivors lack either the technical knowledge or the resources to replace it. The ship was known to be far off normal space lanes when it re-entered normal space from faster than light drive. Accordingly, the survivors recognize that they are marooned and are now colonists.

Happily, the ship was carrying large amounts of farming and construction equipment including seeds, and livestock (mostly in frozen embryo form). The former passengers include a wide variety of specialists and experts. Strangely enough, however, there are no lawyers, an absence that the survivors do not find troubling.

The new colonists come from a wide variety of different cultural and religious backgrounds. In fact they come from at least seven different planets and thirty-five terrestrial nations.

The colonists elect a seven person legislative council and a colony administrator and adopt a basic governing document that specifies that the administrator shall implement the rules made by the council members as the people's annually elected representatives. Neither civil nor criminal laws are legislated as such. Instead, the new government begins an emergency program of exploration, housing construction, and farming.

The planet is named "Bryan" after the deceased starship captain.[1]

The First Homicide

The facts:

About two weeks after the legislative council is elected, it divides the local arable land among the colonists. Jean Waltz's plot is fed by water coming from the land now owned by Sidney West. Jean feels that Sidney is using an unreasonable amount of water. Sidney disagrees and refuses to alter the irrigation pattern. After thinking about the problem for a day or two, Jean takes one of the sharpened farm implements (made from the ship's salvaged structure) and stabs Sidney in the back causing immediate death. There were witnesses to the event.

The legislative council elects a judge and directs that the judge empanel a jury and try Jean Waltz for killing Sidney. Brought before the judge, Jean says, "Sure, I did it. Sid was rotten; he never even smiled. So what? There's no law here against killing someone. You can't touch me!"

---

1. And in honor of the late Honorable Frederick vanPelt Bryan, United States District Judge for the Southern District of New York.

Issue:

Absent some form of enacted law, can society (the State) adjudicate a person responsible for and punish a person for a harmful act?

Assumptions:

By express terms, neither the law of Earth nor that of any other planet applies to a newly colonized world absent advance approval by the Federated Planets.

By contract, every passenger agreed to obey the orders of the ship's captain and officers "while embarked in the vessel."

Criminal laws cannot or should not be given retroactive effect.

Discussion:

Jean has conceded killing another person. Ordinarily, this would be a crime, homicide. However, the legislative council has not affirmatively created a law prohibiting homicide. Was it then against the "law" to kill Sidney? This raises the fundamental question, "What is Law?"

As understood by most lay people, "law" means a body of rules that have been enacted by the legislature and that are applied by judges. Ideally, these rules are, or should be, comprehensible and susceptible to easy interpretation and application. That they are neither is well known, and the function of judicial interpretation is misunderstood, distrusted, and often viewed as a form of judicial usurpation.

Law is far more complex than a simplistic rules formulation suggests, however. It is a dynamic system with two sets of contradictory goals—predictability and certainty on the one hand, and flexibility and adjustability on the other. These disparate goals yield constant tension.

The distinction between social mores (i.e., normative conduct) and law may be debated. Law may be defined to include those customary practices which society expects and impels through social pressure. Such a definition is inadequate, however, to a highly populated technological society. We may say, consequently, that for our purposes law consists in its most basic form of those social rules which will be enforced by the State, usually through the actual use or threat of use of some form of force.

Law may be entirely unpredictable as when the entire legal system consists of the potentially inconsistent decisions of a single person such as a tribal chief who may be unconcerned with consistency. Few societies can tolerate such uncertainty, however, and it is virtually impossible to imagine a complex modern society which could operate with such a structure.

A word of caution: we are understandably oriented toward contemporary legislative law making. Clearly law may be made (or found) by individuals holding coercive power either by the consent of the governed or without it. In our probable emphasis on legislatures we should remember that the English judges who created the common law were in theory exercising power derived from the crown.

The Problem:

We must now turn to our problem. Assume that **YOU** are the judge. As judge, you clearly have the delegated power to hear the case; that is, you have **jurisdiction** over the case. However, if homicide is not against the law you have little to do. Either it is against the law or it isn't. As is usually true of real cases, a decision *must* be made and inaction usually has the same effect of an intentional action.

To rephrase our basic question: Is there *law* without authoritative pronouncement by an individual or institutional body? If there is law, from where is it derived, and what are its limits?

It is possible to conclude that law must consist of some form of positive, affirmative, declaration. That is, someone or something with recognized authority must promulgate a rule. Should you choose this definition, Jean cannot be guilty of homicide. But surely, "law" can mean more than this. Doesn't nearly *everyone* agree that killing another person without some form of significant cause is wrong? If that is so, and if our colonists echo that same belief, wasn't Jean on notice that killing Sid was wrong and potentially punishable?

If this is acceptable, we must ask where this belief, this social norm, came from. It might well be the product of religious doctrine. Should enough people accept a given tenet, a rule of correct behavior will exist. The belief might also stem from non-religious philosophy or logical analysis. One might argue that it is obvious that it is wrong to kill another person without adequate cause if only because that person cannot be readily replaced, and the death will cause economic loss to the community. Rather cold-blooded, isn't it? Perhaps it might be better to say that absent a prohibition on homicide no one's life would be safe, and that self preservation and one's interest in others would compel such a social rule. Any of these approaches might permit one to argue that Jean's actions were obviously wrong because they violated morality, religious doctrine, natural law, or basic economics. Of course, we may still be left with the question of who should decide what these obvious unwritten rules are, a particularly difficult matter if the population has dissimilar cultural backgrounds and may not unanimously agree on the given principle. In our case, however, as is customary the judge will decide what the "law" is.

Note that if you accept this approach, we can conclude that Jean violated an unwritten law and should be punished for it. So be it; Jean goes to trial. But are there limits to this approach? Presumably, we would all agree that rape would also be prohibited. Perhaps we would also agree that hitting someone else without cause would be wrongful. But, suppose one colonist produces a book, likely memoirs, and a second colonist copies it verbatim. Can we hale the second person into our court for the "accepted crime" of copyright infringement?[2]

---

2. If we assume that most of us would argue that unlawful action must be or should

Over the ages, noted commentators have disagreed as to what constitutes law:

Demosthenes: That is law, which all men ought to obey for many reasons, and especially because every law is an invention and gift of the Gods, a resolution of wise men, a corrective of errors intentional and unintentional, a compact of the whole state, according to which all men who belong to the state ought to live.

Cicero: Law is the highest reason implanted in nature, which prescribes those things which ought to be done, and forbids the contrary.

Hooker: A Law is properly that which Reason in such sort defineth to be good that must be done.

Grotius: A rule of moral action obliging to that which is right.

Blackstone: A rule of civil conduct prescribed by the Supreme power in a state, commanding what is right, and prohibiting what is wrong.

Amos: A command proceeding from the supreme political authority of a state and addressed to the persons who are the subjects of that authority.

Jhering: The sum of the rules of constraint which obtain in a state.

Gareis: Law in the objective sense of the term is a peaceable ordering of the external relations of men and their relations to each other.

Tolstoi: Rules established by men who have control of organized power and which are enforced against the recalcitrant by the lash, prison, and even murder.

Russian Penal Code, Article 590: Law is a system of social relationships which serves the interests of the ruling classes and hence is supported by their organized power, the state.[3]

---

be properly declared unlawful, we must discuss the meaning of "wrongful." The criminal law is divided into offenses that are *malum in se* and those that are *malum prohibitum*. This classification says nothing about the seriousness of the offense or the results that may flow from the criminal act. Lederer, *Compliance with the Law*, ASPECTS OF AMERICAN LAW at 31 (Virginia Law Institute).

  3. *See* SEAGLE, THE HISTORY OF LAW 4 (1941) (citations omitted). For reasons of space, our discussion largely omits the *reasons* for law. Professor Burton has written in this respect,

  Members of the legal community generally assume that society would be different if the law did not exist. People generally abide by the law due to a habit of compliance and a sense of obligation, or the practical threat of its sanctions... or both... We also assume that society generally is better off because the law exists. The laws are thought to encourage valued behavior and discourage disvalued behavior and, accordingly, are normative.

S. BURTON, AN INTRODUCTION TO LAW AND LEGAL REASONING 107 (1985) (footnotes omitted).

  Burton adds other justifications including "the promotion of social order by the peaceful settlement of serious disputes" and "contributions to a more just society."

The definition of "law" may thus vary, and one might well argue that the simpler and more homogenous a society, the higher the likelihood and utility of unwritten law based on social norm.

Although overly simplistic, one could say that the origins[4] of the Anglo-American legal system stem from this functional definition of "law." In England the King's judges rode "circuit" and administered the law. Absent royal edict or statutory rule, the judge was required to determine and apply the law without prior authoritative pronouncement.[5] One could argue, of course, that in so doing, the judge was exercising the discretion the King had vested in him. However, if one assumes that it is undesirable or morally wrong (or both) to give criminal laws ex post facto (ie. retroactive) effects, the judge's pronouncements must either state the law as it previously existed or declare it for the future. Accordingly, even though our judge has been delegated some form of authority by the legislative council, the judge must either decide that killing without adequate cause was against the law when done or wasn't. No other option applies.

Note that we have not yet discussed justice, if only because justice is usually in the eye of the beholder. By the standards of most, it would be unjust for Jean to walk free because of the absence of a promulgated rule. Yet, most people would also argue that it would be unjust to punish a person who was not advised in advance that the given conduct was wrong. It is only that we are dealing with a killing, a crime that causes nearly universal abhorrence in the United States, that usually makes most, although not all, lay people opt to find that killing is against the law. If the judge decides that homicide is not illegal on the planet, the issue will be left to the population who would presumably cause the legislative council to speedily enact a rule barring homicide. Jean might escape justice, but planetary society would escape permitting its judges to "make up the law" as they went.

The judge—you—must make a decision. That decision may be verbal or written or both. When a result is accompanied by an explanation of the court's reasoning, we term it an **opinion**. If the opinion is not reported in writing in some way, it is not likely to influence later cases and may be misunderstood by those

---

4. Of course, the origins go back still further, and, absent total isolation, all law is shaped to some degree by other legal systems. The development of legal institutions is a fascinating topic which we heartily recommend to the intellectually curious.

5. The judge was helped by the doctrine of precedent which we will soon discuss.

interested in the court's results. A well reasoned opinion will not only help the community accept the judge's reasoning, giving it social acceptance, but may also be highly persuasive should a similar case arise at a later time.

A legal system which is heavily dependent upon judicial interpretation of the law—one that recognizes judicial opinions themselves as law—is usually said to be a **common law** system. "Common law" has many definitions, however, and no educated person can escape encountering the term in its varied use. We are using two different definitions; initially we are using it in what may be its purest sense:

> [T]he rules of law which are not created or declared by express enactment but developed by the courts from principles founded in the "custom of the realm," or deemed so to be: "such laws as were generally taken and holden for law before any statute was made to alter the same." In this sense common law is opposed to statute law, although many statutes enacted by the Legislature have been and may be, as it is said, "in affirmance of the common law," making no change in the substance of the law, but defining in authoritative terms rules that were already recognized.[6]

Normally, however, we use the more common and far broader definition:

> The term [common law], in its largest sense, now means the whole body of legal principle and usage which is common to all parts of England, and now to all jurisdictions whose law is of English origin.[7]

Our current legal system is a common law system in the sense that our law is composed of constitutions, statutes and regulations *and* their judicial interpretations. Judicial decisions are law just as legislative statutory enactment is law.

YOU ARE THE JUDGE, is homicide against the law on Bryan? Please note, there is no right or wrong answer here. Either choice is reasonable; each embodies different value judgments. You might wish, however, to compare your election with the choice that you make on the remainder of the homicides that follow.

The Second Homicide
The facts:

Subsequent to the Waltz case, the legislative council enacts a statute:[8]

Any person who shall kill another shall be guilty of murder and shall be punished by death or life enslavement as the jury may direct.

---

6. J. SMITH, DEVELOPMENT OF LEGAL INSTITUTIONS 20 (1965) quoting from F. Pollock, "Common Law," 3 ENCYCLOPAEDIA OF THE LAWS OF ENGLAND 304–06 (3d ed. 1938).
7. *Id.* Of course, our definition usually applies either to the law of the United States alone or the combined legal heritage of both the United States and Great Britain.
8. A legislatively created rule.

The law was passed hastily without discussion.

Some months later, Mike Tatem gets into an argument at the makeshift tavern with Bill Schultz. Schultz leaves the tavern vowing to kill Tatem. Later that evening when Tatem leaves to return to his hut he sees Schultz coming towards him. Schultz, 6'2" and 250 pounds, was carrying a large club and yelling that he would use Tatem's dead body for fertilizer. As Schultz lunged towards him with the club, Tatem desperately struck at Schultz with the sharpened wooden spear he usually carried for protection from animals. The spear penetrated Schultz's heart killing him instantly. Neither person was drunk.

Tatem is arrested by the colony constable and brought before the judge for trial on murder charges.

Again, you are the judge.

Issue:

If a statute defines killing another person as murder, is it murder when the defendant knowingly and intentionally killed another person to prevent that person from killing the defendant?

Discussion

We start with the assumption that a statute is binding and must be enforced. However, before dealing with the consequences of that assumption, we must briefly deal with some basic procedure. In the Anglo-American legal system judges and juries have different roles. The judge decides what law is applicable to the given case. The jury first determines the facts; that is, from the evidence presented the jury decides what really happened in the case. Then, the jury applies the law (the rules) announced by the judge (via **instructions** to the jury) to the facts and reaches its ultimate decision. In a criminal case, the jury will decide whether the government has proven that the defendant committed the alleged crime. In a civil case, the jury will decide whether the plaintiff has proven that the defendant was liable for (legally responsible for) a legally improper act and what damages are due the injured plaintiff. Many trials are conducted by judges without juries. In **bench trials** the judge also serves as the **factfinder** but does not instruct himself or herself. Instead, we ordinarily assume that the judge correctly applied the law.[9] In our homicide scenarios, we will, however, assume the American normative standard of jury trials.

As a consequence of this basic criminal procedure, which applies on Bryan, you must decide, as judge, what the new statute means in this context. The situation presents two interpretative alternatives:

---

9. In some, but not all, cases a judge may make findings of fact and announce conclusions of law.

1) As judge, you may consider yourself bound by the literal text of the statute and must instruct the jury that if Tatem killed Schultz he is guilty of murder.

2) As judge, you may attempt to go beyond the literal text of the statute to implement the possible intent of the legislative council to punish only an intentional killing done without adequate justification.

We begin with a simple and yet incredibly important question—how do you interpret a statute? The answer to this question is far more complicated than one might imagine. Yet, again at the risk of over simplification, we can supply adequate answers. We begin with the text of the rule. *When interpreting a statute, always begin with the language of the statute itself!*[10] If there is a **plain meaning**, ordinarily we would apply that meaning. But, what if there is no such meaning or an impossible or unreasonable result would take place? In such a case, we must resort to the **legislative history** of the law.[11] In other words, we would examine the historical record to determine why the law was proposed, what changes were made in it before passage and why they were made, and why the legislators enacted the law as it is now written. Customarily, legislative committee reports and floor debate transcripts are used. At the risk of digressing, we should note that determination of legislative history can be particularly difficult. After all, even if we can ascertain the intent of a law's author, how can we be sure why the individual legislators voted on a bill? Our system is thus imperfect and often permits contrary conclusions as to **legislative intent.** One of the most divisive questions in the law today is when a judge may or should resort to legislative history. Those favoring a limited judicial role encourage reliance on the statutory text; those favoring a more expansive role encourage examination of legislative intent. Further, lawyers and judges would differ on the question of whether judges may ascribe intent to the legislature when there is no evidence of such intent.

The statute with which you are faced has a clear meaning. It provides an absolute rule, one which does not recognize self-defense. Further, even if we attempt to apply legislative intent, we find no evidence at all of such intent. Despite this, could we not argue that no "right thinking person" would mean to disallow self-defense? Note, however, that this position may be flawed. A government, particularly a new colonial government, might wish not to recog-

---

10. Because of the emphasis placed on case analysis by both law school classes and judges, all too often individuals immediately begin analyzing earlier cases dealing with the same issue. This is dangerous and likely to mislead. Start with the statute; then turn to the cases that interpret the statute.

11. This very phrasing is controversial. Many courts analyze legislative history routinely even if an apparent "plain meaning" exists. Given both the imprecision of language and human fallibility, it is readily possible to discover that a law's intent contradicts its text.

nize self-defense[12] in order to ensure that people avoid conflict, thus trying to preserve human life. More importantly, however, we simply don't know what the legislature intended. The Council never even discussed the law let alone pontificated on what should happen in the event of self-defense.

The decision is yours, as judge. Note, however, the systemic consequences of your decision.

If you decide to apply the statute as written, Tatem will be convicted, and, depending upon possible extrajudicial options, Tatem will face death or life enslavement.[13] This may not be as disturbing as it may seem initially. It has the merit of leaving total control of the law in the legislative council; if the judicial result is undesirable, the council should amend the statute. This, of course, creates a judiciary of very limited powers, arguably one that may be unable to function successfully if numerous legal questions are to be resolved by the judiciary. Although this provides absolute predictability, it does so at the price of flexibility. In particular, it may needlessly sacrifice the individual or case before the court in favor of leaving change to the legislative authority. In criminal cases, at least a partial answer may be the grant of some form of discretionary executive pardon or clemency. This approach was used in early England.[14]

Suppose, however, that you decide that the Council surely would have meant to exempt self-defense had it discussed it, and you instruct the jury that Tatem is innocent if the homicide was necessary to prevent Schultz from killing Tatem. This has the virtue of meting out justice to Tatem. It provides the judge with flexibility to adapt the law as necessary. It does so, however, at the cost of shifting significant law making power from the legislature to the judiciary. Not only does power shift, but flexibility increases at the cost of predictability.

YOU ARE THE JUDGE, does Bryan have self-defense? Again, there is no right or wrong answer here. Either choice is reasonable; each embodies different value judgments.

The Third Homicide
The facts:

After much demonstrated anguish, you decide in the Tatem case to apply probable legislative intent and instruct the jury that self-defense is an absolute de-

---

12. Self-defense was not recognized as a defense to homicide in England until sometime in the reign of Edward III (1327–1377); insane defendants received pardons from the crown. PERKINS ON CRIMINAL LAW 851 (1969) citing at n. 4, GLUECK, MENTAL DISORDER AND THE CRIMINAL LAW 125 (1925).

13. One should never underestimate a lawyer. Faced with this problem, one talented William and Mary law student opined that she would interpret the statute according to its plain meaning, but would sentence the defendant to death—to die of natural causes at the end of the defendant's life span.

14. *See, e.g.,* PERKINS ON CRIMINAL LAW 741 n. 15 (1969) quoting 2 POLLOCK & MAITLAND, HISTORY OF ENGLISH LAW 480 (2d ed. 1899) to the effect that the rolls of Henry III (whose reign began in 1216) include pardons for those whose homicides were occasioned by "misadventure, in self-defense, or while of unsound mind. . . . "

fense to a charge of murder. Your decision takes the form of a written decision on the defense request for jury instructions as well as the instructions themselves. Tatem is acquitted. The results appear to have widespread public support. Some members of the Legislative Council, however, voice disapproval of the judge's "creation" of law. The Council does not change the statute. Subsequently, our judge dies during an exploratory trip.[15] The Council elects a replacement.

A few weeks after the verdict, yet another killing takes place. Having argued, Joe Fourth advanced on Sam Boyd with a large club loudly announcing an intent to kill Boyd. Boyd, armed with a bow and arrow, happened to be standing about fifty feet in front of the colony's constable who was armed with a firearm. He could easily and safely have retreated to the protection of the Constable. Instead, Boyd shot Fourth with an arrow killing him. It is clear that absent intervention by others, Fourth would have killed Boyd. Notwithstanding this, Boyd is tried for murder.

Issue:

When the jurisdiction's sole judge has previously recognized a defense of self-defense, in light of a statute that defines killing another person as murder, does self-defense apply when the defendant knowingly and intentionally killed another person to avoid his own death but could have avoided doing so by retreating?

Discussion:

The threshold issue is whether the judge will recognize self defense at all. Although the prior judge did so, it is unclear whether that decision is binding on the incumbent. We might ask:

Is a **court** a corporate institution which is greater than its human components, or is each individual judge independent of his or her predecessors?

Regardless of the basic nature of a court, what effect should be given a prior interpretation of a statute in a current case?

The heart of the Anglo-American common law system is the doctrine of adherence to precedent, **stare decisis**. The doctrine provides that in the normal case a rule of law developed by a court of equal or superior authority in the same jurisdiction must subsequently be applied when identical facts occur. Precedent provides predictability and to some degree promotes judicial efficiency; a judge need not come up with a new rule in every case. As will become apparent later and in chapter 5, the doctrine is so sophisticated that it also

---

15. Sorry; of course, the advantage of role playing is that you can survive such otherwise fatal mishaps.

permits flexibility because the judge may modify the rule when sufficiently dissimilar facts are involved.

Our precedent based system is not a necessity, however. Classical civil law (*e.g.* French law) is code based and rejects our form of precedent. Theoretically, the statute (the code) is the law, and each interpretation of it by a court has no effect beyond that case. This may provide a greater measure of equity than is theoretically present in the common law system. It does so at the expense of less predictability and usually far more detailed statutes than were customary in Anglo-American law. Speaking generally, the greater the degree of legislative detail, the smaller the need for judicial interpretation. In real life, however, the complexity of modern society coupled with the limitations of language and legislative imagination limit the number of cases clearly and readily solved by explicit codal language. This is not to criticize comprehensive legal codifications. Even in the United States a number of critical legal areas have been codified. The primary difference between the civil and Anglo-American systems continues to be the precedential impact of a judicial decision.

Accordingly, our first question is: To what extent is a court bound by a decision in an earlier case with facts that are partially similar to a current case?

Although we could decide either that each case is approached independently, without any consideration of prior cases, or that prior decisions vanish upon the arrival of a new judge, we shall consider the predictability and reasonable efficiency present in the precedential system sufficiently useful to impel its use. Consequently, we will begin with the assumption that we will apply the first judge's legal decisions to the extent appropriate.

If we accept the doctrine of precedent, the judge must recognize self-defense. Inasmuch as the Council has not altered the statute despite its knowledge of the prior decision, one might also infer legislative blessing through inaction.

Recognizing self defense does not, of course, resolve the current case. *Stare decisis* compels application of the same legal rule to facts identical to those in the prior case in which that legal rule was derived. The question here is whether the facts of the present case are close enough to the prior one.

Unlike the prior *Tatem* case in which the defendant had no option to save life but to kill in self defense, Boyd could have avoided killing Fourth had he retreated. This case is thus **distinguishable** (i.e. different) from *Tatem*. Accordingly, the judge is not bound by that case and must address the issue afresh.

To some degree the judge in the *Boyd* case is faced with the same dilemma as that of the first judge. The statute makes killing murder. There is no doubt that Boyd killed Fourth. The judge is faced with the question of how to apply the statute save only that the judge will presumably begin by conceding that because of precedent some self-defense acts constitute a defense to murder. In other words, judge-made law on Bryan recognizes that self-defense is a defense to murder, but that law has not yet fully defined it.

The judge must now determine whether self-defense extends to the current facts. One may recognize an individual's right to defend himself or herself and yet refuse to recognize that as a defense when the threatened person could have safely retreated. Surely, the earlier Bryan self-defense decision has left this issue open. Again, the same policy questions inherent in the earlier decisions apply. Should the judge decide that Boyd acted in proper self-defense, the doctrine of self-defense is extended far beyond anything the Legislative Council considered. Further, by making a difficult policy decision about which reasonable people might differ, it may be argued that the judge would arrogate legislative power to the court.

The judge is faced with a real case, one that must be resolved; the judge can't pass on it. To refuse to consider how the doctrine of self defense should be applied yields a result as real as interpreting and applying it. Different consequences may follow from each judicial option, but neither option is either inherently correct or desirable.

How should the substantive issue be resolved? Can a person kill another in self-defense when the need to do so could be avoided by retreat?

This is an important question in the United States, and the states have split on the issue. The duty to retreat (unless one is in his or her "castle" or home) is recognized as a substantial minority rule, albeit one that has been adopted as a proposed national model rule by the American Law Institute.[16] Under this rule, individuals who are not in their homes or otherwise located on protected property must retreat if possible, and courts will not give a self-defense instruction to the jury if the individual stands his or her grounds and replies with force. States using the majority rule permit an individual to respond with force in self defense even if safe retreat is available. Accordingly, the issue is one of policy, and either result is acceptable.[17]

How should the judge rule?

A digression:

We have thus far established the role of judge made or common law. Note again that if the content of judicial opinions is not preserved and distributed, the doctrine of precedent has limited impact. Those opinions are crucial if one is to learn both how judges interpret and apply the law as well as what the law

---

16. *See, e.g.,* W. LaFave, Modern Criminal Law 469 (2d ed. 1988) citing United States v. Peterson, 483 F.2d 1222 (D.C. Cir. 1973); Perkins on Criminal Law 1009 (1969).

17. Note how the answer to an important legal question varies by state. This illustrates why so many client questions are initially answered by the lawyer's refrain, "I'll have to do some legal research before answering that."

is on any given point. Those opinions are consequently important to law students. They have also proven to be critical to the existence of law schools as we know them. The **case method** of law study gave birth to the modern law school.

In 1886, Professor Christopher Columbus Langdell of Harvard said, "First, that law is a science; secondly, that all the available materials of that science are contained in printed books."[18] Law study has always consisted of an often uneasy combination of intellectual study and skill development. Langdell's argument was that law was a science and judicial opinions the raw material to be studied as if in a laboratory. He observed: "If law be not a science, a university will best consult its own dignity in declining to teach it. If it be not a science, it is a species of handicraft, and may best be learned by serving an apprenticeship to one who practices it."[19] By proclaiming law as science, Langdell justified its study in the university as an academic subject. The modern post-graduate law school was born.

For Langdell, law was and consisted of judicial opinions. Notwithstanding the importance of such opinions, today most of us would view Langdell's views as far too limited. Numerous schools of legal philosophy have evolved to explain what law is, what influences it, and how it influences society. Legal realism, feminist law, and critical legal studies are but some approaches that go far beyond judicial opinions. Nonetheless, constitutions, statutes, judicial opinions, and administrative regulations make up law as we usually define it.

The proper scope of law study continues to be debated. Following Langdell, for many years many if not most law schools avoided any subject that could be said to be training or tradeschool rather than education. As most important judicial opinions were appellate, appellate moot courts were acceptable as were classes in writing appellate briefs. Trial work, however, was too close to real legal practice and either ignored or left to low priority electives. A whole panoply of skills were ignored: interviewing of clients and witnesses, counseling, negotiation, alternative dispute resolution, management, delivery of legal services, etc. For the last two decades, however, law schools have been changing their outlooks. Immense change has taken place in many schools. Ironically, increased attention to skills can enrich traditional academic study, as skills teaching places those subjects in context and enriches the academic study inherent in them. Can one truly study tort law—roughly those acts or omissions for which one may be sued for damages—without some understanding of how trial work warps results? What should be a proper measure of damages in light of the size of contemporary legal fees? Notwithstanding the manifold curricular changes incorporated in recent years, a false and mis-

---

18. H. Jones, Materials for Legal Method 17 (1952).
19. Id.

leading distinction often is maintained by some law faculty and faculties between "skills" courses and "real" courses.[20] Such a distinction may influence
critical resource allocation decisions as well as faculty status and promotion
decisions.

The Fourth Homicide

The facts:

It is 35 years after the colony was accidentally established. It has prospered and
expanded. The government structure has been expanded. The legislative council now is a 50 member House of Delegates. The settled area has been divided
into three judicial districts each served by one judge. Appeals from the districts are taken to the Supreme Court in the capitol.

About a decade ago, the House of Delegates enacted a criminal code. In relevant part, the provisions dealing with homicide, codifying past decisions,
provide:

Section 1.   *Any person who shall kill another with premeditation shall be*
               guilty of murder.

Section 2.   *Any person who shall kill another without premeditation shall be*
               guilty of manslaughter.

Section 3.   *Notwithstanding the above, a person shall not be guilty of murder*
               or manslaughter if that person acted in self-defense, which defense
               was reasonable, except that this defense shall not be available to a
               person who knew or should have known that he or she could have
               avoided the necessity of acting in self-defense by retreating from
               the scene provided that no person need retreat when in his or her
               home.[21]

Recently, the population has expanded into areas in which a hallucinatory
plant grows. At the appropriate stage of its growing cycle, it releases a gas
which causes intense vivid hallucinations which are also incredibly pleasurable. Two cases have resulted from this plant's hallucinatory nature.

---

20. *See, e.g.,* Moliterno, *Goodness and Humanness: Distinguishing Traits?* 19
N.M.L. REV. 203 (1989).
21. We don't pretend that this is a well drafted statute; it isn't. On the other hand, it's
a fairly good example of normal legislative drafting. Note how unnecessarily complex
§ 3 is. "Notwithstanding the above" negates the effect of all prior language while "except" and "provided" add critical modifiers. After you have analyzed this provision you
are likely to agree with us that "legalese" should be avoided to the greatest extent possible—and we haven't even added a single "hereinafter." Substantively, the statute is also
flawed. §§ 1 and 2 ought to require, for example, that the defendant killed another person intentionally unless we want to permit a person to be guilty of manslaughter because
of simple accident.

In the Northern District, Celia Lynd was part of an exploratory party that blundered into a patch of the drug plants. Lynd was caught by the gas and, under the impression that a fellow explorer was a charging wild beast analogous to a tiger, shot and killed him. In the Eastern District, another killing resulted but under different circumstances. Having heard of the plant's effect, Grant Doyle had intentionally sought them out and breathed their hallucinatory gas. While under its effect, Doyle returned to his home, saw another man, and killed him while under the erroneous belief that the deceased was trying to kill him.

Part One

Issues:

Do either §§ 1 or 2 of the statute apply to an individual who under the circumstances did not comprehend reality and killed a person under a mistaken delusion of necessity?

Does a person act with premeditation within the sense of § 1 of the statute when he or she takes action, with premeditation, which might predictably result in dangerous consequences including the unintended killing of another?

Does a person who kills another under accidental or intentional drug induced delusion that the killing is in self-defense act in self-defense within the meaning of § 3 of the statute?

Discussion

Once again, we must interpret and apply a statute. Before proceeding, consider the statute's history. We find its origins in the *Waltz* and *Tatem* cases decided (by you) soon after the founding of Bryan. The planet's first governing body codified the holdings of those cases in Bryan's first criminal statute. The court in the *Boyd* case interpreted the statute in order to decide whether self-defense required a defendant to retreat when retreat was safely possible. The present statute not only adopts the *Waltz* and *Tatem* cases but adds the *Boyd* case decision in modified form. As no constitution applies, we must begin with the present statute; it supersedes all prior versions and all cases decided before it, although we may consider those statutes and cases in seeking to interpret the statute drafters' intent. Note the continual interrelation between legislature and court. One creates law only to have the other modify it. The process continues forever providing the change that is necessary to adapt the law to new situations. Absent overriding constitutional provision, at least theoretically the ultimate power lies in the legislature which could create a statute clear enough in language and intent to forestall any ethical court from modifying it.[22]

---

22. This restates the American belief that the people's elected representatives should

Now look to the statute; let's begin with Celia Lynd. As always, we begin
with the text of the statute. Sections 1 and 2 apply to "Any person who shall
kill another. . . . " There can be no doubt that Lynd killed her fellow explorer
so we begin with the conclusion that she is guilty of some form of homicide
subject to §3.[23] But, as defense counsel would surely argue, "She was unable
to appreciate reality through no fault of her own." Does the statute have an
exception for those who are insane or temporarily deprived of their ability to
appreciate reality? Clearly it does not. May the judge "write it into the statute?" Depending upon the degree of freedom the judge feels appropriate to
the task of statutory interpretation, that is possible. As we have already discussed this basic issue, we will pass it by despite its importance and leave it to
our judge's ultimate decision. Instead we will focus on the language of the
statute and will deal with much the same concern.

Premeditation, normally necessary in the United States for murder, is not
defined by the statute. Let's assume that "premeditation" means after prior
thought. Clearly, that was not present here; Lynd acted instantaneously after
"perceiving" the hallucination. Accordingly, Lynd seems to be guilty of manslaughter under § 2. What of § 3, however?

Section 3 of the statute provides a defense to either murder or manslaughter "if
that person acted in self-defense, which defense was reasonable. . . . " Self-defense,
as such, isn't defined. We now come to grips with our dilemma. Lynd honestly
believed she was acting in self-defense when she killed the deceased. Further, from
her perspective at the time, the killing was both reasonable and absolutely necessary to save her own life. However, from an objective, unaffected, on-looker's
position, Lynd didn't act in self-defense at all; no one was really attacking her.

---

be the law makers. Judges make law only in the sense that they must do so in the process
of interpreting statutes or resolve live disputes that no statute governs. Of course, many
judges are elected. We could argue that they too are the people's representatives and
ought to have independent power to make law. However, that's not the social or legal
understanding in the United States. Although election (and recall) may provide a check
on the judge's actions, nowhere in the United States are judges elected with the assumption that they may freely depart from the legislature's decisions.

23. You might respond, however, "But, the jury makes the final decision. How can we
assume that Lynd would be found guilty?" Remember, that back at the beginning of our
discussion, we asked you to take the facts we supply as true. That's customary in law
school. The professor's hypothetical facts must be taken as true for purposes of discussion. Otherwise, we could not adequately raise many important legal issues. We should
not beg the question ourselves, though. In a jury trial, the jury makes the final decision
on guilt and innocence, and a defendant is innocent until proven guilty beyond a reasonable doubt. Because [under the constitutional right against double jeopardy] an acquittal
is final in the United States (even if erroneous), a jury has the *power* to ignore the law and
acquit a person who is clearly guilty. This is known as **jury nullification**. However, in
most courts the jury cannot be advised of this power; it is extra-legal. Accordingly, if not
given a self-defense instruction a jury might well convict Lynd of manslaughter or
murder.

Which perspective should govern? This is really a question of social policy. Ideally, it ought to be decided by the House of Delegates. Unfortunately, the House didn't address the issue, and the court must make a decision.

If you were the judge, how would you rule? Coin flipping is considered poor form, by the way. If you decide that Lynd's perspective governs, she will be acquitted, and, from the perspective of most people, justice will be done. However, such a decision will expand the definition of self-defense. Is that desirable?

One thing is certain, regardless of how you rule, you'll get your name in the planetary papers, and your mail's going to get larger.

How do you rule, Your Honor?

Now for Grant Doyle. The facts of Doyle's case differ significantly from Lynd's. Lynd breathed the hallucinatory gas accidentally. Doyle intentionally sought out the plants to "get high." Is this difference legally important? It's clearly important emotionally, but emotion ought not to rule in the courtroom, especially not in a precedential system where an emotionally satisfying but flawed ruling might have massive ill effects in later years.

Like Lynd, within the terms of the statute, Doyle is clearly guilty of either murder or manslaughter if we don't consider § 3. Which shall it be? There is surely no evidence that Doyle planned to kill anyone; like Lynd, he killed the deceased under the influence of the hallucination and would not have done so absent the gas. But—and it may be an important "but"—Doyle initially sought out the plants with the foreknowledge that they would cause hallucinations. That's why he wanted to experience them. Although he might not have predicted that he would kill someone under their influence, shouldn't he be charged with the knowledge that under their effects, he might well *do something wrong*? Should that be enough for premeditation? Such an interpretation would seem to require "stretching" premeditation, but perhaps not unreasonably so. Again, this is a policy decision.[24]

What of self-defense under § 3 of the statute? Arguably, the key difference between Lynd and Doyle is twofold:

1) § 3 recognizes self-defense when that "defense was reasonable...."
2) § 3 provides that self-defense is unavailable "to a person who knew or should have known that he or she could have avoided the necessity of acting in self-defense by retreating from the scene...."

---

24. There may be another difference, however, between the two cases. Normal statutory construction in the United States requires that a criminal statute be construed strictly. Because our society prefers the greatest degree of personal liberty possible, when there is doubt as to the meaning of a criminal statute, we give the statute the most limited effect consistent with its language. Applying this principle, "premeditation" ought to be given its more limited meaning.

Does "reasonable" refer to Doyle's subjective understanding; the objective situation immediately after inhaling the hallucinatory gas; or Doyle's entire situation including the fact that he sought out the gas? We have previously dealt with aspects of this issue in Lynd's case. *NOTE*, however, that *Lynd* was decided in the Northern District, and Doyle is being tried in the Eastern District. Because previously decided cases have binding precedential effect *only* when decided by either the same or a higher court within the same jurisdiction, the Eastern District is not bound by the decision of the Northern District. The decision of the Northern District is **persuasive** but not binding. Accordingly, it is possible for the two districts to reach diametrically contradictory interpretations of the statute.[25] Having discussed the issue previously, however, we will leave it to you for resolution.

There is, however, another potentially applicable part of § 3, the retreat provision. Clearly, it is inapplicable if interpreted in its usual fashion; from Doyle's mental perspective he could not know that he could have safely retreated. However, the statute makes the defense unavailable to a person who "should have known" that retreat was possible. From what point shall we calculate this? Obviously, if Doyle had not indulged in the inappropriate act of intentionally subjecting himself to the plant gas, he would have known that he didn't have to kill the deceased.[26] Can—should—the judge decide that Doyle violated his duty to retreat by putting himself in the situation in the first place?

If you were the judge, how would you decide?

Part Two
Assumption:

Construing the statute, both courts decide that self-defense is inapplicable and so instruct the juries. The Northern District jury convicts Lynd of manslaughter on the grounds that she killed without premeditation. The Eastern District jury, however, convicts Doyle of murder reasoning that intentionally seeking out plants with a known dangerous hallucinatory gas constitutes premeditation.[27]

---

25. Resolution of this difference is for an **appellate** court, a matter we will discuss shortly.

26. The current law of voluntary intoxication is that a voluntarily intoxicated person who subsequently commits a crime can be convicted of it if the crime is defined in terms of the act's mere commission (i.e. *actus reus*). Such a person may lack, however, the specific intent necessary to commit crimes such as larceny or murder.

27. We are *not* saying that these decisions were correct; we are merely creating the situation we must resolve. Please note that law school hypotheticals often do not embody the professor's real views. It is the professor's job to make students think and question. Taking difficult, controversial, and creative positions is a long and valued tradition in good law schools.

Procedural posture:

Both defendants appeal to the Supreme Court arguing that the district courts misapplied the statute,[28] and that the judges below should have given self-defense instructions.[29]

Issues:

Did the district courts below err in refusing to give the jury a self-defense instruction because of the courts' holdings that under the statute a person is not acting in self-defense when he or she intentionally kills another person under the honest but mistaken belief that the death was necessary to protect his or her own life?

Did the Bryan District Court for the Eastern District err when it instructed the jury that intentionally seeking out plants known to cause hallucinations could constitute premeditation under § 1 of the statute?

Did the Bryan District Court for the Eastern District err when it refused to give the jury a self-defense instruction on the grounds that intentionally seeking out plants known to cause hallucinations meant that the defendant necessarily "knew or should have known that he or she could have avoided the necessity of acting in self-defense by retreating from the scene" under § 3 of the statute?

Discussion:

We have already discussed the issues themselves. The more important question now is the function of appellate courts in a precedential system. Initially, we must discuss the concept of an appeal based upon an error of law. In the normal appeal, the appellate court will assume that the facts found by the court or jury below were accurate, but will determine whether a legal error was made. In other words, appellate judges do not substitute their factual conclusions for those made below although an appellate court may determine as a matter of law that insufficient admissible evidence was presented at trial to justify the factfinder's result. Few United States appellate courts have the power to determine a case's facts for themselves. Those that do, such as the armed forces' Courts of Military Review, use the power sparingly as they do not have access to the demeanor evidence present at trial.[30] You *must* recog-

---

28. Counsel should also argue that a person may not be guilty of either type of homicide without proof of volitional intent. The statute, of course, does not appear from its text to require intent. Thus, the court would have to interpret the statute in order to decide the question. We have chosen not to directly deal with this matter for reasons of space. In contemporary law, intent is a crucial and complicated matter with substantial constitutional overtones.

29. Ultimately, counsel must *detail* his or her allegations of error. A broadsided "t'aint fair" complaint rarely is successful even if heard in the first place.

30. At trial the factfinder may evaluate and take into account the truthfulness of a witness by observing or her appearance and reactions while testifying.

nize that most appeals are based upon allegations of judicial error below and that such errors usually stem from jury instructions, debate over evidentiary and procedural matters, and motion dispositions.

When an appellate court sustains the result in the court below, it **affirms** that judgment. When it finds that the judgment was sufficiently affected by error,[31] it **reverses** the judgment which normally nullifies the result. Usually, a reversal is accompanied by a **remand**, an order returning the case to the lower court for possible retrial.

Obviously, one of the primary purposes of the appellate court of last resort is to end litigation and to ensure that the law was followed in the given case. At the same time, in the Anglo-American system the appellate court's ability to affirm or reverse the decision of a lower court necessarily requires the lower courts to follow the appellate court's precedents lest reversal be ordered. In addition, appellate courts usually have supervisory authority over subordinate courts, which authority may be used to ensure compliance with the appellate court's procedures or legal interpretations. Accordingly, appellate courts control the system of precedent. Because precedent is so powerful, there are important limitations on it. Perhaps the most important one is that only that part of a judicial opinion is precedential that had to be decided to resolve the case before the court. That part of the opinion is **holding**; the rest of the opinion is **dictum** (*pl.* dicta). The distinction between dictum and holding can be a difficult one and ordinarily you will not be comfortable with it until you have accumulated a fair amount of experience with it.[32] Let's briefly look at an example. In the *Tatem* case, the court determined whether self-defense would be a defense to homicide. The defendant raised the issue, and it had to be decided to resolve the case. The court's holding was that self-defense was a defense under the statute. Suppose, however, the court in its opinion had added, unnecessarily: "Further, self-defense may be asserted even if the accused could have 'turned tail' and run in order to escape and deliberately chose not to do so." Retreat was not part of the *Tatem* case. If the court's superfluous language were to be given precedential effect, courts would truly supersede legislatures. Mere judicial remark in an opinion would have the force of law for future cases. The doctrine of holding and dictum thus limits the precedential reach of opinions.[33] We will return to this in Homicide Five.

The appellate court's importance in the area of precedent can hardly be overstated. Its decisions are binding on its lower courts and necessarily establish precedent throughout its jurisdiction. Our limited scenario does not dis-

---

31. It is virtually impossible to try a case perfectly. Some mistakes always occur. The real question is whether error prejudiced a party to an unacceptable extent.

32. This will be discussed further in chapter 4.

33. Dicta may be important as an indication as to how the court might decide a future case.

cuss the procedural basis for appeal, but we should point out that in the United States appeals may be **of right** or **discretionary** with the appellate court. Most appeals to the first level appellate court are of right, while hearing further appeals are often subject to the discretion of the higher court. Especially when there are two levels of appellate courts, the primary duty of the higher appellate court is apt to be the creation of precedent and resolution of conflicting precedent rather than mere correction of errors made by lower courts. The general public often finds this hard to understand. Under the Constitution, the United States Supreme Court is the ultimate interpreter of the federal constitutional and federal statutes. The Court is far more concerned with clarifying the law for the nation and resolving contradictory lower court precedents than it is with ensuring that the results of any given case were proper. Further, the Court can only hear a limited number of cases. Accordingly, it usually takes only those cases of the greatest national importance,[34] and a refusal to hear a case does not mean that the courts below didn't err.

We should briefly examine the federal court structure[35] in the United States. Each state is home to at least one federal district court; many have more than one district.[36] Each United States Court of Appeals hears appeals from its **circuit**, its multi-state grouping of federal district courts. There are twelve ordinary circuits and a special circuit for matters such as copyright, trademark, and suits against the federal government.[37] Each court of appeals creates binding precedent for the federal district courts within its circuit.[38] All courts of appeals, all district courts, and all state courts are bound by decisions of the United States Supreme Court when it interprets the United States Constitution or other federal law.

Back to our homicide. The colonial Supreme Court is now faced with interpreting the homicide statute in order to supply guidance to all of Bryan's lower courts. The lower court decisions have no precedential impact on the Supreme

---

34. Death penalty cases may be an exception to this general rule. At least in the past such a case was more likely to be heard on the merits of the case because of the ultimate finality of the penalty.

35. Each state has its own judicial system. The federal model is highly useful, however, not only because of the importance of federal law, but also because its basic structure is similar to that of most states.

36. For example, New York has four districts while California has five.

37. There are also other federal courts. The United States Court of Military Appeals, for example, hears cases from the four different intermediate armed forces Courts of Military Review.

38. The federal and state governments are independent sovereigns. Accordingly, although a federal court decision binds the parties in a particular case, absent a Supreme Court decision, a federal judicial opinion does not constitute binding precedent in a state court. However, this conclusion is misleading. The decision of the United States court of appeals, for example, is so persuasive on a question of federal constitutional or statutory law that ordinarily a state court within that circuit would defer to it.

Court. The court must deal with significant policy questions, ones which ideally should have been decided by the legislature. Again the question of deference to the legislature is raised. This may be particularly important as the statute has been revised and modernized by the legislature. Presumably, it should be entitled to more respect than a statute which has been left to languish without legislative attention. With this in mind, the court must approach the issues in the same manner as we have previously discussed.

Presume, however, that Earth has rediscovered the colony but recognized its independence. Posit that defense counsel present various Earth precedents in their favor. Would a United States Supreme Court decision on point be binding? Would a decision of the High Judicial Tribunal of Proxima Centauri apply? Note that although decisions of both courts would be persuasive, they would not be binding as they are not higher courts in the same jurisdiction.

If you were acting on behalf of the Bryan Supreme Court, how would you decide the cases before it?

The Fifth Homicide
Assumption:

The colonial Supreme Court in the preceding cases issued an opinion resolving both cases. In relevant part, it wrote:

> *The degree of intent required to make out a criminal offense is within the province of the legislature. Accordingly, manslaughter may exist when a person kills another without premeditation but with intent. The legislature has, however, provided for self defense, and we hold that should a person reasonably believe that killing another person is necessary to preserve his or her own life in a situation not of the defendant's own making, the accused may raise a defense of self-defense.*

The facts:

Two years after the Bryan Supreme Court's decision in the *Lynd* and *Doyle* cases, the populace is shocked by news of a maritime disaster and rescue. A deep sea fishing boat sank suddenly leaving eight crew members to survive in the ship's boat without provisions. After ten days at sea, despite efforts to catch fish the survivors were dehydrated and starving and were at the point of death. That night, seven of the survivors decided that one should be sacrificed for the others and decided to kill the 8th. He was chosen because he, the cabin boy, was comatose and closest to death, and because he had no known family. He was killed and eaten. Within 24 hours the survivors were fortuitously rescued at sea. Experts agree that the crew had no reason to expect rescue and that had they not eaten the cabin boy, they would have died within 36 to 48 hours after they killed him. The survivors are tried in the Eastern District.

Issues:

In light of the Bryan Supreme Court's decisions in the *Lynd* and *Doyle* cases, is a homicide defendant who killed and ate another in order to survive entitled to a self-defense jury instruction?

Discussion:

We begin by applying the statute. Under § 1, it is clear that the killing with premeditation of the cabin boy by the survivors constituted murder subject only to the § 3 self-defense provision. Although we must now turn to § 3, we must also consider the Bryan Supreme Court's decision in the *Lynd* and *Doyle* cases because that court's interpretation of § 3 is binding and constitutes law as well as the statute it interprets. The court's opinion stated, "we hold that should a person reasonably believe that killing another person is necessary to preserve his or her own life in a situation not of the defendant's own making, the accused may raise a defense of self-defense." The survivors believed that killing the cabin boy was necessary to preserve their own lives; experts have testified that their belief was correct, let alone reasonable; the sinking and shortage of food was surely not the fault of the survivors. Consequently, we must conclude that under the strict language of the Supreme Court's decision, the survivors are entitled to a self-defense instruction and ought to be acquitted by the jury. Case closed; let's quit for the day and adjourn to Pomerey's Pub to socialize with Rumpole of the Bailey and Perry Mason. Are you pleased with the result?

Unfortunately for Rumpole and Perry, both of whom would certainly have liked our preliminary result, our analysis is inadequate. Yes, the opinion contains the language we've quoted. That language may not, however, constitute binding precedent. Remember that we've already discussed the difference between holding and dictum. What did the court *have* to decide in the *Lynd* and *Doyle* cases? Presumably, it had to decide whether a killing in the mistaken hallucinating belief that the death was necessary for the self-defense of the defendant constituted self-defense under §3 of the statute in light of the unique facts of each case. The court's sweeping language was unnecessary to resolve the cases before it. As a result, that part of the opinion which can be viewed as **surplusage is** *dictum* without precedential effect. Further, the present case is distinguishable from all prior cases. Unlike the normal self defense case, there was no actual attacker who arguably consented by conduct to an attack in self defense. Unlike the *Lynd* and *Doyle* cases, the defendants were fully aware of reality and were not attempting to defend against a perceived attacker. The prior cases did not involve a ship sinking, a planned killing, a non-delusional killing, or the intentional conscious decision to kill and eat another to survive additional time at sea. The policies underlying the prior decisions do not apply to the present facts.

Let us suppose for a moment, however,[39] that the Supreme Court's prior language had not been dicta, that it had been required to resolve the cases. It would then constitute holding and binding precedent, and the District Court for the Eastern District would be bound by it. If that court believed the result inappropriate, what could it do? Is there no escape from these chilling facts? If the district court decides that it must give a self-defense instruction and the accused is acquitted, the acquittal is final and cannot be reopened. Suppose, however, that the district court decides that the Bryan Supreme Court could not possibly have intended for its decision to reach this type of case, and refuses to give the instruction yielding a conviction. The defendant would appeal the conviction to the Bryan Supreme Court. The Supreme Court might well reverse the conviction because the district court failed to follow precedent. However, because it decided the precedent in question, the Supreme Court has one power not available to the lower courts, it can **overrule** the precedent.

Under the Anglo-American system of precedent, a court has the power to overrule its own precedents. If a court decides that a prior precedent was wrongly decided, it overrules the case,[40] and announces a new rule. Because a court is not supposed to make law freely as a legislature can (and often must), courts are loathe to overrule their precedents. Such an abrupt change—based only on the grounds that the court made a mistake or that circumstances have changed so much as to make that prior result wrong in modern times—sends shockwaves through the community. Too many overrulings would destroy the predictability of precedent. Here, the Supreme Court could overrule its prior decision if it decided that it was bound by it and that it had been wrong. As the critical language in that opinion was dictum, however, the court should have no need to even consider the issue.

Since the Supreme Court's applicable language is dictum, and all prior cases are distinguishable, we must interpret the statute directly. It sheds no light on whether the survivors' action constitutes self-defense. Its plain meaning, however, would strongly suggest that it did not. "Self-defense" usually connotes taking physical action to repel an attacker's immediate physical assault. Absent some unusual form of legislative history, a judge would have to reach quite far on his or her own to decide that the crew's cannibalism constituted self-defense. What message would such a decision send to society?

Was the killing of the cabin boy something that should be unlawful? A brief excursion into the reason for criminal law may be desirable here. Convinced

---

39. In law school or court we often say, "assume *arguendo*," assume for the sake of argument.

40. It is important to distinguish between overruling and reversal. Overruling of a case voids its legal effect as a rule of law; it has no effect at all on the actual result of that case. Reversal changes the result in an appellate case and may have no precedential effect at all.

of impending death if they do not kill the cabin boy, would the crew have been deterred by clear statute and court decision? You may wish to distinguish between laws that actually seek to govern human behavior and laws that establish or recognize norms of human behavior to reenforce them. This case is nearly identical with the famous decision of *Regina v. Dudley & Stephens* decided by the House of Lords in England in 1884.[41] The House of Lords condemned the killing of the cabin boy and sustained the death sentences adjudged for murder. We believe that the defendants were later pardoned by the Crown,[42] however, thus leaving the normative law intact but recognizing the existence of extraordinary circumstances.

Given the controversial nature of a crime such as the one in *Regina v. Dudley & Stephens*, should a court attempt to cope with highly unusual circumstances of this type or leave the case to the executive for clemency and the law to the legislature?

If you were the district court judge, would you give a self-defense instruction to the jury?

Conclusion

Via the unfortunate homicide history of the planet Bryan, we have:

1. Probed the meaning and definition of *law*;
2. Introduced the concept of common law;
3. Explored the way in which law is created and changed in the United States as well as aspects of the general structure of the American legal system;
4 Introduced the concept of legal analysis and reasoning.

It often takes some time to appreciate the brilliance of *stare decisis*, of precedent. It permits the law to evolve, usually slowly, via judicial decision. Predictability is protected while the concepts of distinguishing cases and dicta permit reasonable flexibility. Precedent is not well suited, however, for rapidly changing circumstances, either social or technological, and such matters usually require legislative action. The relationship between the courts and legislatures is one of continuing interplay and tension. After one has created a legal rule, the other is free to modify it, with the first institution able to take yet another "shot" at the rule, and so on forever in most cases. Through this continuing process, the law adapts to unique facts and changes with society.

---

41. L.R. 14 Q.B.D. 273 (1884).

42. After serving less than one year in prison. Blat, *Law, Science, and Narrative: Reflections on Brain Science, Electronic Media, Story, and Law Learning*, 40 J. LEGAL. EDUC. 19, 21 n.2 (1990).

Case analysis is crucial to the law and lawyers. It is sometimes a difficult skill to master, but mastery is necessary. Having laid the foundations, we now turn to some of the mechanics of analysis, and then to a detailed analysis of a famous line of New York cases.

4

Law as a Literary Profession

The Writing of Law Students and Lawyers

The law is a literary profession, and lawyers must be professional writers. The legal profession lives and breathes through the written word: letters, briefs, opinions, contracts, memoranda, and other products. If you are or will be a law student, your study of law will involve that literary focus as well. You will become, if you are not already, a professional writer.

Compare the practice of law with other professions. One difference that stands out is the law's dependence on the art of communication. A surgeon, for example, applies professional knowledge through skillful hands. While a patient would certainly feel better with a doctor who could explain procedures carefully and fully, the measure of the surgeon is the performance of the operation. A lawyer, however, can only operate through communication. Virtually every aspect of the lawyer's craft involves transmitting legal knowledge and ideas to someone else: a client, another party, a judge, or even future lawyers. Like a surgeon with crippled hands, a lawyer who cannot communicate cannot fully perform.

Contrary to the impression you might have from watching popular fictional lawyers such as Sandy Stern, Grace Van Owen, or Perry Mason, most of a lawyer's communication is in writing. Certainly, oral advocacy is a valuable skill for a lawyer, but before the lawyer ever makes it to court,[1] stacks of written work must first be performed. Complaints must be drafted, answers filed, letters written, motions submitted. Then, long after the courtroom is empty and silent, only the written opinion of the judge may bear testimony to the results of the legal event.

The Need for Precision

If you have not yet strolled through a law library, do so. No one who has walked through the stacks could argue with the proposition that law is a

---

1. And most legal matters never go to court.

profession of words. Much of the collection in the library consists of court opinions that resolve disputes between parties and make law. In many of those opinions, courts are engaged in determining the proper meaning of a particular word or phrase. That word or phrase most often will be from a statute, or from a contract, a will, or some other document. In most cases, the document or statute at issue will have been written by lawyers. Why is it a document written by lawyers—professional writers—should end up in litigation to determine its meaning? In some cases, the answer is that no amount of foresight by the lawyer could have predicted the dispute that arose. In too many cases, though, the answer is that the lawyer was not precise enough with language to prevent challengers from arguing a plausible meaning not intended by the drafter. No matter how litigious we may be as a society, people do not litigate over questions that can only be answered in one way; people rarely litigate over questions that are not arguable. If drafting lawyers were more precise, more careful with the expression of the ideas that they try to convey, fewer cases would be litigated, fewer words would be needed in the library, and the ones that were needed would be more useful.

Good Legal Writing is Simply Good Writing

Good legal writing is, first of all, good writing. It should be a precise communication of intended meaning. As a group though, lawyers are not very good at being precise in conveying intended meanings. Much of the legal writing that you will read, which will be primarily judicial opinions for now, will be dull, wordy, and pompous. It will be unclear and redundant; some of it will be musty. Some of it will seem as if the writer was trying to hide the intended meaning rather than convey it. You may not be worried yet about the damage that such a lack of clarity does to the state of the law; you will be able to see, however, as a very immediate concern, that such poor writing makes your job of reading case opinions far more burdensome than it needs to be. Those poorly written opinions damage the state of the law in the same way that they frustrate you. Just as you must do the best you can with them to learn the law, practicing attorneys must read the cases to provide sound advice to clients with real and serious concerns. When you are prevented from understanding the law in an opinion by poor writing, you may be able to find answers to your questions in class. For the legal profession, however, the result is confusion, avoidable litigation, and a failure of the law to function as a reliable predictor of safe conduct for the public.

When you read a passage in an opinion that is unclear, your first reaction may be to assume that the fault lies with you. Many times, though, that will not be the case. Some legal writing is difficult to read because law is complex. Some of it is difficult to read because the analysis and the reasoning process involved are difficult. Some of it is difficult to read because there are special words that have legal meanings that are quite different from their ordinary English meaning. But to the extent that legal writing is difficult to read because of its generally turgid style and its use of old formalisms, the difficulty is needless.

Why should the language of law continue to be inaccessible to so many? There are many reasons, but among them is one that you might not expect: lawyers, as a group, are insecure.

If two non-lawyers were to get together in a room, and wanted to make an agreement, they might begin with something profound like, "We agree...." But if they were in that same room and a lawyer or two got involved, rather than "We agree," the document might begin instead, "In consideration of the agreements herein contained, the parties hereto have entered into agreements represented by the following particulars...."

In fact, "We agree" would have done quite well. The words that the lawyer might have chosen do not work any special magic. At one time, a few hundred years ago, "legalistic" words did work a kind of magic, and legal transactions, such as land transfers, were a kind of ceremony, complete with symbols and chants. Strangely, the language of law retains that notion, even though the conditions of medieval England have faded into history. Lawyers, insecure people that we are, seem to believe that when a particular pattern of words operates to make a transaction work once, they will do so for all time, and they are the only words that will do so. As a result, the legal profession has traditionally perceived little need to develop new language. The premise has been that if the "magic words" worked before, fifty, one hundred, or four hundred years ago, they will still work as well today.

That confidence in the old language is wrong. Society and law are interrelated. Both have changed, and changes in the law require matching language changes. The law is a dynamic, important part of modern society that needs to be accessible to that society; it must not be buried under the encrusted and mildewed forms of traditional legal incantations.

We encourage and challenge you to make your own writing at the least accessible, and to the extent possible, even pleasant to read. We offer this encouragement not only for your own good, but for the good of the language, the legal profession, and your clients. As you will see, we serve clients poorly when we fail to write and speak clearly as lawyers.

Writing in Law School

If you are a law student, you will do a great deal of writing in law school and in practice. In law school, you will write exams, outlines, and casebriefs; and you will write an array of law practice-oriented documents in your writing or skills courses. Once you are an attorney, you will write letters to clients, adversaries, and courts, legal documents such as business contracts, wills, and settlement contracts, intra-office documents such as memoranda of law, court documents such as pleadings, motion papers, discovery requests, and persuasive memoranda and briefs to courts.

The relationship between the writing you will do in law school writing or skills courses and the writing you will do as a lawyer is clear: they produce the same kinds of documents. What may be less clear, but equally important, is the relationship between the law school exams, outlines, and casebriefs you will write and the writing you will do in practice. The exams, outlines, and casebriefs are not only important vehicles for learning the law, they are also opportunities to practice the process of legal analysis that will find its way into all of your writing as a lawyer.

You will be responsible for all of the writing that you do in law school; you will no longer be able to regard the teacher as the one who fixes the framework of your writing. While you will have opportunities to have your writing critiqued by teachers, critiques will take on a form that may be new to you. They will not be so much compliance and grading experiences as they will be critiques of one professional writer's work by another.

Many students regard the teacher's role in a writing course as that of an editor.[2] Such students regard the teacher's critique as a list of corrections to be made on revision. Revision thus becomes simple proofreading and word processing practice (add the comma where the teacher said to add the comma, and so forth) without any thought or analysis of why the teacher made the suggestions given, or the effect of changes on the meaning of the writing.

You will benefit by abandoning that sort of teacher-student relationship. Instead, adopt the posture of a professional writer and expect the teacher to be an interested, helpful reader of your professional work. The teacher will give you a critique, will comment on your work, and will advise you of ways in which your work may be improved. While the teacher may do some line editing, view it not as an order to make specific typographical changes, but as an example of improvements that might be useful to you in that piece and in all of your future writing. Ultimately, your teachers are trying to enable you to read your own writing, critique it, revise it, and improve it from one draft to the next.

Much of your writing in law school will be outside the context of your writing or skills courses. That writing will be valuable far beyond its worth as preparation for the writing you will do as a lawyer. Because your writing of exams, casebriefs, and outlines will be a written exposition of your understanding of particular aspects of the law, the more of this type of writing that you do, the deeper will be your understanding of those aspects. For most of

---

2. At least one author of this book would count himself as having been among this group as a beginning law student some years ago.

your courses, you should prepare written outlines of the course material. The process of writing itself reveals your level of understanding. If you force yourself throughout the term to write about your courses, such as torts, contracts, civil procedure, and so on, in a form of an outline of the material, revising earlier portions as you make your way through the course, you will better appreciate the relationships among the various topics you are learning about. In addition, you will force yourself to identify particular aspects that may be unclear, while you have the time and opportunity to clarify them. Thus, you will be able to weave your own strong understanding of the law, one thread at a time.

The Casebrief

As you know from chapter 3, important court decisions are usually expressed in the form of judicial opinions (cases). Particularly because of their style, those opinions can be complex and difficult to understand. Issues can be resolved on procedural grounds, substantive grounds, or both. Dicta may be camouflaged as holding, or holding as dicta. The critical facts may be buried in remote aspects of the case. Consequently, reading a case is more difficult than it ought to be, and skillful reading and analysis requires a "roadmap" for the journey. A **casebrief** is nothing more than a written analysis of a case using a generally accepted framework for that analysis. Casebriefs are essential for new law students who must read cases in preparation for class.

Read the following judicial opinion from our mythical planet of Bryan. Pause for a moment and reflect on what the court has decided in the opinion and why. Then turn to the two sample briefs of the case that follow it. They differ in style but not in substance. Do the briefs and their formats make it easier to understand the case? Following the briefs are several pages of explanation.[3]

---

3. In chapter 8 you will find a sample of another kind of writing often required of first semester law students, the intra-office memorandum of law. In footnotes to that sample, we have provided some information useful to drafters of office memoranda. Despite the helpfulness of the information we provide there, this book is not designed to teach writing skills themselves. That teaching will undoubtedly be provided for you through other sources early in your law school career.

IN THE SUPREME COURT OF
THE PLANET OF BRYAN

GRAVEY C. CLAYTON, Petitioner
v.
JOAN K. FORT, Superintendent,
Bryan Department of Corrections

25 Br. 497

[No. 2233-196] Argued July 13, 2233. Decided November 6, 2233

Opinion of the Court

Justice Nagle delivered the opinion of the Court.

On August 3, 2231, petitioner, Gravey C. Clayton, was operating a "bullzer," a large four track nuclear powered Caryn class exploratory mining vehicle in the Sullivan Mountains approximately three days cruising range from the town of Dunnigan. Clayton was accompanied by Sam Maxwell, the navigator/mechanic. At the time of this tragic event Clayton and Maxwell, close friends, had been "on the track" for six weeks without any significant human contact. The bullzer's radio system had been inoperable for the last 12 days, and the life support systems were malfunctioning. At trial, the prosecution and defense conceded that both petitioner and the deceased had been functioning in 103 degree conditions for at least three days.

At approximately 10:00 A.M. on August 3rd, Clayton suddenly stopped the bullzer and announced that, "We're rich; we've struck the motherlode." He then donned his environment suit and cycled out of the bullzer running toward a rock outcrop. Confused by events, Maxwell followed. As clearly documented by the bullzer's automatic videolog, Maxwell examined the outcrop and calmly told Clayton that all he had found was glass. Clayton twice good naturedly told Maxwell to stop joking, that the outcrop showed a huge vein of energy rich Hanumeit.

After Maxwell's third effort to correct Clayton, Clayton's attitude changed sharply. He began to accuse Maxwell of planning to cheat him; to steal the Hanumeit. Maxwell denied this, treating it as a poor attempt at humor. Clayton, however, began to advance on Maxwell waving his sharp edged mining probe in the air. Maxwell began to retreat; turned and ran, and fell on a small boulder. Clayton then clubbed him (braking his helmet) and then stabbed him in the back with the probe, killing him instantly.

Apparently dazed, Clayton dropped to his knees for 15 minutes. When he rose, he shook his head from side to side and triggered the bullzer's mayday signal. A rescue aircraft found both petitioner and deceased and retrieved them. Perhaps ironically, Clayton proved correct; the Hanumeit deposit is the largest ever found in the history of the colony.

Petitioner was charged with manslaughter pursuant to Bryan Code § 100.9996. The prosecution's case was succinct and consisted primarily of the bullzer's recordings. Petitioner defended on the grounds of insanity and presented expert testimony to the effect that situational environmental factors had deprived Clayton of his ability to distinguish right from wrong and to adhere to the right. Specifically, he claimed that at the time of the killing he lacked any understanding of reality, did not realize what he was doing, and was incapable of controlling his actions. He alleged total ignorance of his fatal actions.

After presentation of the evidence, the defense requested that the jury be instructed that it could not lawfully convict the defendant unless it found beyond a reasonable doubt that at the time of death Clayton had been able to distinguish right from wrong and to adhere to the right. The trial judge denied the request. In so doing, she held that an inability to distinguish right from wrong must stem from mental disease or defect and not temporary environmental factors, and that the burden of proof on the question of insanity belongs to the defendant.

With the issue of sanity removed from the case, the jury convicted Petitioner, and the judge sentenced him to eight years penal servitude in the Billy Mines. Petitioner then appealed as of right to the 2nd Circuit Court of Appeals which affirmed his conviction. He then requested and received this court's consent to pursue his discretionary appeal here pursuant to Bryan Code § 28-901. He seeks an order to the Superintendent declaring his conviction void and ordering his release from custody. The Bryan Attorney General, the real party in interest in the case, represents the Superintendent.

Because the Court of Appeals held moot Clayton's claim that the trial judge reversed the burden of proof on the question of sanity, our grant of review extends solely to whether Petitioner was potentially entitled to a jury instruction raising an insanity defense.

We will presume for purposes of this appeal that Petitioner killed deceased solely because his mind was temporarily deranged because of the unusually strenuous, cumulative, environmental factors pressing on Petitioner and that he lacked both understanding of his conduct and the ability to consciously control it.

As one would expect for a lost colony begun without benefit of law books or lawyers, our legal system remains immature and unburdened by significant precedential authority. We have long recognized, however, that under the Bryan Constitution no person may be lawfully convicted of a crime if that person is insane at the time of the offense. Bryan v. Bistard, 2 Br. 201 (2117). Since the legislature has failed to define "sanity" for purposes of the criminal law, the applicable definition is one to be resolved by resort to the common law.

When the original settlers arrived, such little authority as existed on this point came from the United States. It indicated significant disagreement on the question. Apparently, the first major test stemmed from an old English case. Called the M'Naghten Rule, this doctrine provided that a defendant could not be held criminally responsible if at the time of the incident in question he was suffering from a mental disease or defect such that he did not know either the nature and quality of the act or that the act was wrong. In later years, some jurisdictions expanded the test to permit acquittal for a defendant who knew the difference but was unable to "adhere to the right," a modification known as the irresistible impulse rule. By the 1980s, most courts had adopted the American Law Institute's Model Penal Code provision requiring acquittal if the defendant at the time of the act as a result of mental disease or defect lacked substantial capacity either to appreciate the criminality of the conduct or to conform his or her conduct to the law. This modification was rejected for federal offenses by the United States Congress after an attempt to kill an American President. At the same time, federal law was amended to require a federal defendant to prove insanity rather than requiring the government to prove sanity beyond a reasonable doubt once the issue was raised.

Our law makes it plain that a defendant may not be convicted if due to mental disease or defect he or she lacked substantial capacity to know the nature of his or her actions or to act in conformity with the law, *"Mad Dog" Fatzsimmons v. Bryan*, 4 Br. 1 (2153). Although this test is fairly liberal, we note in passing that during much of this planet's history a killer was unlikely to have much opportunity to raise such a defense, summary executions by vigilante groups being fairly common.

The question before us is whether our legal system permits the conviction of a person whose condition would clearly constitute insanity if caused by a mental disease or defect when the condition is instead caused by extraordinary environmental stress.

It is an item of faith that no person should be convicted of an act committed when for no reason of his or her own making he or she was incapable of appreciating the nature of the act or conforming behavior to moral and legal propriety. Further, a person unable to appreciate the nature of an act or to conform to the law can hardly be deterred from improper conduct.

We recognize that extraordinary stress is a continuous risk in a frontier environment, and that some people will succumb to it. Does that justify inflicting the rigors of the criminal law upon them? Should the happenstance of proving more susceptible to extreme pressure than others merit punishment? It is not sufficient to argue that unusual cases may receive executive clemency.

The dissent argues that to permit Clayton to raise an insanity defense without evidence of mental disease or defect is to "open the floodgates" to perjurers and to encourage groundless acquittals. Nothing could be farther from the truth. The traditional "parade of horrors" proves little, particularly as our decision this day is hardly so broad. We hold only that when a person is subjected to such extraordinary environmental stress that through no personal fault he or she lacks the capacity to appreciate the wrongfulness of his or her conduct or to conform conduct to the law, that person may not be held criminally responsible for an act committed in that mental state.

As this case may be retried, we note in passing that it is perfectly constitutional to place the burden of proof on the defendant when asserting an affirmative defense. Such a defense, of course, admits the completion of the basic act (here homicide) but argues that the act was accompanied by circumstances that legally excuse that act. So long as the prosecution proves the basic act beyond a reasonable doubt, it is constitutional to make the defendant prove that the conduct was excusable. Given the nature of this type of insanity defense, it would not be inappropriate for the trial judge to require the defendant to raise the issue of "stress insanity" and to prove its existence by clear and convincing evidence. Given that the legislature has not acted on this issue, however, and that it has not been briefed and argued, we express no opinion on what the law might require in this case.

Reversed; petitioner's motion for an order directing his release from custody is **granted** and shall issue. A retrial is permitted.

So ordered (Concurring: Filton, Orton, Bainwohl, Alyssa, JJ)

Separate Opinion
Justice Diane, with whom
Justice Ring joins, dissenting.

The majority reaches its result with its heart rather than its head. Insanity defenses have always been difficult to bring successfully. This is hardly surprising given the uncertainty of psychiatry and the quite legitimate suspicion ordinary citizens bring to an assertion of lack of mental capacity on the part of a person charged with serious harm.

On a frontier world who can escape extraordinary stress? What actions should a pioneer be responsible for given the likelihood of encountering inhuman conditions? It is hard enough to determine whether a defendant at a prior moment suffered from a mental disease or defect. How should a jury determine how much stress is enough? How much pressure is so extraordinary that the criminal acts of a defendant will be excused if the jury accepts the proposition that the stress caused the defendant to lose contact with reality? The majority has needlessly opened the floodgates to perjurers and rival claimants to treasure. The vigilantes may yet return if we continue to abdicate our sworn responsibility in this fashion.

I respectfully dissent.

Sample casebrief # 1

Clayton v. Planet of Bryan, 25 Br. 497 (2233). Criminal
Law Text at page 24

Facts

Defendant-Petitioner killed the victim while the two
were on an exploratory mining mission. The two had
been living under extraordinarily difficult conditions,
e.g., 103 degree temperatures, away from all other
humans for six weeks, no radio contact with civilization.
While under these conditions the two sharply disagreed
about a possible mineral find. Defendant-Petitioner
became highly agitated believing that the victim intended
to steal the mineral find from D-P. D-P chased, struck,
and killed the victim.

Procedural History

D-P was charged with manslaughter and he raised an
insanity defense based upon extreme environmental
stress. The trial court denied D-P's request for an
instruction that would require acquittal unless the jury
found that D-P had been able to distinguish right from
wrong and to adhere to right. The trial court ruled that
an insanity defense must be based upon mental disease
or defect and not environmental stress. D-P was convicted. Ct. of Appeals affirmed. Supreme Court granted
petition for discretionary review.

Issue

May an insanity defense, which requires demonstration that the defendant was incapable of distinguishing
right from wrong or incapable of adhering to the right,
be based solely upon extraordinary environmental
stress?

Disposition

Reversed, retrial permitted.

Holding

Yes, an insanity defense may be based solely upon
extraordinary environmental stress.

Reasoning

In our society, in spite of its relative lack of sophistication and rigorous lifestyle, no one should be punished for an act when the person was unable, through no fault of his or her own, to distinguish between right or wrong or to conform to the right. No deterrent effect would accrue by penalizing such an act. There is no sound reason for distinguishing an inability to distinguish right from wrong or to conform to the right that results from mental disease or defect and the same inability that results from extraordinary environmental stress.

Dicta

It is appropriate for the court to place the burden of proving insanity upon the defendant.

Separate Opinion

Dissent. The majority opinion will permit too many defendants to escape punishment in a frontier world such as this. Ordinary life in such world is itself subject to extraordinary stress.

Why did I read this opinion?

Sample casebrief # 2

Clayton v. Planet of Bryan, 25 Br. 497 (2233). Criminal Law Text at page 24

Facts

1. The case of the murderous miner.
2. D (defendant) killed V (victim) while on exploratory mining mission.
3. D and V had been under extraordinary environmental stress (e. stress) conditions:
   a. High temperatures (103 +) (3 days)
   b. Isolation from others (6 weeks)
   c. No radio contact (12 days)
   d. Life support systems malfunctioning.
4. D and V sharply disagreed about a possible mineral find. D believed that V intended to steal from him, "went crazy" and killed V.

Procedural History

1. D charged with manslaughter, asserted affirmative defense of insanity due to e. stress.

2. TC (trial court) denied D's request for jury instruction that D must have been able to tell right from
wrong to convict. TC ruled that insanity defense
could only be based on mental disease or defect, not
e. stress.
3. D was convicted.
4. Ct. of Appeals aff'd (affirmed).
5. To Supreme Ct. on discretionary review.

Issue

1. May insanity defense (that D was incapable of distinguishing right from wrong or was incapable of
adhering to the right) be based solely on extraordinary e. stress?

Disposition

Reversed, retrial permitted.

Holding

Yes, an insanity defense may be based solely upon
extraordinary e. stress.

Reasoning

1. In our society, despite relative lack of sophistication
and rigorous lifestyle, no one should be punished for
an act when the person was unable, through no fault
of his or her own, to distinguish between right or
wrong or to conform to the right.
2. No deterrent effect by penalizing such an act.
3. No sound reason for distinguishing between mental
disease or defect and extraordinary e. stress WRT
(with regard to) a D's inability to distinguish right
from wrong or to conform to the right.

Dicta

1. It is appropriate for the court to place the burden of
proving insanity upon the defendant.

Separate Opinion

Dissent:
1. In a frontier world like this, too many D's will escape
punishment.
2. Ordinary life itself is subject to extraordinary stress.

Why did I read this opinion?

1. Competing values in affirmative defense of no mental
   responsibility: shouldn't punish when D's are unable
   to know/conform to right. On other hand, life is
   stressful: need strict standards of behavior, can't
   allow all D's to claim stress as an excuse.

Briefing cases, an introduction

As with every other writing that you do in the law, the first thing you should
do when preparing to write a casebrief is identify why you are creating the
writing; ask yourself the question, "What am I trying to accomplish here?" In
almost all instances, a casebrief is solely for your own use; few law professors
will ask you to submit a casebrief as part of your coursework. Writing a casebrief serves several purposes. The most obvious reason for writing a casebrief
is to enable you to participate in class. The law school class is a very important
experience. It is not like many large-room undergraduate classes in which you
can either read the reading or sit through the lecture and pretty much get the
same thing. You are in the law school classroom to engage yourself with the
professor and the other students in the process of discovering what the law is
all about, how it works, and how it fits with other things you have studied.[4] If
you expect the rich understanding of law necessary to practice more than just
rudimentary, mechanical law, you must be ready to participate in that learning
process. The casebrief is the tool that enables you to engage in the classroom
dialogues, by providing the essence of the case, and your analysis of the
opinion.

The predicate to participating in class is your effort in digesting and understanding the cases that will be discussed there. The casebrief provides a
valuable structure for that process. Implicitly, your preparation of casebriefs is
part of your learning of the course material. By forcing yourself to identify and
summarize the key facts, the issues and holdings, and the reasons for each
decision, you will develop the analytical skills necessary to understand and
apply the law as a lawyer.

Lastly, your casebriefs will serve as the foundation for your course outline
or synthesis. Taken collectively, they will be your synopsis of your casebook.
They will permit you to identify the subtle balances of the law: what a court
means by "the reasonable person," what a proximate cause is, why some
actions indicate a binding agreement and others do not. Reviewing your casebriefs as you prepare your course outline will enable you to develop the
sensitivity necessary to appreciate why some fact patterns indicate a legal
cause of action and others do not.

---

4. See the discussion of the socratic method in chapter 9, *infra*.

Because the casebrief is for your own benefit, it is up to you to find the style and format that best suits you, in order to achieve the purposes of the casebrief. Although you have just read two examples of ways to structure the casebrief,[5] you have free rein to choose and adapt your own format. If you start out with a particular format, but find that it is of little value to you, either for understanding the material or for participating in class, then you will need to consider how to modify it. If you choose a style that is so cumbersome that it hampers your understanding, or that you simply don't have time to generate, then you should adopt a simpler, more workable style. Just as an artist selects and customizes a brush to fit the hand as well as the canvas, you must customize your casebriefs to fit your own style as well as the course subject and format involved. Note, however, that although nomenclature and sequence may vary, the casebrief examples above reflect the generally accepted basic components of a casebrief.

Parts of the casebrief

Each part of the casebrief serves a different purpose. The particular names that we have chosen for the various parts are not cast in stone anywhere; different writers have used many different names for their casebrief sections. Regardless of the section headings, all casebriefs should address each of the topics described below. We will describe the parts of the casebrief in their order of appearance in the sample casebriefs.

Heading: The heading of a casebrief is straightforward. You should give the name of the case, the citation[6] to it, and the page on which the opinion may be found in your casebook. Additionally, you will find it helpful to list the parties by their procedural titles (for example, plaintiff, appellee, respondent) and, when possible, by a characterization that has legal significance to the opinion (for example, buyer, injured person, father, finder of lost goods). In the sample brief, the only characterization of legal significance happens to coincide with a procedural title, "criminal defendant."

---

5. In particular, you will notice that the sample casebriefs are done on only half the page. This format feature allows the student to generate classnotes from discussion of the case on the same page as the casebrief itself.

6. See chapter 7 for information on locating the full text of a reported case opinion. As you might expect, casebook editors provide an edited version of most included cases; the edit is designed to highlight the court's discussion of the issues being addressed at that part of the casebook. Although time would not permit you to examine the full reported text of every opinion that is found in your casebooks and doing so would often be *counterproductive* because of the possible loss of focus that the casebook editor had hoped to achieve with the edit, occasionally (particularly when you feel confused by a particular opinion) you may find it useful to examine the full reported text of some of the opinions in your casebooks.

Statement of Facts: The casebrief's statement of facts is a short rendition of the story of the opinion. Keep the section brief! You can do that by limiting the facts you include to those actually discussed by the court when it applies the legal rules to the case facts, and those necessary to fill in a coherent story. All the other detail, no matter how interesting, should be excluded. For example, in the sample casebrief, the facts do not include a description of what a bullzer is, or describe the particulars of the mineral find beyond saying that it was a possible valuable mineral find.

Using the legal roles of the parties in lieu of their names will often help you to clarify the facts and issues. You will be reading many case opinions, and the parties' names will begin to blur into each other before too long. You should also resist the temptation to simply quote extensively from the case when writing the statement of facts. Summarizing in your own words will help you significantly in remembering the facts of each case, in focusing on the key facts, and in making your statement of facts more concise. You are going to use some language directly out of the opinion of course, and that is fine, but try not to make your statement of facts a cut and paste from a couple of paragraphs from the opinion.

Procedural History: The procedural history section of the casebrief is more important to you than it may seem at first. The procedural history (or the procedural posture) of the case shows the path that the controversy followed through the judicial system to the point at which this court wrote the opinion that you are briefing. It will clarify the nature of the proceeding involved. You will most often be reading opinions of appellate courts ruling on actions taken by lower courts. The procedural history briefly explains the steps that led to the appeal. It answers questions such as: "Who filed the complaint?" "What defenses were raised?" "How was the case resolved in the lower courts?" "Did the trial court rule for the plaintiff or the defendant?" "Was there a jury verdict or were the trial court proceedings resolved on some particular kind of motion presented to the court?" "Did it dismiss the plaintiff's complaint?" "Did it rule for the defendant on a motion for summary judgment?"

After reading and analyzing a few appellate opinions, you will see that the way in which the trial court resolved the case determines the framework within which the appellate court must analyze the issues involved. That framework particularly affects the perspective on the facts that the appellate court must adopt. As we saw in Chapter Three, trial courts find facts, appellate courts do not. As a result, an appellate court must use the facts as developed in the trial court. Whether the appellate court applies the law to the plaintiff's version of the facts or the defendant's version of the facts or the facts as found by the jury is determined by the procedural history of the case.

Issue Statement: The issue statement of the casebrief should focus you on the precise legal question that the appellate opinion answers. Different profes-

sors vary considerably in the form of issue statements they use. Some are
interested in a procedurally cast statement of the issue. For example, a professor might be interested in hearing an issue statement cast as follows: "should
the trial court have granted plaintiff's motion to dismiss under these circumstances?" Some courses, notably Civil Procedure, or parts of courses lend
themselves to this procedurally cast type of issue statement. Other professors
will be more interested in a purer form of legal question. An example of such
an issue statement is in the sample casebrief:

> May an insanity defense, which requires demonstration that the defend-
> ant was incapable of distinguishing right from wrong or incapable of
> adhering to the right, be based solely upon extraordinary environmental
> stress?

This kind of question does not ask about what the trial court did, or
whether the decision under review is correct or not. It asks a purely legal question: does the law recognize the defense as it was raised? The answer to that
question implicitly answers that procedurally cast question as well.[7] If the
appellate court says that the defense can be raised under these circumstances,
then the trial court erred in refusing to allow it to be raised. The pure legal
question underlies the procedurally cast question.

Notice that issue statements will usually not include references to the parties
by their names. In framing a pure legal question, we really do not care whether
the defendant's name is Clayton, or Jones, or Crusher; what matters is the parties' respective roles in the legal controversy. In property class, for example,
you might write an issue statement that says something like, "May a 'finder of
lost goods' do x, y, and z?"

Notice the precision in the casebrief example. In the next to last line, the
question asks whether an insanity defense "may be based *solely* upon extraordinary environmental stress." What if the word "solely" were not used: "may
be based on extraordinary environmental stress?" If "solely" were not used,
the issue statement would not accurately describe the issue before the court.
We might then be describing a case in which a *partial* basis of the insanity
defense was environmental stress coupled with some mental defect or disease
that the court identifies as a more traditional basis for the insanity defense.
The person writing the example casebrief recognized the need to focus very
precisely on the exact legal question presented.

Disposition: The disposition of the case is what you might expect it to be,
and no more. It is merely the immediate result for the parties of the appellate
court's opinion, the statement of what the appellate court did to dispose of the

---

7. In this case the procedurally cast question might have been something like, "Did
the trial court properly refuse to give defendant's insanity instruction?"

controversy. Because you will usually be reading an appellate court opinion, the disposition will usually be expressed in terms of approval or disapproval of the lower court's earlier disposition of the case. The appellate court may **reverse** or **affirm** the lower court's disposition. When the appellate court reverses the lower court, it may **remand** for specified further proceedings or enter judgment for the prevailing party on appeal; the alternative that is appropriate in a particular case will depend upon the procedural history of the case and the reasons for the appellate court's reversal of the lower court.

Holding: The holding is straightforward if you have drafted an issue statement of the "pure" variety described earlier. Under those circumstances, the holding will simply be the answer to that question. For example, the court's holding in the *Clayton* case is "Yes, the insanity defense may be based solely on extraordinary environmental stress." If the question had been framed procedurally, the holding would be the reason behind the yes or no answer to the issue statement "[Yes, the conviction should be reversed *because*] an insanity defense may be based solely on extraordinary environmental stress."

Reasoning: The reasoning section identifies why the court ruled as it did. It is the "because why" for the court's holding and should provide you with the underpinnings of the court's decision. As you saw from your work in chapter 3 and will see again in chapter 5, the court's reasoning will usually be based not merely on the authority of earlier pronouncements of the law, but also on the policies that underlie those prior decisions and the rule of law itself. As you may infer, the reasoning that supports a court's opinion generally says more about what the law *is* than the specific words of the rule of law applied or announced by the court.

Because precisely identical fact patterns occur so rarely in the law, it is less important that a court finds certain facts to call for a particular result, than it is *why* the court so found. For example, understanding the "why" of the *Clayton* case will enable you to understand other situations in which persons may or may not be held criminally responsible, beyond situations involving mineral finds and long nights in a bullzer. As a result, your work in generating the reasoning section of the casebrief is likely to be the most important casebriefing work you do. Early in your legal education, you should probably opt for over-inclusiveness in the reasoning section, waiting to narrow and refine your focus until you become more practiced at legal analysis.

In the reasoning section, you provide the answers to questions such as: "Why did the court do what it did?" "Why did the court apply the rule to the facts as it did?" "What policies underlie the rule that this court announced?" "What policies are furthered by the particular application of the rule?" "How does the court's action in the case make the law work better, provide more justice, or make the world a more sensible place?" "Was the court correct in its disposition?" "Do the policies that underlie the rule really support the court's particular use of the rule?" As you draft the reasoning section, force yourself to use the word "because." Force yourself to avoid glossing over the underlying reasons for things being the way they were in the opinion.

Obiter Dicta: The notion of dicta seems to give beginning law students nightmares, but it is not that bad. As we saw in chapter 3, courts make law because of the power that they have to resolve disputes. When a court resolves a dispute, it does so, and then announces its opinion. That opinion is law to the extent that what the court said was necessary to resolve the dispute before it. When the court speaks in asides, or when the court talks about matters that do not logically form a part of the path to a decision in the case, the court is speaking in dicta. Dicta is extra material not logically related to the disposition of the dispute that the court makes.

Often what the court says in dicta is perfectly accurate as a statement of what the law really is. But because the statement of law was unnecessary, it is not the law because this particular court said it. The statement would be law only because some other court had to establish that law to resolve a dispute, and made the statement as a logical part of its decision.[8] A good example may be found in the *Clayton* case. Near the end of the court's opinion are passages regarding the burden of proof in insanity defense cases. The court was not faced with the issue of the burden of proof in such cases; therefore, a decision on the allocation of the burden of proof in those cases was unnecessary to resolve the issue that was before it. As a result, the court's gratuitous remarks on burden of proof, while they may be accurate, are not the law because of anything that the *Clayton* court said. As a lawyer trying to convince a later court that the burden of proof must be allocated in the manner described by the *Clayton* court, the *Clayton* opinion would not be mandatory authority for the proposition urged.

Why am I reading this? This section is not often a formal part of a recommended casebrief format, but we think that this question can be one of the most important parts of your casebrief, particularly as a study aid. It is worth noticing that when editors put casebooks together, they arrange the materials in a particular order, and edit the cases to emphasize particular points of law. Even so, many cases may address a wide range of legal issues, or may be difficult to decipher because of complexity or turgid prose. By focusing on the reason your professor has had you read *this* case at *this* time, you will be better able to focus on and grasp the point of law the case is intended to illustrate.

Further, if you take advantage of the opportunity offered by trying to figure out why they have placed the materials in a particular order, you will find

---

8. It may also be the law because it is a legislative pronouncement, but we do not ordinarily think of dicta as a statement of statutory law unnecessary to the court's reasoning; ordinarily we think of dicta in the context of common law decisions.

insights about the large-scale organization of the field of law you are studying, and about the relationships between particular parts of that field. Ask yourself, "Why is the case in the book at all?" "What was the editor's purpose in including this particular case for me?" "How does it contribute to my understanding of the law of torts (or contracts, or whatever)?" "Why is it *here* in the book rather than *there*?" "How does it fit together with the surrounding material?" Some casebooks are better constructed than others, and the benefits you derive from this inquiry will vary according to how carefully the materials have been constructed. In any event, the exercise is well worth the effort.

Separate opinions: Often, judges of an appellate court do not agree unanimously upon a disposition or the reasons that should underlie a disposition. Sometimes casebook editors will include the separate opinions of the dissenting or concurring judges. When a majority of the court joins in an opinion for the court, the separate opinions are not the law; but they are important. In particular, dissenting opinions demonstrate that reasonable, bright minds can differ. They can disagree about the proper legal analysis to be applied to these cases, or about the proper result of an agreed-on analysis to the facts involved.

This point is an important one, particularly in the context of the law school classroom experience, in which any number of sound views on a question may be expressed. Those views may not be the law, but they may be worthy of consideration. You should regard the high frequency of vigorous dissents as a signal that you are empowered to be an independent thinker, creative about the way that you look at the law.

Dissents are included in your law study materials sometimes because they later became the law, but more often because they frame the most controversial legal questions that were resolved by that particular case. Indeed, this process of framing the controversial question is probably more important to your legal education than is the learning of particular rules of law. By thinking about the arguments that are presented on both sides of a particular question, you may better understand how to reason to a sensible conclusion on a similar question. In the long run, the ability to reason to a sensible conclusion is more important than knowing the usually illusory "right answer."

Ordinarily, you would include some reference to separate opinions in your casebrief, because they often provide the framework for the classroom discussion of the particular case. Indeed, although time may not often permit, it can be valuable to go to the library to read a dissenting opinion in a particularly important case, when the dissent is not included in your casebook.

5

Common Law Development and the Classroom Experience

As we saw in chapter 3, the law, particularly the common law, develops in steps, usually small ones. We move from our hypothetical world of Bryan to a line of real case opinions that demonstrates the way in which the common law develops. These are, you will notice, one-hundred year old opinions, and you may wonder why we would not prefer to place a more recent line of cases here. We are concerned here with the process of common law development rather than your learning any particular rule of substantive law, and this particular line of cases represents a classic demonstration of that process. Your learning of that process, as opposed to your learning the law of these cases is the utility of studying them. For those of you who are law students and think that efficiency requires that you learn some useful substantive law here as well, check your Torts casebook (and later perhaps your Products Liability casebook) for references to some of these cases. We suspect that you will be seeing them again.

Besides illustrating how law changes via judicial opinion, this chapter serves another purpose as well. It shows how a typical first year law course might be structured. Much of the material in this chapter is arranged as if these same materials were a part of a Torts or Products Liability casebook covering this area of the substantive law. Our purpose in so arranging the material is to allow you to become familiar with the manner of study required in law school, and to allow you to become more comfortable with it. We will refer back to this chapter, particularly the Notes sections that follow each opinion. You will find those sections in your substantive law casebooks to be quite important to your drive to understand the concepts that are presented in casebooks.

Additional material that may help you focus on your beginning efforts to become acclimated to the study of law but that would not be common to the standard casebook is included in the footnotes to the opinions found in this chapter. That footnote material should help guide you through your consideration of these materials in two ways. First, it is meant to help you understand the requirements of precise reading of law school assignments, and second, it is meant to help you discover the way in which judge-made law develops.

As you read, you will naturally be in the role of student, trying to become familiar with difficult subject matter and new vocabulary. Try also to consider your reaction to the materials from two other perspectives. First consider yourself to be the lawyer to whom one of the parties originally brought the matter being addressed by the appellate court in its opinion: How would you have learned the facts of the case? What would your reaction have been? How would you have gone about advising your client? We will return to this perspective in chapter 8. Second, consider yourself to be counsel to a business, and react to each case by considering its effect on your client's affairs: How would you explain the effect of each case to your client? What would you advise your client to do based on the incremental increase in your legal knowledge represented by your reading of each case? We hope that the insights provided by your consideration of the opinions in this chapter will help you to understand all of your law school coursework, and give you a client-based perspective on the law itself.

The Appendix to this book contains illustrative casebriefs for each of the cases that follow as well as explanatory "lecture type" commentary on them. Before you refer to the Appendix, give yourself full opportunity to work through the analysis of these materials on your own, with the assistance of classmates, or in a classroom experience if one is available to you.

Seixas v. Woods

Supreme Court of New York
2 Caines 48, 2 Am. Dec. 215 (1804)

This was an action on the case for selling peachum wood for brazilletto. The former worth hardly anything, the latter of considerable value. The defendant had received the wood in question from a house in New Providence, to whom he was agent, and in the invoice it was mentioned as brazilletto. He had also advertised it as brazilletto, had shown the invoice to the plaintiffs, and had made out the bill of parcels for brazilletto. But it was not pretended that he knew that it was peachum, nor did the plaintiffs suspect it to be so, as it was delivered from the vessel, and picked out from other wood by a person on their behalf. In short, neither side knew it to be other than brazilletto, nor was any fraud imputed. On discovery, however, of the real quality of the wood it was offered to the defendant, and the purchase money demanded. On his refusal to accept the one or return the other, as he had remitted the proceeds, the present action was brought, in which a verdict was taken for the plaintiffs, subject to the opinion of the court.

* * *

KENT, J. This is a clear case for the defendant. If upon a sale, there be neither a warranty nor deceit, the purchaser purchases at his peril.[1] This seems to have been the ancient, and the uniform language of the English law, and the only writer of authority, that calls this doctrine in question is Professor Woodeson, in his Vinerian Lectures, and he does not cite any judicial decision as the basis of his opinion. In the case of Chandelor v. Lopus, (Cro. Jac. 4) it was determined a jewel, which was affirmed to be a bezoar stone, when it was not, no action lay, unless the defendant knew it was not a bezoar stone, or had warranted it to be one. This appears to me to be a case in point and decisive.[2] And in the case of Parkinson v. Lee, 2 East 315, it was decided that a fair merchantable price did not raise an implied warranty, and that if there was no warranty and the seller sells the thing, such as he believes it to be without fraud, he will not be liable for a latent defect.[3] These decisions are two centuries apart, and the intermediate cases, are to the same effect. Co. Litt. 102 a. Cro. J. 197, 1 Sid. 146 Yelv. 21.1 L. Raym. 1121. Per Holt, C.J. Doug. 20. Alleyn. 91, cited 2 East 298, notis. By the civil law, says L. Coke, every man is bound to warrant the thing that he selleth, albeit there be no express warranty; but the common law bindeth him not, unless there be a warranty in deed, or law. So Fitzherbert, (N.B. 94 C.) says, that if a man sells wine that is corrupted, or a horse that is diseased, and there be no warranty, it is at the buyer's peril, and his eyes and his taste ought to be his judges in that case.[4] In the case cited from 2 East, the judges were unanimous that the rule applied to sales of all kinds of commodities. That without a warranty by the seller, or fraud on his part, the buyer must stand to all losses arising from latent defects, and that there is no instance in the English law of a contrary rule being laid down. The civil law is more rigorous toward the seller, and makes him responsible in every case for a latent defect, (see the Dig. lib. 1. tit. 2, ch. 13. n. 1. which gives the very case

---

1. Is this the rule that governs in this case? As you read on, try to determine from where the rule came, and by what process the court applies it to the facts of the current case.

2. What does the court mean in describing the prior case in this way?

3. Notice the way in which the court uses different prior cases to explain or apply different parts of the governing legal rule. Although you might intuit that there will usually be a single prior decision that is applicable on all points to the current case, this is rarely true. More often, a court (and the advocates who have made these arguments to the court) must piece the governing law together from various sources of legal authority.

4. Consider the implications of this rule on the relationship between buyer and seller. Assuming that businesspeople operate with at least some understanding of the legal rules, their conduct will be affected by those rules. They will know what risks they take in sending others to do their inspecting, they will know how to protect themselves from their own lack of careful inspection, and presumably, they will know that the price of the goods will be affected by the terms of the contract.

of selling vitiated wood) and, if the question was res integra[5] in our law, I confess I should be overcome by the reasoning of the civilians.[6] And yet the rule of the common law has been well and elegantly vindicated by Fonblanque, as most happily reconciling the claims of convenience, with the duties of good faith. It requires the purchaser to apply his attention to those particulars, which may be supposed, within the reach of his observation and judgment, and the vendor to communicate, those particulars, and defects, which cannot be supposed to be immediately within the reach of such attention. And even against his want of vigilance, the purchaser may provide, by requiring the vendor expressly to warrant the article. The mentioning of the wood, as brazilletto wood, in the bill of parcels and in the advertisement some days previous to the sale, did not amount to a warranty to the plaintiffs. To make an affirmation at the time of the sale, a warranty, it must appear by evidence to be so intended, and not to have been a mere matter of judgment and opinion, and of which the defendant did not have particular knowledge. Here it is admitted, the defendant was equally ignorant with the plaintiffs, and could have had no such intention.

* * *

LEWIS, C. J. contra.[7]

Notes on *Seixas v. Woods*, 2 Cai. R. (N.Y.) 48, 2 Am. Dec. 215 (1805).

1. One question presented in this case was whether in the absence of an express warranty, the law would annex to the contract an implied one. For more on this question, *see, e.g., Bertram v. Lyon*, 3 F. Cas. 296, 1 McAll. 53 (1855).
2. What if the defendants-sellers were negligent in their description of the word 'brazilletto'? Could the plaintiff-buyer have recovered then? Consider the opinion of the court in *Withers v. Green*, 50 U.S. 213 (1850).
3. One of the other judges writing an opinion in the *Seixas* case described the buyer-seller relationship this way:
   "Fonblanque, in his valuable *Treatise of Equity*, speaking of the justice and propriety of this principle says, 'To excite that diligence which is necessary

---

5. What does this mean? Get used to routinely consulting both legal and standard English dictionaries as you read cases.

6. If free to do so, Judge Kent seems to say that he would apply the civil law rule. Why can he not do so? Are these constraints good? What would we call a judge who did not openly confess preference for a rule that was contrary to the jurisdiction's law (as Judge Kent did), but rather found a way to make the result be what it would be under that preferred but contrary to law rule? Would we call that judge creative, unprincipled, just, undisciplined, or something else?

7. Judge Kent said this was "a clear case." How can this be so if the chief judge disagrees?

to guard against imposition, and to secure that good faith which is necessary to justify a certain degree of confidence, is essential to the intercourse of society. These objects are attained by those rules of law which require the purchaser to apply his attention to those particulars, which may be supposed to be within the reach of his observation and judgment; and the vendor to communicate those particulars and defects, which cannot be supposed to be immediately within the reach of such attention. If the purchaser be wanting of attention to those points, where attention would have been sufficient to protect him from surprise or imposition, the maxim caveat emptor ought to apply. But even against this maxim he may provide, by requiring the vendor expressly to warrant that which the law would not imply to be warranted. If the vendor be wanting in good faith, fides servanda is the rule of law, and may be enforced, both in equity and at law.' "

Consider further the contractual relationship between the buyer and the seller. How do its attributes affect your evaluation of the following question: Assuming for the moment that Woods and the House in New Providence were no more than buyer and seller of the wood in this case, could Seixas have collected from the House in New Providence if it had been careless in its delivery to Woods of the peachum wood for brazilletto? What if the House had intentionally deceived Woods? What if it had made a warranty to Woods?

4. For a recent application of the rule in this *Seixas* case, *see In re: Dakota Country Food Stores, Inc.*, 107 Bankr. 977 (D.S.D. 1989).

Thomas and Wife v. Winchester

Court of Appeals of New York, 1852.
6 N.Y. 397.

Action in the supreme court, commenced in August, 1849, against Winchester and Gilbert, for injuries sustained by Mrs. Thomas, from the effects of a quantity of extract of belladonna, administered to her by mistake as extract of dandelion.

In the complaint it was alleged,[8] that the defendants from the year 1843, to the first of January, 1849, were engaged in putting up and vending certain vegetable extracts, at a store in the city of New York, designated as "108 John-

---

8. Why should we care what the Plaintiff's complaint said? How did the Thomases' case traverse the court system to reach the point at hand? Determining the procedural history of a case is crucial to understanding the significance of statements made in an opinion and the factual basis upon which the opinion is rendered. By what process did this dispute reach the decision-makers who are writing the opinion? Carefully examine this and every case to determine its procedural history, being careful not to confuse procedural facts with the facts of the parties' dispute.

street," and that the defendant Gilbert had for a long time previous thereto TO THAT
been so engaged, at the same place. That among the extracts so prepared and
sold by them, were those respectively known as the "extract of dandelion,"
and the "extract of belladonna;" the former a mild and harmless medicine,
and the latter a vegetable poison, which, if taken as a medicine in such quantity as might be safely administered of the former, would destroy the life, or
seriously impair the health of the person to whom the same might be administered. That at some time between the periods above mentioned, the defendants put up and sold to James S. Aspinwall, a druggist in the city of New York,
a jar of the extract of belladonna, which had been labeled by them as the extract of dandelion, and was purchased of them as such by said Aspinwall. That
said Aspinwall afterwards, and on the 10th day of May, 1845, relying upon the
label so affixed by the defendants, sold the said jar of belladonna to Alvin
Foord, a druggist of Cazenovia, in the county of Madison, as the extract of
dandelion. That afterwards, and on the 27th of March, 1849, the plaintiff
Mrs. Thomas, being sick, a portion of the extract of dandelion was prescribed
for her by her physician, and the said Alvin Foord, relying upon the label affixed by the defendants to said jar of belladonna, and believing the same to be
the extract of dandelion, did on the application of the plaintiff, Samuel
Thomas, sell and deliver to him from the said jar of belladonna, a portion of
its contents, which was administered to the plaintiff, Mrs. Thomas, under the
belief that it was the extract of dandelion; by which she was greatly injured,
so that her life was despaired of, etc. The plaintiffs also alleged that the whole
injury was occasioned by the negligence and unskillfulness of the defendants
in putting up and falsely labeling the jar of belladonna as the extract of dandelion, whereby the plaintiffs, as well as the druggists, and all other persons
through whose hands it passed before being administered as aforesaid, were
induced to believe, and did believe that it contained the extract of dandelion.
Wherefore, etc.

The defendants in their answers, severally denied the allegations of the complaint, and insisted that they were not liable for the medicines sold by Aspinwall and Foord.

The cause was tried at the Madison circuit, in December 1849, before Mason, J. The defendant Gilbert was acquitted by the jury under the direction of
the court, and a verdict was rendered against Winchester, for eight hundred
dollars. A motion for a new trial made upon a bill of exceptions taken at the
trial, having been denied at a general term in the sixth district, the defendant
Winchester, brought this appeal. The facts which appeared on the trial are sufficiently stated in the opinion of RUGGLES, Ch.J.

* * *

RUGGLES, Ch.J., delivered the opinion of the court.

This is an action brought to recover damages from the defendant for negligently putting up, labeling, and selling as and for the extract of dandelion, which is a simple and harmless medicine, a jar of the extract of belladonna, which is a deadly poison; by means of which the plaintiff Mary Ann Thomas, to whom, being sick, a dose of dandelion was prescribed by a physician, and a portion of the contents of the jar, was administered as and for the extract of dandelion, was greatly injured, etc.

The facts proved were briefly these: Mrs. Thomas being in ill health, her physician prescribed for her a dose of dandelion. Her husband purchased what was believed to be the medicine prescribed, at the store of Dr. Foord, a physician and druggist in Cazenovia, Madison County, where the plaintiffs reside.

A small quantity of the medicine thus purchased was administered to Mrs. Thomas on whom it produced very alarming effects; such as coldness of the surface and extremities, feebleness of circulation, spasms of the muscles, giddiness of the head, dilation of the pupils of the eyes, and derangement of mind. She recovered however, after some time, from its effects, although for a short time her life was thought to be in great danger. The medicine administered was belladonna, and not dandelion. The jar from which it was taken was labeled "1/2 lb. dandelion, prepared by A. Gilbert, No. 108 John-street, N.Y. Jar 8 oz." It was sold for and believed by Dr. Foord to be the extract of dandelion as labeled. Dr. Foord purchased the article as the extract of dandelion from Jas. S. Aspinwall, a druggist at New York. Aspinwall bought it of the defendant as extract of dandelion, believing it to be such. The defendant was engaged at No. 108 John-street, New York, in the manufacture and sale of certain vegetable extracts for medicinal purposes, and in the purchase and sale of others. The extracts manufactured by him were put up in jars for sale, and those which he purchased from others were put up by him in like manner. The jars containing extracts manufactured by himself and those containing extracts purchased by him from others, were labeled alike. Both were labeled like the jar in question, as "prepared by A. Gilbert." Gilbert was a person employed by the defendant at a salary, as an assistant in his business. The jars were labeled in Gilbert's name because he had been previously engaged in the same business on his own account at No. 108 John-street, and probably because Gilbert's labels rendered the articles more salable. The extract contained in the jar sold to Aspinwall, and by him to Foord, was not manufactured by the defendant, but was purchased by him from another manufacturer or dealer.

The extract of dandelion and the extract of belladonna resemble each other in color, consistence, smell, and taste; but may on careful examination be distinguished the one from the other by those who are well acquainted with these articles. Gilbert's labels were paid for by Winchester and used in his business with his knowledge and assent.

The defendant's counsel moved for a nonsuit on the following grounds:

1. That the action could not be sustained, as the defendant was the remote vendor of the article in question: and there was no connection, transaction, or privity between him and the plaintiffs, or either of them.

* * *

The case depends on the first point taken by the defendant on his motion for a nonsuit; and the question is, whether the defendant, being a remote vendor of the medicine, and there being no privity or connection between him and the plaintiffs, the action can be maintained.

If, in the labeling of a poisonous drug with the name of a harmless medicine, for public market, no duty was violated by the defendant, excepting that which he owned to Aspinwall, his immediate vendee, in virtue of his contract of sale, this action cannot be maintained. If A builds a wagon and sells it to B, who sells it to C, and C hires it to D, who in consequence of the gross negligence of A in building the wagon is overturned and injured, D cannot recover damages against A, the builder. A's obligation to build the wagon faithfully, arises solely out of his contract with B. The public have nothing to do with it. Misfortune to third persons, not parties to the contract, would not be a natural and necessary consequence of the builder's negligence; and such negligence is not an act imminently dangerous to human life.

So, for the same reason, if a horse be defectively shod by a smith, and a person hiring the horse from the owner is thrown and injured in consequence of the smith's negligence in shoeing, the smith is not liable for the injury. The smith's duty in such case grows exclusively out of his contract with the owner of the horse; it was a duty which the smith owed to him alone, and to no one else. And although the injury to the rider may have happened in consequence of the negligence of the smith, the latter was not bound, either by his contract or by any considerations of public policy or safety, to respond for his breach of duty to any one except the person he contracted with.

This was the ground on which the case of Winterbottom v. Wright, 10 Mees. & Welsb. 109, was decided. A contracted with the postmaster general to provide a coach to convey the mail bags along a certain line of road, and B and others also contracted to horse the coach along the same line. B and his cocontractors hired C, who was the plaintiff, to drive the coach. The coach, in consequence of some latent defect, broke down; the plaintiff was thrown from his seat and lamed. It was held that C could not maintain an action against A for the injury thus sustained. The reason of the decision is best stated by Baron Rolfe. A's duty to keep the coach in good condition, was a duty to the postmaster general, with whom he made his contract, and not a duty to the driver employed by the owners of the horses.[9]

---

9. Here the court seems to be offering the rationale for the general rule to prepare for

But the case in hand stands on a different ground. The defendant was a dealer in poisonous drugs. Gilbert was his agent in preparing them for market. The death or great bodily harm of some person was the natural and almost inevitable consequence of the sale of belladonna by means of the false label.[10]

Gilbert, the defendant's agent, would have been punishable for manslaughter if Mrs. Thomas had died in consequence of taking the falsely labeled medicine.[11] Every man who, by his culpable negligence, causes the death of another, although without intent to kill, is guilty of manslaughter. 2 R.S. 662, Section 19. A chemist who negligently sells laudanum in a phial labeled as paregoric, and thereby causes the death of a person to whom it is administered, is guilty of manslaughter. Tessymond's case, 1 Lewin's Crown Cases, 169. "So highly does the law value human life that it admits of no justification wherever life has been lost and the carelessness or negligence of one person has contributed to the death of another." Regina v. Swindall, 2 Car. & Kir. 232-3. And this rule applies not only where the death of one is occasioned by the negligent act of another, but where it is caused by the negligent omission of a duty of that other. 2 Car. & Kir. 368, 371. Although the defendant Winchester may not be answerable criminally for the negligence of his agent, there can be no doubt of his liability in a civil action, in which the act of the agent is to be regarded as the act of the principal.

In respect to the wrongful and criminal character of the negligence complained of, this case differs widely from those put by the defendant's counsel. No such imminent danger existed in those cases. In the present case the sale of the poisonous article was made to a dealer in drugs, and not to a consumer. The injury therefore was not likely to fall on him, or on his vendee who was also a dealer; but much more likely to be visited on a remote purchaser as actually happened.[12] The defendant's negligence put human life in imminent[13]

---

its application of that rule. As we shall see, the reasons supporting a common law rule are crucial to an understanding (and application of) that rule.

10. Consider as you read on whether this is the reason supporting the distinction that the court draws.

11. Or is this the reason?

12. The court distinguishes this case from Winterbottom v. Wright. Are the comparisons and analogies drawn reasonable? Are not both injured parties among the group of people most likely to be injured by the maker's negligence? If they are among this group, then the court's use of Winterbottom should tell us that the Thomas rule is not that "a party has a right of action against a negligent maker of goods when the negligence results in the party's injury and the party is among those most likely to be injured by the maker's negligence." The rule must be different or at the least require more.

13. The precise use of language (and from the opposite end of the communication process, careful reading) is vital to legal communication. What if the court had said "inherent danger" rather than "imminent danger" here. Notice that the word "imminent" allows for a focus on the defendant's conduct, while the word "inherent" here would focus the reader more on the thing sold. Think about this subtle but important distinction as you read this and the next few cases.

danger. Can it be said that there was no duty on the part of the defendant, to avoid the creation of that danger by the exercise of greater caution? Or that the exercise of that caution was a duty only to his immediate vendee, whose life was not endangered? The defendant's duty arose out of the nature of his business and the danger to others incident to its mismanagement. Nothing but mischief like that which actually happened could have been expected from sending the poison falsely labeled into the market; and the defendant is justly responsible for the probable consequences of the act. The duty of exercising caution in this respect did not arise out of the defendant's contract of sale to Aspinwall. The wrong done by the defendant was in putting the poison, mislabeled, into the hands of Aspinwall as an article of merchandise to be sold and afterwards used as the extract of dandelion, by some person then unknown. The owner of a horse and cart who leaves them unattended in the street is liable for any damage which may result from his negligence. Lynch v. Nurdin, 1 Ad. & Ellis, N.S. 29; Illidge v. Goodwin, 5 Car. & Payne, 190. The owner of a loaded gun who puts it into the hands of a child by whose indiscretion it is discharged, is liable for the damage occasioned by the discharge.[14] 5 Maule & Sel. 198. The defendant's contract of sale to Aspinwall does not excuse the wrong done to the plaintiffs. It was a part of the means by which the wrong was effected. The plaintiff's injury and their remedy would have stood on the same principle, if the defendant had given the belladonna to Dr. Foord without price, or if he had put it in his shop without his knowledge, under circumstances which would probably have led to its sale on the faith of the label.

The defendant, on the trial, insisted that Aspinwall and Foord were guilty of negligence in selling the article in question for what it was represented to be in the label; and that the suit, if it could be sustained at all, should have been brought against Foord. The judge charged the jury that if they, or either of them, were guilty of negligence in selling the belladonna for dandelion, the verdict must be for the defendant; and left the question of their negligence to the jury, who found on that point for the plaintiff.[15] If the case really depended on the point thus raised, the question was properly left to the jury. But I think it did not. The defendant by affixing the label to the jar, represented its contents to be dandelion; and to have been "prepared" by his agent Gilbert. The

---

14. Notice that these last two examples are absent the element of a sale. Is the court drawing poor analogies, or could it be that the contract of sale is less important in the context of this new rule?

15. We know that Foord and Aspinwall were not negligent because the trial jury said so. For purposes of this appeal, the court must operate on that basis. Consider the journey that a fact takes from being, to being explained by a client or witness to a lawyer, to being synthesized from various sources by a lawyer, to being presented to a trial court, to being found by a trial jury, to being relied on as truth by an appellate court.

word "prepared" on the label, must be understood to mean that the article was manufactured by him, or that it had passed through some process under his hands, which would give him personal knowledge of its true name and quality. Whether Foord was justified in selling the article upon the faith of the defendant's label, would have been an open question in an action by the plaintiffs against him, and I wish to be understood as giving no opinion on that point. But it seems to me to be clear that the defendant cannot, in this case, set up as a defense, that Foord sold the contents of the jar as and for what the defendant represented it to be. The label conveyed the idea distinctly to Foord that the contents of the jar was the extract of dandelion; and that the defendant knew it to be such. So far as the defendant is concerned, Foord was under no obligation to test the truth of the representation. The charge of the judge in submitting to the jury the question in relation to the negligence of Foord and Aspinwall, cannot be complained of by the defendant.

GARDINER, J. concurred in affirming the judgment, on the ground that selling the belladonna without a label indicating that it was a poison, was declared a misdemeanor by statute (2 R.S. 694, Section 23;) but expressed no opinion upon the question whether, independent of the statute, the defendant would have been liable to these plaintiffs.

* * *

Judgment affirmed.

Notes on *Thomas v. Winchester*, 6 N.Y. 397 (1852).

1. It has been said that *Winterbottom v. Wright*, 10 M. & W. 109, 152 Eng. Rep. 402 (1842), was misinterpreted to state a general rule of nonliability of any contractor, including the supplier of a product, to third parties, whether in contract or tort. See, e.g., Bohlen, *The Basis of Affirmative Obligations in the Law of Torts*, 53 U. PA. L. REV. 209 (1905).

2. Courts have continued to cite *Thomas v. Winchester* as the point of origin of the "dangerous instrumentality" theory (that is, with a focus more on the product than on the defendant's conduct). For example, Note, *Tort Liability to Third Parties Arising from Breach of Contract*, 14 MD. L. REV. 77 (1954), discusses the further extension of the *Thomas* theory in the context of *Otis Elevator v. Embert*, 198 Md. 585, 84 A.2d 876 (1951). The author stated that New York doctrine had developed so well that it was held that "an elevator is a dangerous instrumentality within the doctrine of *Thomas* and that one who contracted to repair an elevator owed the same duty to third persons as a manufacturer."

3. The decision in *Winterbottom* reflected the original common law rule. For a statement of the current law, *see* RESTATEMENT (SECOND) OF TORTS § 395 (1989 Supp.) (Negligent Manufacture of Chattel Dangerous Unless Carefully Made).

Loop v. Litchfield

Court of Appeals of New York, 1870.
42 N.Y. 351.

Appeal from a judgment of the General Term in the fourth district, reversing a judgment entered upon a verdict in favor of the plaintiffs, and ordering a new trial.[16]

* * *

The complaint alleged that in 1861 the defendants were partners in manufacturing iron castings and machinery, and made a cast-iron balance wheel to be used with a circular saw. That the balance wheel had a large hole in its rim, occasioned by negligence in casting it, by which its thickness and strength were diminished, and by defendants' wrongful act this hole was concealed by filling it with lead and finishing the surface of the rim so as to resemble a sound wheel. The strength of the rim was further diminished by boring through it, so as to insert a rivet to hold the lead in the hole, and by the wrongful act of defendants they sold this wheel to Leverett Collister as a sound wheel and fit for use. That in 1864 Collister leased to Jeremiah Loop a frame for a circular wood saw, to be used with a circular saw for the purpose of sawing wood, to the arbor shaft on which frame said balance wheel was attached. That Loop put a saw on the arbor, and used the saw, balance wheel and frame in sawing wood for himself and Collister and for others, without knowledge of the hole in the rim of the balance wheel, and in the belief that it was a sound balance wheel and fit for use. That in October 1866, Loop was so using the saw and balance wheel attached in sawing wood for one Van Rensselaer Loop, in a careful and prudent manner, when the balance wheel burst in the hole in its rim and directly through the hole made to insert the rivet to hold the lead in its place. That such bursting was caused by said hole and boring in the rim, and that a fragment of the wheel when it burst hit Jeremiah Loop in his side and inflicted a mortal wound of which he died on the 29th of October 1866. That such death was occasioned by said wrongful act and negligence of defendants, and plaintiffs bring this action as his legal representatives, for the benefit of his widow and next of kin. There was a motion for a nonsuit at the close of the plaintiffs' evidence and also at the close of all the evidence in the case, on the ground, amongst others, that the plaintiffs had failed to make out a case entitling them to recover; and to the refusal of the court denying this motion, the defendants excepted. There was evidence tending to show that

---

16. In 1870, New York law required plaintiffs to stipulate that if the Court of Appeals agreed with the General Term, judgment should be entered for the defendants and no new trial conducted.

when the defendants sold the wheel to Collister they pointed out to him the defect in the rim of the wheel, and that lead was fastened in the hole by means of a rivet, and that Collister selected and purchased it with full knowledge of such effect, because it was lighter and cheaper than heavier balance wheels which the defendants were accustomed to put upon horse-power for sawing wood, and after he was informed of that fact. The judge stated that the only question upon which counsel could go to the jury would be, whether, in the manufacture and sale of the balance wheel, the defendants were guilty of negligence which negligence produced the injury complained of.

* * *

HUNT, J. A piece of machinery already made and on hand, having defects which weaken it, is sold by the manufacturer to one who buys it for his own use. The defects are pointed out to the purchaser and are fully understood by him. This piece of machinery is used by the buyer for five years, and is then taken into the possession of a neighbor, who uses it for his own purposes. While so in use, it flies apart by reason of its original defects, and the person using it is killed. Is the seller, upon this state of facts, liable to the representatives of the deceased party?

* * *

To maintain this liability, the appellants rely upon the case of Thomas v. Winchester (6 N.Y., 2 Seld., 397).

* * *

The appellants recognize the principle of this decision, and seek to bring their case within it, by asserting that the fly wheel in question was a dangerous instrument.[17] Poison is a dangerous subject. Gunpowder is the same. A torpedo is a dangerous instrument, as is a spring gun, a loaded rifle, or the like. They are instruments and articles in their nature calculated to do injury to mankind, and generally intended to accomplish that purpose. They are essentially, and in their elements, instruments of danger.[18] Not so, however, an iron wheel, a few feet in diameter and a few inches in thickness although one part may be weaker than another. If the article is abused by too long use, or by applying too much weight or speed, an injury may occur, as it may from an ordinary carriage wheel, a wagon axle, or the common chair in which we sit. There is scarcely an object in art or nature, from which an injury may not oc-

---

17. Is this what is required to make the Thomas rule operate? Was the inherent danger of the article (poison) the reason that supported the Thomas court in creating the rule?

18. Notice this court's focus on the nature of the item that seems to have caused the harm. Consider again the choice of words, "imminent" or "inherent."

cur under such circumstances. Yet they are not in their nature sources of danger, nor can they, with any regard to the accurate use of language, be called dangerous instruments. That an injury actually occurred by the breaking of a carriage axle, the failure of the carriage body, the falling pieces of a chair or sofa, or the bursting of a fly wheel, does not in the least alter its character.

It is suggested that it is no more dangerous or illegal to label a deadly poison as a harmless medicine than to conceal a defect in a machine and paint it over so that it will appear sound. Waiving the point that there was no concealment, but the defect was fully explained to the purchaser, I answer, that the decision in Thomas v. Winchester was based upon the idea that the negligent sale of poisons is both at common law and by statute an indictable offence.[19] If the act in that case had been done by the defendant instead of his agent, and the death of Mrs. Thomas had ensued, the defendant would have been guilty of manslaughter, as held by the court. The injury in that case was a natural result of the act. It was just what was to have been expected from putting falsely labeled poisons in the market, to be used by whoever should need the true articles. It was in its nature an act imminently dangerous to the lives of others. Not so here. The bursting of the wheel and the injury to human life was not the natural result or the expected consequence of the manufacture and sale of the wheel. Every use of the counterfeit medicines would be necessarily injurious, while this wheel was in fact used with safety for five years.

It is said that the verdict of the jury established the fact that this wheel was a dangerous instrument. I do not see how this can be, when there is no such allegation in the complaint, and no such question was submitted to the jury. "The court stated to the counsel that the only question on which they would go to the jury would be that of negligence. Whether in the manufacture and sale of this article, the defendants are guilty of negligence, which negligence produced the injury complained of." If the action had been for negligence in constructing a carriage, sold by the defendants to Collister, by him lent to the deceased, which had broken down, through the negligence of its construction, it might have been contended with the same propriety, that the finding of those facts by the jury established that a carriage was a dangerous instrument, and thereby the liability of the defendants became fixed. The jury found simply that there was negligence in the construction of the wheel and that the injury resulted there-from. It is quite illogical to deduce from this, the conclusion that the wheel was itself a dangerous instrument.

Upon the facts as stated . . . I am of the opinion that the verdict cannot be sustained. The facts constitute no cause of action.

---

19. Now the court seems to be relying on a different rationale for the Thomas rule as the basis for distinguishing the present case from the facts of the Thomas case. To what extent was this rationale important in Thomas? Will it be important in subsequent cases?

Notes on *Loop v. Litchfield,* 42 N.Y. 351 (1870).

1. The court in this case attempted to clarify and restrict its earlier decision in *Thomas v. Winchester* by conditioning liability on the "imminently dangerous" nature of the flywheel. Examine how the court characterizes the defective wheel. Does the acceptance of the characterization suit the differing results in *Winterbottom v. Wright* and *Thomas v. Winchester?*
2. Did the court change the privity rule and its exception or did it merely apply the existing rule to new facts? Does this application-function alone serve to change the rule?

Losee v. Clute

Commission of Appeals of New York, 1873.
51 N.Y. 494.

Appeal from judgment of the General Term of the Supreme Court in the fourth judicial district, affirming a judgment entered upon an order dismissing plaintiff's complaint on the trial.[20]

The action was brought to recover damages caused to the property of the plaintiff by the explosion of a steam boiler while the same was owned and being used by the Saratoga Paper Company at their mill situated in the village of Schuylerville, Saratoga County and State of New York, on the thirteenth day of February, 1864, by means whereof the boiler was thrown onto the plaintiff's premises and through several of his buildings, thereby injuring and damaging the same.

The defendants, Clute, were made parties defendants to the action with the Saratoga Paper Company and Coe S. Buchanan and Daniel A. Bullard, trustees and agents of said company, on the grounds that they were the manufacturers of the boiler, and made the same out of poor and brittle iron and in a negligent and defective manner, in consequence of which negligence said explosion occurred.

At the close of the evidence the complaint was dismissed as to the defendants Clute.

* * *

LOTT, Ch. C. It appears by the case that the defendants Clute manufactured the boiler in question for the Saratoga Paper Company . . . for the purposes and uses to which it was subsequently applied by it; and the testimony tended to show that it was constructed improperly and of poor iron, that the said de-

20. Again, consider the procedural history. To which set of facts is the appellate court tied? Is the appellate court tied to one particular version of the facts? Why or why not?

fendants knew at the time that it was to be used in the immediate vicinity of and adjacent to dwelling houses and stores in a village, so that, in case of an explosion while in use, it would be likely to be destructive to human life and adjacent property, and that, in consequence of the negligence of the said defendants in the improper construction of the boiler, the explosion that took place occurred and damaged the plaintiff's property. The evidence also tended to show that the boiler was tested by the company to its satisfaction, and then accepted, and was thereafter used by it for about three months prior to the explosion, and that after such test and acceptance the said defendants had nothing whatever to do with the boiler, and had no care or management of it at the time of the explosion, but that the company had the sole and exclusive ownership, management, and conduct of it.

In determining whether the complaint was properly dismissed, we must assume all the facts which the evidence tended to show as established, and the question is thereby presented whether the defendants have incurred any liability to the plaintiff. They contracted with the company and did what was done by them for it and to its satisfaction, and when the boiler was accepted they ceased to have any further control over it or its management, and all responsibility for what was subsequently done with it devolved upon the company and those having charge of it, and the case falls within the principle decided by the Court of Appeals in The Mayor, etc., of Albany v. Cunliff, 2 Comst., N. Y., 165, which is, that the mere architect or builder of a work is answerable only to his employees for any want of care or skill in the execution thereof, and he is not liable for accidents or injuries which may occur after the execution of the work; and the opinions published in that case clearly show that there is no ground of liability by the defendants to the plaintiff in this action. They owed him no duty whatever at the time of the explosion either growing out of contract or imposed by law.

It may be proper to refer to the case of Thomas v. Winchester, 2 Selden 397, 57 Am. Dec. 455, cited by the appellant's counsel, and I deem it sufficient to say that the opinion of Hunt, J., in Loop v. Litchfield, 42 N. Y. 351, 1 Am. Rep. 513, clearly shows that the principle decided in that case has no application to this.[21]

It appears from these considerations that the complaint was properly dismissed, and it follows that there was no case made for the consideration of the jury and, consequently, there was no error in the refusal to submit it to them.

---

21. Notice the court's shorthand way of using and applying authority. As a law student or lawyer trying to interpret this case, one can only assume that this court had in mind the rule and its rationale from the prior case when making this sort of statement. Apparently the court deems the analogy from the Loop case to the present case and the distinction between the Thomas case and the present case so clear as to require no explanation.

There was an exception taken to the exclusion of evidence to show that two persons were killed by this boiler in passing through a dwelling house in its course, but as it is not urged on this appeal, it is, I presume, abandoned; but if not, it was matter, as the judge held at the trial, wholly immaterial to the issue between the parties in this action.

There is, for the reasons stated, no ground for the reversal of the judgment. It must, therefore, be affirmed, with costs.

All concur.

* * *

Notes on *Losee v. Clute*, 51 N.Y. 494 (1873).

1. Consider a similar case in which it was held that no contractual relationship existed between the manufacturer of defective natural gas fixtures and the installers of such fixtures; therefore, the manufacturer was not held liable for injuries sustained when the fixtures exploded because, in the eyes of the court, natural gas is not in and of itself dangerous. *Bailey v. Gas Co.*, 4 Ohio Cir. Ct. R. 471. *See also Burdick v. Cheadle*, 26 Ohio St. 393 (1875); *Roddy v. Missouri Pac. Ry. Co.*, 204 Mo. 234, 15 S.W. 1112 (1891).

2. The boiler in *Losee* took 3 months to explode, the *Loop* wheel 5 years. What does "imminent" mean?

3. The court seems interested in the inspection that buyers did of the boiler. If it did, why should the inspection by the buyer of the boiler diminish the manufacturer's liability to the plaintiff? *See Richmond and D. R. Co. v. Elliot*, 149 U.S. 266 (1893). In that case the court did not hold defendant company liable to an injured third party because a reasonable inspection of the subject engine was conducted by the company and inspection did not expose the dangerous latent defect.

4. Dr. Thompson in the first volume of his work on Negligence states that "[*Losee*] seems not only clearly at variance with *Thomas v. Winchester*, but unsound in principle." THOMPSON ON NEGLIGENCE, Chapter IV, §2 (1880). Dr. Thompson reasoned that steam boilers are highly dangerous, even when properly constructed, and when defectively constructed, are likely to explode, posing a likely threat to innocent persons. Does Thompson regard the appropriate analogies to examine in these cases as being between poisons and boilers or between mislabelled poisons and defective boilers?

Devlin v. Smith

Court of Appeals of New York, 1882.
89 N. Y. 470

Appeal from judgment of the General Term of the Supreme Court, in the second judicial department, entered upon an order made December 12, 1881, which affirmed a judgment entered upon an order dismissing plaintiff's complaint on trial. (Reported below, 25 Hun, 206.)

This action was brought to recover damages for alleged negligence, causing the death of Hugh Devlin, plaintiff's intestate.

Defendant Smith entered into a contract with the supervisors of the county of Kings, by which he agreed to paint the inside of the dome of the court-house in that county. Smith was not a scaffold-builder, and knew nothing of that business. He entered into a contract with defendant Stevenson, who was an experienced scaffold-builder, and had been previously employed by Smith, to build the necessary scaffold. This was to be of the best materials, and first-class in every way. Stevenson built the scaffold of poles were lashed with roped; these were called ledgers. Upon these ledgers, plank were placed, and upon the top of each section so constructed, was placed another, similarly constructed. When the scaffolding reached the curve of the dome, it was necessary to lessen the width of the upper section. For this purpose a strip of plank was used as an upright to support the end of the shorter ledger. This upright was called a cripple; but instead of fastening the ledger to it by lashing, it was fastened by nailing. The scaffold was ninety feet in height.

Devlin was a workman in Smith's employ. He was working on the curve of the dome, and sitting on a plank laid upon a ledger which was nailed to an upright or cripple, as above described, when the ledger gave way and broke. He was precipitated to the floor below, and so injured that he died soon after.

RAPALLO, J. Upon a careful review of all the testimony in this case, we are of opinion that there was sufficient evidence to require the submission to the jury of the question, whether the breaking down of the scaffold was attributable to negligence in its construction. It appears that the ledger which supported the plank upon which the deceased was sitting broke down without any excessive weight being put upon it, and without any apparent cause sufficient to break a well constructed scaffold. One witness on the part of the plaintiff, accustomed to work on scaffolds and to see them built, testified that the upright which supported the end of the ledger should have been fastened to it by lashing with ropes, instead of by nailing, and that lashing would have made it stronger, giving as reasons for this opinion, that the springing of the planks when walked upon was liable to break nails or push them out, whereas lashings would only become tighter, and the witness testified that the kind of scaffold in question was generally fastened by lashing and that it was not the proper way to support the end of the ledger which broke with an upright nailed to the ledger, and that the ledger in question was fastened by nailing.

* * *

[W]e think that on the whole evidence it was a question of fact for the jury, and not of law for the court, whether or not the injury was the result of the negligent construction of the scaffold.

* * *

[T]he remaining question is, whether, if those facts should be found, the defendants, or either of them, should be held liable in this action.

The defendant Smith claims that no negligence on his part was shown.

[The Court decided to affirm the dismissal of the complaint as to the defendant Smith. Ed.]

If any person was at fault in the matter it was the defendant Stevenson. It is contended, however, that even if through his negligence the scaffold was defective, he is not liable in this action, because there was no privity between him and the deceased, and he owed no duty to the deceased, his obligation and duty being only to Smith, with whom he contracted.

As a general rule the builder of a structure for another party, under a contract with him or one who sells an article of his own manufacture, is not liable to an action by a third party who uses the same with the consent of the owner or purchaser, for injuries resulting from a defect therein, caused by negligence. The liability of the builder or manufacturer for such defects is in general , only to the person with whom he contracted. But, notwithstanding this rule, liability to third parties has been held to exit when the defect is such as to render the article in itself imminently[22] dangerous, and serious injury to any person using it is a natural and probable consequence of its use. As where a dealer in drugs carelessly labeled a deadly poison as a harmless medicine, it was held that he was liable not merely to the person to whom he sold it, but to the person who ultimately used it, though it had passed through many hands. This liability was held to rest, not upon any contract or direct privity between him and the party injured, but upon the duty which the law imposes on every one to avoid acts in their nature dangerous to the lives of others. Thomas v. Winchester, 6 N.Y. 397, 57 Am.Dec. 455. In that case Mayor, etc., v. Cunliff, 2 N.Y. 165 was cited as an authority for the position that a builder is liable only to the party for whom he builds. Some of the examples there put by way of illustration were commented upon, and among others the case of won who builds a carriage carelessly and of defective materials, and sells it and the pur-

---

22. Here we have the word choice again. Here the court uses "imminent" to describe the danger and talks of the defect rather than the inherent nature of the article.

chaser lends it to a friend, and the carriage, by reason of its original defect, breaks down and the friend is injured, and the question is put, can he recover against the maker? The comments of Ruggles, Ch. J., upon this suppositious case, in Thomas v. Winchester, and the ground upon which he answers the question in the negative, show clearly the distinction between the two classes of cases. He says that in the case supposed, the obligation of the maker to build faithfully arises only out of his contract with the purchaser. The public having nothing to do with it. Misfortunes to third persons, not parties to the contract, would not be a natural and necessary consequence of the builder's negligence, and such negligence is not an act imminently dangerous to human life.

Applying these tests to the question now before us, the solution is not difficult. Stevenson undertook to build a scaffold ninety feet in height,[23] for the express purpose of enabling the workmen of Smith to stand upon it to paint the interior of the dome. Any defect or negligence in its construction, which should cause it to give way, would naturally result in these men being precipitated from that great height. A stronger case where misfortune to third persons not parties to the contract would be a natural and necessary consequence to the builder's negligence, can hardly be supposed, nor is it easy to imagine a more apt illustration of a case where such negligence would be an act imminently dangerous to human life. These circumstances seem to us to bring the case fairly within the principle of Thomas v. Winchester.

The same principle was recognized in Coughtry v. The Globe Woolen Co. (56 N.Y. 124), and applied to the case of a scaffold. It is true there was in that case the additional fact that the scaffold was erected by the defendant upon its own premises, but the case did not depend wholly upon that point. The scaffold was erected under a contract between the defendant and the employers of the person killed. The deceased was not a party to that contract, and the same argument was made as is urged here on the part of the defendant, that the latter owed no duty to the deceased; but this court held that in view of the facts that the scaffold was upwards of fifty feet from the ground, and unless properly constructed was a most dangerous trap, imperiling the life of any person who might go upon it, and that it was erected for the very purpose of accommodating the workmen, of whom the person killed was one, there was a duty toward them resting upon the defendant, independent of the contract under which the structure was built, to use proper diligence in its construction. The additional fact that the structure was on the premises of the defendant was relied upon, but we think that, even in the absence of that feature, the liability can rest upon the principle of Thomas v. Winchester.

---

23. The Loop court talked about the metal wheel, five feet in diameter, not about its place in the machine and the speed at which it might be spinning. Why should the Devlin court talk about the scaffold being ninety feet high rather than being some rope, wood and nails?

Loop v. Litchfield (42 N.Y. 351, 1 Am. Rep 543) was decided upon the grounds that the wheel which caused the injury was not in itself a dangerous instrument, and that the injury was not a natural consequence of the defect or one reasonably to be anticipated. Losee v. Clute (51 N.Y. 494, 10 Am. Rep. 638) was distinguished from Thomas v. Winchester, upon the authority of Loop v Litchfield.[24]

We think there should be a new trial as to the defendant Stevenson, and that it will be for the jury to determine whether the death of the plaintiff's intestate was caused by negligence on the part of Stevenson in the construction of the scaffold.

The judgment should be affirmed, with costs, as to the defendant Smith, and reversed as to the defendant Stevenson, and a new trial ordered as to him, costs to abide the event.

Judgment accordingly.[25]

* * *

Notes on *Devlin v. Smith*, 89 N.Y. 470 (1882).

1. Was defendant negligent? Consider if he would have been negligent under the rule of *Goullon v. Ford Motor Company*, 44 F.2d 310 (6th Cir. 1930), in which the court ruled that a manufacturer of an article reasonably certain to imperil life and limb if negligently made, who knows it will be used without new tests by persons other than the purchaser, must make the item carefully, irrespective of contract.
2. For a thorough discussion of the duty of care owed to recipients of unreasonably dangerous chattels, *see* James, *Products Liability*, 34 TEX. L. REV. 44 (1955).
3. For a general discussion of duty of care, review PROSSER, HANDBOOK OF THE LAW OF TORTS §53 (5th ed. 1984).
4. The case of *Goodlander Mill Co. v. Standard Oil Co.*, 63 F. 400 (7th Cir. 1894), provides an interesting discussion as to whether crude petroleum properly may be classified as a "dangerous agency" within the meaning of the rule set forth in *Devlin v. Smith*.

---

24. Notice again (and begin to feel the frustration presented by) a court's shorthand use of authority to replace analysis.
25. Review the procedural history. Do Hugh Devlin's kin get their money after this opinion is rendered?

MacPherson v. Buick Motor Co.

Court of Appeals of New York, 1916.
217 N.Y. 382, 111 N.E. 1050.

Appeal, by permission, from a judgment of the Appellate Division of the
Supreme Court in the third judicial department, entered January 8, 1914, affirming a judgment in favor of plaintiff entered upon a verdict.

* * *

CARDOZO, J. The defendant is a manufacturer of automobiles. It sold an
automobile to a retail dealer. The retail dealer resold to the plaintiff. While the
plaintiff was in the car, it suddenly collapsed. He was thrown out and injured.
One of the wheels was made of defective wood, and its spokes crumbled into
fragments. The wheel was not made by the defendant; it was bought from another manufacturer. There is evidence, however, that its defects could have
been discovered by reasonable inspection, and that inspection was omitted.
There is no claim that the defendant knew of the defect and wilfully concealed
it. The case, in other words, is not brought within the rule of Kuelling v. Lean
Mfg. Co., 183 N.Y. 78, 75 N.E. 1098, 2 L.P.A., N.S. 303, 111 Am. St. Rep.
691, 5 Ann. Cas. 124. The charge is one not of fraud, but of negligence. The
question to be determined is whether the defendant owed a duty of care and
vigilance to any one but the immediate purchaser.

The foundations of this branch of the law, at least in this state, were laid in
Thomas v. Winchester, 6 N.Y. 397. A poison was falsely labeled. The sale was
made to a druggist, who in turn sold to a customer. The customer recovered
damages from the seller who affixed the label. "The defendant's negligence,"
it was said, "put human life in imminent danger." A poison falsely labeled is
likely to injure any one who gets it. Because the danger is to be foreseen, there
is a duty to avoid the injury. Cases were cited by way of illustration in which
manufacturers were not subject to any duty irrespective of contract. The distinction was said to be that their conduct, though negligent, was not likely to
result in injury to any one except the purchaser. We are not required to say
whether the chance of injury was always as remote as the distinction assumes.
Some of the illustrations might be rejected today. The principle of the distinction is for present purposes the important thing.[26]

Thomas v. Winchester became quickly a landmark of the law. In the application of its principle there may at times have been uncertainty or even error.

---

26. Have you found these first two paragraphs of Justice Cardozo's opinion easier to
read than the previous opinions? Notice the use of verbs that convey a significant part of
the meaning in nearly every sentence, the shorter, simpler sentences and the absence of
unnecessarily formal language.

There has never in this state been doubt or disavowal of the principle itself. The chief cases are well known, yet to recall some of them will be helpful. Loop v. Litchfield, 42 N.Y. 351, 1 Am. Rep. 513, is the earliest. It was the case of a defect in a small balance wheel used on a circular saw. The manufacturer pointed out the defect to the buyer, who wished a cheap article and was ready to assume the risk. The risk can hardly have been an imminent one, for the wheel lasted five years before it broke. In the meanwhile the buyer had made a lease of the machinery. It was held that the manufacturer was not answerable to the lessee. Loop v. Litchfield was followed in Losee v. Clute, 51 N.Y. 494, 10 Am. Rep. 638, the case of the explosion of a steam boiler. That decision has been criticized (Thompson on Negligence, 233; Shearman & Redfield on Negligence [6th ed.], § 117); but it must be confined to its facts. It was put upon the ground that the risk of injury was too remote. The buyer in that case had not only accepted the boiler, but had tested it. The manufacturer knew that his own test was not the final one. The finality of the test has a bearing on the measure of diligence owing to persons other than the purchaser. Beven, Negligence (3d ed.). pp. 50, 51, 54; Wharton, Negligence (2d ed.) §134.

These early cases suggest a narrow construction of the rule. Later cases, however, evince a more liberal spirit. First in importance is Devlin v. Smith, 89 N.Y. 470, 42 Am. Rep. 311. The defendant, a contractor, built a scaffold for a painter. The painter's servants were injured. The contractor was held liable. He knew that the scaffold, if improperly constructed, was a most dangerous trap. He knew that it was to be used by the workmen. He was building it for that very purpose. Building it for their use, he owed them a duty, irrespective of his contract with their master, to build it with care.

From Devlin v. Smith we pass over intermediate cases and turn to the latest case in this court in which Thomas v. Winchester was followed. That case is Statler v. Ray Mfg. Co., 195 N.Y. 478, 480, 88, N.E. 1063. The defendant manufactured a large coffee urn. It was installed in a restaurant. When heated, the urn exploded and injured the plaintiff. We held that the manufacturer was liable. We said that the urn "was of such a character inherently that, when applied to the purposes for which it was designed, it was liable to become a source of great danger to many people if not carefully and properly constructed."

It may be that Devlin v. Smith and Statler v. Ray Mfg. Co. have extended the rule of Thomas v. Winchester. If so, this court is committed to the extension. The defendant argues that things imminently dangerous to life are poisons, explosives, deadly weapons—things whose normal function it is to injure or destroy.[27] But whatever the rule in Thomas v. Winchester may once have

---

27. Appreciate this court's direct confrontation of the difference between the two interpretations that have troubled us in the earlier opinions. We have seen that courts do not always explain the way they approach the questions they face.

been,[28] it has no longer that restricted meaning. A scaffold (Devlin v. Smith, supra) is not inherently a destructive instrument. It becomes destructive only if imperfectly constructed. A large coffee urn (Statler v. Ray Mfg. Co., supra) may have within itself, if negligently made, the potency of danger, yet no one thinks of it as an implement whose normal function is destruction. What is true of the coffee urn is equally true of bottles of aerated water, Torgeson v. Schultz, 192 N.Y. 156, 84 N.E. 956, 18 L.R.A., N.S., 726, 127 Am. St. Rep. 894. We have mentioned only cases in this court. But the rule has received a like extension in our courts of intermediate appeal. In Burke v. Ireland, 26 App. Div. 487, 50 N.Y.S. 369, in an opinion by Culen, J., it was applied to a builder who constructed a defective building; in Kahner v. Otis Elevator Co., 96 App. Div. 169, 89 N.Y.S. 185, to the manufacturer of an elevator; in Davies v. Pelham Hod Elevating Co., 65 Hum 573, 20 N.Y.S. 523, affirmed in this court without opinion, 146 N.Y. 363, 41 N.E. 88, to a contractor who furnished a defective rope with knowledge of the purpose for which the rope was to be used. We are not required at this time either to approve or to disapprove the application of the rule that was made in these cases. It is enough that they help to characterize the trend of judicial thought.

Devlin v. Smith was decided in 1882. A year later a very similar case came before the Court of Appeal in England (Heavan v. Pender, L.R. [11 Q.B.D.] 503). We find in the opinion of Brett, M.R., afterwards Lord Esher (p.510), the same conception of a duty, irrespective of contract, imposed upon the manufacturer by the law itself: "Whenever one person supplies goods, or machinery or the like, for the purpose of their being used by another person under such circumstances that every one of ordinary sense would, if he thought, recognize at once that unless he used ordinary care and skill with regard to the condition of the thing supplied, or the mode of supplying it, there will be danger of injury to the person or property of him for whose use the thing is supplied, and who is to use it, a duty arises to such thing." He then points out that for a neglect of such ordinary care or skill whereby injury happens, the appropriate remedy is an action for negligence. The right to enforce this liability is not to be confined to the immediate buyer. The right, he says, extends to the persons or class of persons for whose use the thing is supplied. It is enough that the goods "would in all probability be used at once [...] before a reasonable opportunity for discovering any defect which might exist," and

---

28. Do you think the rule was ever this restricted? Had prior courts misinterpreted it? If so, weren't their decisions, even if somehow wrong, the rule in the sense that they governed the relationship between the parties and no doubt many others who never went to court but conducted themselves according to the rule as those courts interpreted it? Or is it that the Loop and Losee courts understood the rule and simply had other reasons in those cases for deciding that Thomas did not apply, but failed to tell us what those reasons were?

that the thing supplied is of such a nature "that a neglect of ordinary care or skill as to its condition or the manner of supplying it would probably cause danger to the person or property of the person for whose use it was supplied, and who was about to use it." On the other hand, he would exclude a case "in which the goods are supplied under circumstances in which it would be a chance by whom they would be used or whether they would be used or not, or whether they would be used before there would probably be means of observing any defect," or where the goods are of such a nature that "a want of care or skill as to their condition or the manner of supplying them would not probably produce danger of injury to person or property." What was said by Lord Esher in that case did not command the full assent of his associates. His opinion has been criticized "as requiring every man to take affirmative precautions to protect his neighbors as well as to refrain from injuring them." Bohlen Affirmative Obligations in the Law of Torts, 44 Am. Law Reg., N.S., 341. It may not be an accurate exposition of the law of England. Perhaps it may need some qualification even in our own state. Like most attempts at comprehensive definition, it may involve errors of inclusion and of exclusion. But its tests and standards, at least in their underlying principles, with whatever qualification may be called for as they are applied to varying conditions, are the tests and standards of our law.[29]

We hold then, that the principle of Thomas v. Winchester is not limited to poisons, explosives, and things of like nature, to things which in their normal operation are implements of destruction. If the nature of a thing is such that it is reasonably certain to place life and limb in peril when negligently made, it is then a thing of danger. Its nature gives warning of the consequences to be expected. If to the element of danger there is added knowledge that the thing will be used by persons other than the purchaser, and used without new tests, then, irrespective of contract, the manufacturer of this thing of danger is under a duty to make it carefully. That is as far as we are required to go for the decision of this case. There must be knowledge of a danger, not merely possible, but probable. It is possible to use almost anything in a way that will make it dangerous if defective. That is not enough to charge the manufacturer with a duty independent of his contract. Whether a given thing is dangerous may be sometimes a question for the court and sometimes a question for the jury. There must also be knowledge that in the usual course of events the danger will be

---

29. This statement is the essence of the common law. As important as language is, a common law rule is what its underlying policies say it is. When a court applies a common law rule (or when a lawyer answers a client's question based on analysis of a common law rule), the analysis of every step or part of the rule's application is controlled by the policies that the rule is meant to further. Restricted by the doctrine of precedent, when a court determines that a rule's policies are not furthered by a uniform application of the rule, rules change and exceptions to rules are created.

shared by others than the buyer. Such knowledge may often be inferred from the nature of the transaction. But it is possible that even knowledge of the danger and of the use will not always be enough. The proximity or remoteness of the relation is a factor to be considered. We are dealing now with the liability of the manufacturer of the finished product, who puts it on the market to be used without inspection by his customers. If he is negligent, where danger is to be foreseen, a liability will follow. We are not required at this time to say that it is legitimate to go back to the manufacturer of the finished product and hold the manufacturers of the component parts.[30] To make their negligence a cause of imminent danger, an independent cause must often intervene; the manufacturer of the finished product must also fail in his duty of inspection. It may be that in those circumstances the negligence of the earlier members of the series is too remote to constitute, as to the ultimate user, an actionable wrong. Beven on Negligence (3d ed.) 50, 51, 54; Wharton on Negligence (2d ed.) § 134, Leeds v. N.Y. Tel. Co., 178 N.Y. 118, 70 N.E. 219; Sweet v. Perkins, 196 N.Y. 482, 90 N.E. 50; Hayes v. Hyde Park, 153 Mass. 514, 516, 27 N.E. 522, 12 L.R.A. 249. We leave that question open. We shall have to deal with it when it arises. The difficulty which it suggests is not present in this case. There is here no break in the chain of cause and effect. In such circumstances, the presence of a known danger, attendant upon a known use, makes vigilance a duty. We have put aside the notion that the duty to safeguard life and limb, when the consequences of negligence may be foreseen, grows out of contract and nothing else. We have put the source of the obligation where it ought to be. We have put its source in the law.[31]

From this survey of the decisions, there thus emerges a definition of the duty of a manufacturer which enables us to measure this defendant's liability. Beyond all question, the nature of an automobile gives warning of probable danger if its construction is defective. This automobile was designed to go fifty miles an hour. Unless its wheels were sound and strong, injury was almost certain. It was as much a thing of danger as a defective engine for a railroad. The defendant knew the danger. It knew also that the car would be used by persons other than the buyer. This was apparent from its size; there were seats for three persons. It was apparent also from the fact that the buyer was a dealer in cars, who bought to resell. The maker of this car supplied it for the use of pur-

---

30. The court refrains from giving a sort of advisory opinion on matters not before it. Without interested parties to argue this issue (the wheel-maker is not a party to the case), the court is in no position to answer this question, and it says so. Further, because a court's power to make law is limited to the predictive value of its resolution of disputes brought to its attention by parties, a ventured answer to this question would not be binding authority on any other court: it would not be law.

31. What does the court mean here? Think about what it means to say that the law, rather than an agreement between the parties, imposes an obligation.

chasers from the dealer just as plainly as the contractor in Devlin v. Smith supplied the scaffold for use by the servants of the owner. The dealer was indeed the one person of whom it might be said with some approach to certainty that by him the car would not be used.[32] Yet the defendant would have us say that he was the one person whom it was under a legal duty to protect. The law does not lead us to so inconsequent a conclusion. Precedents drawn from the days of travel by stagecoach do not fit the conditions of travel today. The principle that the danger must be imminent does not change, but the things subject to the principle do change. They are whatever the needs of life in a developing civilization require them to be.

In reaching this conclusion, we do not ignore the decisions to the contrary in other jurisdictions. It was held in Cadillac M. C. Co. v. Johnson, 221 F.801, 137 C.C.A. 279, L.R.A. 1915E, 287, that an automobile is not within the rule of Thomas v. Winchester. There was, however, a vigorous dissent. Opposed to that decision is one of the Court of Appeals of Kentucky. Olds Motor Works v. Shaffer, 145 Ky. 616, 140 S.W. 1047, 37 L.R.A., N.S., 560, Ann. Cas. 1913B, 689. The earlier cases are summarized by Judge Sanborn in Huset v. J.I. Case Threshing Machine Co., 120 F. 865, 57 C.C.A. 237, 61 L.R.A. 303. Some of them, at first sight inconsistent with our conclusion, may be reconciled upon the grounds that the negligence was too remote, and that another cause had intervened. But even when they cannot be reconciled, the difference is rather in the application of the principle than in the principle itself. Judge Sanborn says, for example, that the contractor who builds a bridge, or the manufacturer who builds a car, cannot ordinarily foresee injury to other persons than the owner as the probable result. 120 F. 865, at p. 867, 57 C.C.A. 237, at page 239, 61 L.R.A. 303. We take a different view. We think that injury to others is to be foreseen not merely as a possible, but as an almost inevitable result. See the trenchant criticism in Bohlen, supra, at p. 351. Indeed, Judge Sanborn concedes that his view is not to be reconciled with our decision in Devlin v. Smith, supra. The doctrine of that decision has now become the settled law of this state, and we have no desire to depart from it.   _supra - "written above / before_

In England the limits of the rule are still unsettled. Winterbottom v. Wright, 10 M. & W. 109, is often cited. The defendant undertook to provide a mail coach to carry the mail bags. The coach broke down from latent defects in its construction. The defendant, however, was not the manufacturer. The court held that he was not liable for injuries to a passenger. The case was decided on a demurrer to the declaration. Lord Esher points out in Heaven v. Pender, supra, at p. 513, that the form of the declaration was subject to criticism. It did

---

32. Notice the court's use of the facts of the case in developing its argument. You will find it necessary to do the same as a student taking an exam or as a student and a lawyer in writing both objective and persuasive legal memoranda.

Demurrer - a claim by the defendant in a legal action that the plaintiff does not have sufficient grounds to proceed.

not fairly suggest the existence of a duty aside from the special contract which was the plaintiff's main reliance. See the criticism of Winterbottom v. Wright, in Bohlen, supra, at pp. 281, 283. At all events, in Heaven v. Pender, supra, the defendant, a dock owner, who put up a staging outside a ship, was held liable to the servants of the shipowner. In Elliott v. Hall, 15 Q.B.D. 315, the defendant sent out a defective truck laden with goods which he had sold. The buyer's servants unloaded it, and were injured because of the defects. It was held that the defendant was under a duty "not to be guilty of negligence with regard to the state and condition of the truck." There seems to have been a return to the doctrine of Winterbottom v. Wright in Earl v. Lubbock, L. R. [1905] 1 K.B. 253. In that case, however, as in the earlier one, the defendant was not the manufacturer. He had merely made a contract to keep the van in repair. A later case, White v. Steadman, L.R. [1913], 3 K.B. 340, 348, emphasizes that element. A livery stable keeper who sent out a vicious horse was held liable not merely to his customer but also to another occupant of the carriage, and Thomas v. Winchester was cited and followed. White v. Steadman, supra, at pp. 348, 349. It was again cited and followed in Dominion Natural Gas Co. v. Collins, L. R. [1909] A.C. 640, 646. From these cases a consistent principle is with difficulty extracted. The English courts, however, agree with ours in holding that one who invites another to make use of an appliance is bound to the exercise of reasonable care. Caledonian Ry. Co. v. Mulholland, L. R. [1898] A.C. 216, 227; Indermaur v. Dames, L. R. [1 C.P.] 274. That at bottom is the underlying principle of Devlin v. Smith. The contractor who builds the scaffold invites the owner's workmen to use it. The manufacturer who sells the automobile to the retail dealer invites the dealer's customers to use it. The invitation is addressed in the one case to determinate persons and in the other to an indeterminate class, but in each case it is equally plain, and in each its consequences must be the same. *Departing from a general rule*

There is nothing anomalous in a rule which imposes upon A, who has contracted with B, a duty to C and D and others according as he knows or does not know that the subject matter of the contract is intended for their use. We may find an analogy in the law which measures the liability of landlords. If A leases to B a tumble-down house he is not liable, in the absence of fraud, to B's guests who enter it and are injured. This is because B is then under the duty to repair it, the lessor has the right to suppose that he will fulfill that duty, and, if he omits to do so, his guests must look to him. Bohlen, supra, at p. 276. But if A leases a building to be used by the lessee at once as a place of public entertainment, the rule is different. There injury to persons other than the lessee is to be foreseen, and foresight of the consequences involves the creation of a duty. Junkermann v. Tilyou R. Co., 213 N.Y. 404, 108 N.E. 190, L.R.A. 1915F, 700, and cases there cited.

In this view of the defendant's liability there is nothing inconsistent with the theory of liability on which the case was tried. It is true that the court told the jury that "an automobile is not an inherently dangerous vehicle." The meaning, however, is made plain by the context. The meaning is that danger is not to be expected when the vehicle is well constructed. The court left it to the jury to say whether the defendant ought to have foreseen that the car, if negligently constructed, would become "imminently dangerous." Subtle distinctions are drawn by the defendant between things inherently dangerous and things imminently dangerous, but the case does not turn upon these verbal niceties. If danger was to be expected as reasonably certain, there was a duty of vigilance, and this whether you call the danger inherent or imminent. In varying forms that thought was put before the jury. We do not say that the court would not have been justified in ruling as a matter of law that the car was a dangerous thing. If there was any error, it was none of which the defendant can complain.

We think the defendant was not absolved from a duty of inspection because it bought the wheels from a reputable manufacturer. It was not merely a dealer in automobiles. It was a manufacturer of automobiles. It was responsible for the finished product. It was not at liberty to put the finished product on the market without subjecting the component parts to ordinary and simple tests. Richmond & Danville R. R. Co. v. Elliott, 149 U.S. 266, 272, 13 S.Ct. 837, 37 L.Ed. 728. Under the charge of the trial judge nothing more was required of it. The obligation to inspect must vary with the nature of the thing to be inspected. The more probable the danger, the greater the need of caution. There is little analogy between this case and Carlson v. Phoenix Bridge Co., 132 N.Y. 273, 30 N.E. 750, where the defendant bought a tool for a servant's use. The making of tools was not the business in which the master was engaged. Reliance on the skill of the manufacturer was proper and almost inevitable. But that is not the defendant's situation. Both by its relation to the work and by the nature of its business, it is charged with a stricter duty.

Other rulings complained of have been considered, but no error has been found in them.

The judgment should be affirmed with costs.

WILLARD BARTLETT, C. J. (dissenting). The plaintiff was injured in consequence of the collapse of a wheel of an automobile manufactured by the defendant corporation which sold it to a firm of automobile dealers in Schenectady, who in turn sold the car to the plaintiff. The wheel was purchased by the Buick Motor Company, ready made, from the Imperial Wheel Company of Flint, Mich., a reputable manufacturer of automobile wheels which had furnished the defendant with 80,000 wheels, none of which had proved to be made of defective wood prior to the accident in the present case. The defendant relied upon the wheel manufacturer to make all necessary tests as to the strength of the material therein, and made no such test itself. The present suit is an action for negligence, brought by the subvendee of the motor car against the manufacturer as the original vendor. The evidence warranted a finding by the jury that the wheel which collapsed was defective when it left the hands of the defendant. The automobile was being prudently operated at the time of the accident, and was moving at a speed of only eight miles an hour. There was no allegation or proof of any actual knowledge of the defect on the part of the defendant, or any suggestion that any element of fraud or deceit or misrepresentation entered into the sale.

The theory upon which the case was submitted to the jury by the learned judge who presided at the trial was that, although an automobile is not an inherently dangerous vehicle, it may become such if equipped with a weak wheel; and that if the motor car in question, when it was put upon the market was in itself inherently dangerous by reason of its being equipped with a weak wheel, the defendant was chargeable with a knowledge of the defect so far as it might be discovered by a reasonable inspection and the application of reasonable tests. This liability, it was further held, was not limited to the original vendee, but extended to a subvendee like the plaintiff, who was not a party to the original contract of sale.

I think that these rulings, which have been approved by the Appellate Division, extend the liability of the vendor of a manufactured article further than any case which has yet received the sanction of this court. It has heretofore been held in this state that the liability of the vendor of a manufactured article for negligence arising out of the existence of defects therein does not extend to strangers injured in consequence of such defects, but is confined to the immediate vendee. The exceptions to the general rule which have thus far been recognized in New York are cases in which the article sold was of such a character that danger to life or limb was involved in the ordinary use thereof; in other words, where the article sold was inherently dangerous. As has already been pointed out, the learned trial judge instructed the jury that an automobile is not an inherently dangerous vehicle.

The late Chief Justice Cooley of Michigan, one of the most learned and accurate of American law writers, states the general rule thus:

> The general rule is that a contractor, manufacturer, vendor or furnisher of an article is not liable to third parties who have no contractual relations with him, for negligence in the construction, manufacture, or sale of such article. 2 Cooley on Torts (3d Ed.) 1486.

The leading English authority in support of this rule, to which all the later cases on the same subject refer, is Winterbottom v. Wright, 10 Meeson & Welsby, 109, which was an action by the driver of a stagecoach against a contractor who had agreed with the postmaster general to provide and keep the vehicle in repair for the purpose of conveying the royal mail over a prescribed route. The coach broke down and upset, injuring the driver, who sought to recover against the contractor on account of its defective construction. The

Court of Exchequer denied him any right of recovery on the ground that there was no privity of contract between the parties, the agreement having been made with the postmaster general alone.

If the plaintiff can sue, said Lord Abinger, the Chief Baron, every or even any person passing along the road who was injured by the upsetting of the coach might bring a similar action. Unless we confine the operation of such contracts as this to the parties who enter into them the most absurd and outrageous consequences, to which I can see no limit, would ensue.

The doctrine of that decision was recognized as the law of this state by the leading New York case of Thomas v. Winchester, 6 N.Y. 397, 408, 57 Am.Dec. 455, which, however, involved an exception to the general rule. There the defendant, who was a dealer in medicines, sold to a druggist a quantity of belladonna, which is a deadly poison, negligently labeled as extract of dandelion. The druggist in good faith used the poison in filling a prescription calling for the harmless dandelion extract, and the plaintiff for whom the prescription was put up was poisoned by the belladonna. This court held that the original vendor was liable for the injuries suffered by the patient. Chief Judge Ruggles, who delivered the opinion of the court, distinguished between an act of negligence imminently dangerous to the lives of others and one that is not so, saying:

If A. build a wagon and sell it to B., who sells it to C., and C. hires it to D., who in consequence of the gross negligence of A. in building the wagon is overturned and injured, D. cannot recover damages against A., the builder. A.'s obligation to build the wagon faithfully arises solely out of his contract with B. The public having nothing to do with it.

* * *

So, for the same reason, if a horse be defectively shod by a smith, and a person hiring the horse from the owner is thrown and injured in consequence of the smith's negligence in shoeing, the smith is not liable for the injury.

In Torgensen v. Schultz, 192 N.Y. 156, 159, 84 N.E. 956, 18 L.R.A. (N.S.) 726, 127 Am.St.Rep. 894, the defendant was the vendor of bottles of aerated water which were charged under high pressure and likely to explode unless used with precaution when exposed to sudden changes of temperature. The plaintiff, who was a servant of the purchaser, was injured by the explosion of one of these bottles. There was evidence tending to show that it had not been properly tested in order to insure users against such accidents. We held that the defendant corporation was liable notwithstanding the absence of any contract relation between it and the plaintiff—

> under the doctrine of Thomas v. Winchester, supra, and similar cases based upon the duty of the vendor of an article dangerous in its nature, or likely to become so in the course of the ordinary usage to be contemplated by the vendor, either to exercise due care to warn users of the danger or to take reasonable care to prevent the article sold from proving dangerous when subjected only to customary usage.

The character of the exception to the general rule limiting liability for negligence to the original parties to the contract of sale, was still more clearly stated by Judge Hiscock, writing for the court in Statler v. Ray Manufacturing Co., 195 N.Y. 478, 482, 88 N.E. 1063, where he said that:

> In the case of an article of an inherently dangerous nature, a manufacturer may become liable for a negligent construction which, when added to the inherent character of the appliance, makes it imminently dangerous, and causes or contributes to a resulting injury not necessarily incident to the use of such an article if properly constructed, but naturally following from a defective construction.

In that case the injuries were inflicted by the explosion of a battery of steam-driven coffee urns, constituting an appliance liable to become dangerous in the course of ordinary usage.

The case of Devlin v. Smith, 89 N.Y. 470, 42 Am.Rep. 311, is cited as an authority in conflict with the view that the liability of the manufacturer and vendor extends to third parties only when the article manufactured and sold is inherently dangerous. In that case the builder of a scaffold 90 feet high, which was erected for the purpose of enabling painters to stand upon it, was held to be liable to the administratrix of a painter who fell therefrom and was killed, being at the time in the employ of the person for whom the scaffold was built. It is said that the scaffold, if properly constructed, was not inherently dangerous, and hence that this decision affirms the existence of liability in the case of an article not dangerous in itself, but made so only in consequence of negligent construction. Whatever logical force there may be in this view it seems to me clear from the language of Judge Rapallo, who wrote the opinion of the court that the scaffold was deemed to be an inherently dangerous structure, and that the case was decided as it was because the court entertained that view. Otherwise, he would hardly have said, as he did, that the circumstances seemed to bring the case fairly within the principle of Thomas v. Winchester.

I do not see how we can uphold the judgment in the present case without overruling what has been so often said by this court and other courts of like authority in reference to the absence of any liability for negligence on the part of the original vendor of an ordinary carriage to any one except his immediate vendee. The absence of such liability was the very point actually decided in the English case of Winterbottom v. Wright, supra, and the illustration quoted from the opinion of Chief Judge Ruggles in Thomas v. Winchester, supra, assumes that the law on the subject was so plain that the statement would be accepted almost as a matter of course. In the case at bar the defective wheel on an automobile, moving only eight miles an hour, was not any more dangerous to the occupants of the car than a similarly defective wheel would be to the occupants of a carriage drawn by a horse at the same speed, and yet, unless the courts have been all wrong on this question up to the present time, there would be no liability to strangers to the original sale in the case of the horse-drawn carriage.

The rule upon which, in my judgment, the determination of this case depends, and the recognized exceptions thereto, were discussed by Chief Judge Sanborn, of the United States Circuit Court of Appeals in the Eighth Circuit, in Huset v. J. I. Case Threshing Machine Co., 120 Fed. 865, 57 C.C.A. 237, 61 L.R.A. 303, in an opinion which reviews all the leading American and English decisions on the subject up to the time when it was rendered (1903). I have already discussed the leading New York cases, but as to the rest I feel that I can add nothing to the learning of that opinion or the cogency of its reasoning. I have examined the cases to which Judge Sanborn refers, but if I were to discuss them at length, I should be forced merely to paraphrase his language, as a study of the authorities he cites has led me to the same conclusion; and the repetition of what has already been so well said would contribute nothing to the advantage of the bench, the bar, or the individual litigants whose case is before us.

A few cases decided since his opinion was written, however, may be noticed. In Earl v. Lubbock, [1905] L.R. 1 K.B.Div. 253, the Court of Appeal in 1904 considered and approved the propositions of law laid down by the Court of Exchequer in Winterbottom v. Wright, supra, declaring that the decision in that case, since the year 1842, had stood the test of repeated discussion. The Master of the Rolls approved the principles laid down by Lord Abinger as based upon sound reasoning; and all the members of the court agreed that his decision was a controlling authority which must be followed. That the federal courts still adhere to the general rule, as I have stated it, appears by the decision of the Circuit Court of Appeal in the Second Circuit, in March, 1915, in the case of Cadillac Motor Car Co. v. Johnson, 221 Fed. 801, 137 C.C.A. 279, L.R.A. 1915E, 287. That case, like this, was an action by a subvendee against a manufacturer of automobiles for negligence in failing to discover that one of its wheels was defective, the court holding that such an action could not be maintained. It is true there was a dissenting opinion in that case, but it was based chiefly upon the proposition that rules applicable to stagecoaches are archaic when applied to automobiles, and that if the law did not afford a remedy to strangers to the contract, the law should be changed. It [sic] this be true, the change should be effected by the Legislature and not by the courts. A perusal of the opinion in that case and in the Huset case will disclose how uniformly the courts throughout this country have adhered to the rule and how consistently they have refused to broaden the scope of the exceptions. I think we should adhere to it in the case at bar, and therefore I vote for a reversal of this judgment.

HISCOCK, CHASE, and CUDDEBACK, J.J., concur with CARDOZO, J., and HOGAN, J., concurs in result. WILLARD BARTLETT, C. J., reads dissenting opinion. POUND, J., not voting.

Judgment affirmed.

* * *

Notes on *MacPherson v. Buick Motor Co.*, 217 N.Y. 382, 111 N.E. 1050 (1916).

1. This case states simply in the context of foreseeability what may have been the essence of the rule from the time of *Thomas v. Winchester.* None of the prior cases we read, including *Thomas*, do so in such simple terms. Read the words that the Thomases' lawyer used in arguing their case some sixty-seven years before *MacPherson*:

    > N. Hill, Jun. for respondents [the Thomases] . . .
    > To entitle the aggrieved party to sue in such case, no privity is necessary, except such as is created by the unlawful act, and the consequential injury; privity of contract being out of the question. . . .
    > The injury is not rendered too remote to sustain a recovery because separated from the unlawful act by intervening events, however numerous, or of whatever kind, provided they are the natural and probable consequences of the act; i.e. such as would be likely to follow and might be easily foreseen. . . .
    > The rule contended for, does not extend the sphere of accountability to impracticable or unjust limits, but confines it to consequences so proximate as to be expected or readily foreseen, and for which every wrongdoer is and ought to be answerable. . . .
    > The rule contended for by the defendant, that each vendor is liable only to his immediate vendee, has no application to the present case.
    > 1. This rule is founded on the principle that a right or duty wholly created by contract, can only be enforced between the contracting parties. (5 Mees. & Welsb. 283, 286, 288-9.) The case of Wright v. Winterbottom, (10 Mees. & Welsb. 109,) was decided on this principle; the declaration being expressly on a duty created by contract,

and not by law. In The Mayor, & c. v. Cunliff, (2 Const. 165,) each count was on an alleged duty created by law; but the law being void, the allegation as to the duty could not be maintained.

2. Nothing was decided in either of the above cases which interferes with the right to maintain the present action. The duty violated by the defendant was not created by contract, but by law; every one being under an obligation to abstain from acts tending naturally and probably to endanger human life.... Besides, both cases contain dicta which show that the principles on which the present action is based were not intended to be denied....

Thomas v. Winchester, 6 N.Y. 397, 401-404 (1852) (Argument of Counsel).

2. Interestingly, it is actually a duty to inspect that was breached since Buick bought the wheels from an outside manufacturer. For more on the story of the *MacPherson* case, and in particular an argument that Buick could not have performed an inspection under the prevailing circumstances because the wheels arrived at Buick's factory already painted, *see generally* D. PECK, DECISION AT LAW 38–69 (1961).

3. Consider the dissent's position that automobiles capable of traveling at 8 miles per hour are really not different from the coach in *Winterbottom v. Wright*, and note that Cardozo talks about the vehicle's capability of traveling 50 miles per hour. Which is correct? Should the capability of the car or its actual speed at the time of the failure be the relevant fact? Or could it be that both are relevant facts, each for a different reason?

4. *MacPherson* has become a leading case accepted in all American jurisdictions. *Johnson v. Cadillac Motors*, 261 F. 878 (2nd Cir. 1919) is a decision issued soon after, and based soundly on, the decision in *MacPherson*.

5. The *MacPherson* decision provided additional incentive to manufacturers to produce safer products. For a public policy argument in support of placing the burden of protecting the public on the manufacturer, *see* Davis, *Reexamination of the Doctrine of MacPherson v. Buick Motor Co. and Its Application and Extension in the State of New York*, 24 FORDHAM L. REV. 204 (1955).

6. Recovery from a manufacturer for injuries sustained by persons with whom they were not in privity of contract may be based in either contract or tort. Note, *Manufacturers' Liability to Ultimate Consumers*, 37 MARQ. L. REV. 356 (1954), provides insight into the arguments both for and against each approach and identifies areas of confusion. Note that although Contracts, Torts, and Property are usually taught as separate law school courses, at times their subject matter is shared by all three courses.

7. For a concise discussion focusing on the application of traditional legal analysis to the theory of products liability developed by the New York

courts, *see* Hermann, *Phenomenology, Structuralism, Hermeneutics, and Legal Study: Application of Contemporary Continental Thought to Legal Phenomena*, 36 U. MIAMI L. REV. 379, 393 (1982).

*   *   *

Case Analysis Reprised: Examinations

In many respects, law school examinations are similar to the problems that face judges. Just as a judge must determine the correct, or at least best, answer to the legal problem pending before the court, a law student faced with a set of hypothetical facts must determine the best legal answer available. The very same analytical skills that are used in case analysis and opinion writing are used in examination question analysis and answer construction.

After reading a line of cases such as you have, you might reasonably wonder what sort of examination question a law teacher might pose on such material. We have provided a shortened version of what we think would be a highly appropriate exam question to follow the reading of *MacPherson* and its predecessors. You will notice that the question asks what the court has not yet answered; as a result, mere memorization of the materials will be insufficient preparation for an exam. Rather, in addition to being familiar with the materials themselves, you will want to have formed an understanding, a theory, of the underlying principles that drive decisions in the area of law being tested. That theory, rather than a sort of stock response that you might expect to be among the choices available on an objective exam, will advise your own exam answering process just as it would advise a court facing the unanswered question posed by the examiner. Give some thought to how you would answer the sample question, or better still, give yourself an hour to write an answer, before taking a look at the sample answer that we have provided.

Sample examination question

A manufactures steering mechanisms for automobiles. B buys A's product and uses it in manufacturing his product, B's-mobiles. B sells the cars to dealers who sell them to users. C buys a B's-mobile from a dealer. One month later, while driving through town, C's B's-mobile experiences steering problems and veers onto a sidewalk, striking D whose life was despaired of, etc. D lived but was badly injured. A's negligence in manufacturing the steering mechanism caused D's injury.

Does D have a cause of action against A?

Sample examination answer

Even though A may have been negligent, for A to be held liable to D, A must have had some duty to D. A does not have such a duty from any contractual relationship, because A is not in privity with D. A may still have a duty under the principles of manufacturer's liability set out in *MacPherson*. The general rule from *MacPherson* is that the duty to be applied is based upon the risk to be perceived by the defendant. Unlike *MacPherson*, however, D was not a foreseeable *user* of the negligently made automobile part. A could argue that making it liable to *any* person injured as a result of manufacturer negligence would in effect establish unlimited liability for manufacturers.

On the other hand, D could reasonably assert that a manufacturer should foresee that a a negligently made steering mechanism will render an automobile dangerous to pedestrians such as D. If a steering mechanism is improperly made, an automobile will be likely to get out of the control of the driver. If an auto does get out of control, it is certainly foreseeable that the auto may collide with other cars or run up on a sidewalk and injure people. Therefore, the risk that the vehicle would cause an injury to someone like D was foreseeable, and A should be liable to D.

Further, in such a situation, where the danger is foreseeable as to type of accident and type of victim, but not foreseeable as to the particular person injured, a court may refer to the policies underlying *MacPherson*. In that case, the court upheld the manufacturer's liability to the consumer of the product, even though the specific consumer was not foreseeable to the manufacturer. The underlying policy was that if a product could pose a danger to others who would not have the opportunity to guard against the danger, then the manufacturer would be under a duty to those others to make the thing carefully. In this case, D had no opportunity to guard against the danger posed by the negligently made steering mechanism: only A could have guarded against that hazard. Although B and C may have had a limited opportunity to test the finished automobile, they could not have completely guarded against the full range of A's potential negligence. Any such limited tests by B and C, expected by A, could have reduced the likelihood of harm foreseen by A. Yet, because of the limited effectiveness of those tests, A would not have been relieved of the ultimate duty to protect D from the foreseeable harm of an automobile operating without steering control. The policies of manufacturer liability would therefore be furthered by allowing D to state a claim against A. Therefore, D should have a cause of action against A.

6

A Return to Judicial Interpretation

In chapter 3, *The Nature of Law*, we devised our own legal system. We did so through judicial reaction to five homicides on the mythical planet of Bryan. You may recall that after the first such homicide the result in each case rested on the judge's interpretation of the statute and its application to the facts before the court. chapter 3 not only illustrated how law is made in a common law system, it graphically demonstrated the need for judicial interpretation of statutory law. chapter 5, on the other hand, introduced you to a line of real cases. Via their study you learned how to read and analyze cases and saw how law actually developed in one area in New York. The cases in chapter 5 did not include statutory interpretation as codification came later.

Before we move on to the critical question of how real cases begin and the lawyer's entrance into them, we thought you might wish to read a truly unusual exhibit of judicial interpretation. As you know, subject to constitutional law, statutes are binding and must be followed. However, as our make believe statutes demonstrated in chapter 3, the proper meaning of a statute may be hard to determine. Yet, once faced with a case, a judge must interpret the statute in order to apply it. It may be that you thought that we overstated the case with our overly erroneous statutes in chapter 3. The case that follows shows the scope of the responsibility placed on our judiciary. *People v. Gibbons* is a real California criminal case with unusual facts. Faced with a unique interpretation of a statute, the majority of the California Court of Appeals interpreted the statute in one fashion while the dissent reached an opposite conclusion. Read the case, carefully consider the reasoning in both the majority and dissenting opinions, and decide for yourself what the right answer should have been. Ponder what the case symbolizes insofar as the allocation of power between legislature and judiciary is concerned. Ask yourself what the case tells us about the judiciary's powers and responsibilities.

People v. Gibbons[†]

215 Cal. App. 3d 1204; 263 Cal. Rptr. 905 (1989)

OPINION: HOLLENHORST, J.

Pursuant to California Rules of Court, rule 62 et seq., we accepted a transfer of this case from the Appellate Department of the Riverside Superior Court. In this appeal, we are asked for the first time to decide whether the surreptitious videotaping of sexual activity violates California's privacy statutes, Penal Code sections 630 and 632. The trial court overruled defendant's demurrer and a jury convicted defendant. Defendant appeals arguing the conduct in question is not prohibited by these sections. We agree with the trial court's determination and affirm.

SECRETLY

FACTS

On three different occasions, defendant invited young women to his residence. In the bedroom, with the door closed and window curtains drawn, defendant and the three women engaged in sexual activity including sexual intercourse. Without obtaining the consent of the women, defendant videotaped these encounters utilizing a video camera which he had hidden in the closet. The women were never advised of the existence of the camera until being subsequently informed by police who recovered the videotapes.

DISCUSSION

1. *Videotaping May Violate the Right of Privacy.*

Penal Code sections 630 and 632 define the purpose of the privacy act and its proscriptions.[1] Neither side has provided controlling authority dealing di-

---

† Most citations have been omitted for reasons of brevity and clarity. Thus, the sources of quotations are not shown, something that would be improper in normal legal writing. In addition, some of the remaining citations have been edited for form.

1. Penal Code section 630 provides:

"The Legislature hereby declares that advances in science and technology have led to the development of new devices and techniques for the purpose of eavesdropping upon private communications and that the invasion of privacy resulting from the continual and increasing use of such devices and techniques has created a serious threat to the free exercise of personal liberties and cannot be tolerated in a free and civilized society.

"The Legislature by this chapter intends to protect the right of privacy of the people of this state.

"The Legislature recognizes that law enforcement agencies have a legitimate need to employ modern listening devices and techniques in the investigation of criminal conduct and the apprehension of lawbreakers. Therefore, it is not the intent of the Legislature to place greater restraints on the use of listening devices and techniques by law enforcement agencies than existed prior to the effective date of this chapter."

Penal Code §632 provides:

"(a) Every person who, intentionally and without the consent of all parties to a confi-

rectly with videotaping; however, as we discuss, the language of the statute and cases make it clear that the Legislature intended to control the activity underlying this case.

The purpose of the statutes is clear and unambiguous. Initially, in section 630, the legislature recognized that technology had advanced to the extent that privacy could be imperiled unless the legislature intervened. The privacy statutes were enacted after a series of hodgepodge regulations dealing with privacy in communications had been amended and reamended. It was out of recognition that the entire privacy area needed overhaul that the privacy statutes were adopted . . . We note in the text of section 630, no reference is made to a specific device or instrument for eavesdropping. Rather, the prohibition is based on the purpose for which the device or instrument is used. In § 632, the

---

dential communication, by means of any electronic amplifying or recording device, eavesdrops upon or records the confidential communication, whether the communication is carried on among such parties in the presence of one another or by means of a telegraph, telephone or other device, except a radio, shall be punished by a fine not exceeding two thousand five hundred dollars ($2,500), or imprisonment in the county jail not exceeding one year or in the state prison, or by both that fine and imprisonment. If the person has previously been convicted of a violation of this section or § 631, 632.5, or 636, the person shall be punished by a fine not exceeding ten thousand dollars ($10,000), by imprisonment in the county jail not exceeding one year or in the state prison, or by both that fine and imprisonment.

"(b) The term 'person' includes an individual, business association, partnership, corporation, or other legal entity, and an individual acting or purporting to act for or on behalf of any government or subdivision thereof, whether federal, state, or local, but excludes an individual known by all parties to a confidential communication to be overhearing or recording the communication.

"(c) The term 'confidential communication' includes any communication carried on in circumstances as may reasonably indicate that any party to the communication desires it to be confined to the parties thereto, but excludes a communication made in a public gathering or in any legislative, judicial, executive or administrative proceeding open to the public, or in any other circumstance in which the parties to the communication may reasonably expect that the communication may be overheard or recorded.

"(d) Except as proof in an action or prosecution for violation of this § no evidence obtained as a result of eavesdropping upon or recording a confidential communication in violation of this § shall be admissible in any judicial, administrative, legislative, or other proceeding.

"(e) This section shall not apply (1) to any public utility engaged in the business of providing communications services and facilities, or to the officers, employees or agents thereof, where the acts otherwise prohibited by this section are for the purpose of construction, maintenance, conduct or operation of the services and facilities of the public utility, or (2) to the use of any instrument, equipment, facility, or service furnished and used pursuant to the tariffs of such a public utility, or (3) to any telephonic communication system used for communication exclusively within a state, county, city and county, or city correctional facility.

"(f) This section does not apply to the use of hearing aids and similar devices, by persons afflicted with impaired hearing, for the purpose of overcoming the impairment to permit the hearing of sounds ordinarily audible to the human ear."

statute provides against the use of "any electronic amplifying or recording device" for the purpose of eavesdropping or recording private communications. We find that a video recorder is an instrument which, if used in manner proscribed under section 632, is a recording device for purposes of the privacy act. "If the words of the statute are clear, the court should not add to or alter them to accomplish a purpose that does not appear on the face of the statute or from its legislative history." . . . "The dominant objective of the act, as reflected in its preamble, is 'to protect the right of privacy of the people of this state.' " . . .

Defendant contends that even if a video recorder is a device or instrument covered by the privacy act, the statute only prohibits the surreptitious recording of oral communications, i.e., conversations, and does not extend to the recording of sexual acts or other forms of communication. We disagree. While communication and conversation are similar in their meaning, conversation refers to a *spoken* exchange of thoughts, opinions, and feelings while communication refers more broadly to the exchange of thoughts, messages or information by any means. . . . Additionally, we note that in the federal wiretapping provisions, Congress expressly limited the application of its statute to the nonconsensual recording of *oral* communications. . . . No such similar express limitation is found in the privacy act.

In other contexts, communication has been recognized to include not only oral or written communication but communication by conduct as well. For example, in the area of attorney-client privilege, it has been recognized that "[t]he privilege embraces not only oral or written statements but actions, signs, or other means of communicating information by a client to his attorney. . . . '[A]lmost any act, done by the client in the sight of the attorney and during the consultation, may conceivably be done by the client as the subject of a communication, and the only question will be whether, in the circumstances of the case, it was intended to be done as such.' " . . . That sexual relations is a form of communication, be it communication of love, simple affection, or, simply of oneself, cannot be readily disputed.[2]

We acknowledge that certain terms used in the privacy act, such as "eavesdropping," "amplifying device" and "telephone," might suggest a narrow

---

2. The dissent contends that, *unlike other conduct such as flag burning,* sexual conduct is not communication because the message being conveyed by sexual conduct is often difficult to decipher or understand. Implicit in this contention is the concession that communication is not limited to conversations and that at least some conduct is included in its definition. The suggestion, however, that "communication" should be limited to only those communications which are understood, be they words or conduct, is not only a strained construction of the word but one without support as well. The statute is not limited to effective communication and we cannot believe the Legislature would intend such a restriction. Just as the dissent recognizes that words can often be used to conceal rather than convey information, it can be said that people "hear" what they want to "hear." To attempt to define communication by whether the message conveyed is accurately received would lead to absurd results.

definition of communication, synonymous with conversation. However, section 630 expressly states the intent of the Legislature to protect the right of privacy of the people of this state. Consistent with the express declaration of intent and in the absence of any express statutory limitations, we find that "communication" as used in the privacy act is not limited to conversations or oral communications but rather encompasses any communication, regardless of its form, where any party to the communication desires it to be confined to the parties thereto. If the act covers eavesdropping on or recording of a telephone call, it surely covers the nonconsensual recording of the most intimate and private form of communication between two people.

2. *Due Process.*

Having determined that the privacy statute proscribes the nonconsensual recording of any confidential communication, regardless of the content of the communication or its form, we must next determine whether this determination and its application to defendant violates due process. *Bouie v. City of Columbia*, 378 U.S. 347 (1964). The Due Process Clause of the Fourteenth Amendment of the U.S. Constitution includes the concept that statutes must be written with sufficient definiteness and certainty so as to provide fair notice or fair warning of what conduct is either required or proscribed by the statute .... Similarly, "[t]here can be no doubt that a deprivation of the right of fair warning can result not only from vague statutory language but also from an unforeseeable and retroactive judicial expansion of narrow and precise statutory language."...

The concept of fair notice is not intended "to convert into a constitutional dilemma the practical difficulties in drawing criminal statutes both general enough to take into account a variety of human conduct and sufficiently specific to provide fair warning that certain kinds of conduct are prohibited.'..." In the case of judicial construction, due process is not violated merely because the language of the statute is being applied to a particular situation for the first time. Thus, in *Granite Construction Co. v. Superior Court*, 149 Cal. App. 3d 465, 470, 197 Cal. Rptr. 3 (1983), the fact that a corporation previously had never been prosecuted for manslaughter did not result in a lack of due process. Nor do due process concerns of fair warning arise where the language of the statute is not being expanded in an unforeseeable manner even though the case is one of first impression and even if dicta in prior decisions suggested a narrower application. Thus in *People v. Sobiek*, 30 Cal. App. 3d 458, 473–475, 106 Cal. Rptr. 519 (1973), the court found no due process violation in applying the grand theft statute to a partner for the wrongful taking of partnership property even though dicta in prior decisions suggested otherwise.

" 'This is not a case where an act clearly not criminal at the time of its occurrence, is so declared to be at some subsequent time. Nor is it a case where criminal responsibility should not attach because the actor could not reasonably understand that his contemplated conduct was proscribed.' . . . 'It is not always true that where the definition of a crime is extended by judicial construction, a conviction which results therefrom is a denial of due process'. . . . '[T]he law is full of instances where a man's fate depends on his estimating rightly, that is, as the jury subsequently estimates it, some matter of degree. If his judgment is wrong, not only may he incur a fine or a short imprisonment, as here; he may incur the penalty of death . . . . *The criterion in such cases is to examine whether common social duty would, under the circumstances, have suggested a more circumspect conduct.*" ' " . . .

Whether our action today in applying the privacy act to defendant's conduct is viewed as an enlargement of the statutory language or merely an application of first impression, we are convinced defendant received fair warning. There can be little doubt defendant knew that in recording the sexual activity without the woman's consent, he was violating her right of privacy and that "common social duty" would suggest a "more circumspect conduct." Additionally, this is not a case of punishing conduct which *clearly* was not criminal previously or a situation of expanding the language of the statute in an unforeseeable or unreasonable fashion. Rather, as noted previously, the interpretation is consistent with the Legislature's intent to protect individual privacy. Accordingly, we find the statute on its face and as interpreted gave fair warning to the defendant that his conduct was proscribed.

DISPOSITION

Judgment is affirmed.

DABNEY, J., concurs.

CAMPBELL, Presiding Justice, dissenting.

I disagree with the majority's strained construction of Penal Code section 632,[3] and therefore dissent.[4]

---

3. Section references are to the Penal Code unless otherwise indicated.

4. My review of the record causes me to question whether the central issue of this appeal is correctly before us. The case was presented to the jury in the prosecuting attorney's argument as being based on verbal communication in the alternative: "I would submit to you and I'm sure you would agree with me that the act of human sexual relations is [an] act of communicating feelings. You'll also remember in the tapes we saw there was some verbal communication [—] the defendant and the three victims spoke to each other. As such we have communication for the purposes of this proceeding." Counsel for the defendant did not contend that there were no verbal communications with each of the victims or that any verbal communications were any less confidential than the sexual conduct. The defense was that the circumstances indicated that none of the victims considered the sexual and verbal conduct between each of them and the defendant to have

Construing a penal statute so that it fails to give an ordinary person fair notice of the act or acts punished violates due process.... Fair notice that a particular act violates a statute is deemed to have been given to a particular defendant by the words of the statute, the legislative intent, or cases construing the statute.... A construction which does not comport with statutory language, legislative intent, or case law also violates the foundational constitutional principle of the separation of powers, except when the construing court overrules a previous judicial construction.... The exception is not applicable here because there is no previous judicial construction of § 632 as to the meaning of "communication"; therefore, in this case if the majority's construction of that term is not supported by any of the three elements of statutory construction, both due process and the separation of powers have been violated by an act of judicial legislation. Neither language, nor legislative intent, nor case law supports the majority's construction of that key term.

The statutory language gives a defendant fair notice that the defendant's acts violated a statute as long as the language is construed "according to the fair import of [its] terms' " not going "so far as to create an offense ... by giving the terms used ... unusual meanings." ... "Penal statutes will not be made to reach beyond their plain intent; they include only those offenses coming clearly within the import of their language." ...

The majority holds that sexual conduct is a form of communication in the sense that it conveys the thoughts and emotions of the participants. This strained construction of "communication" attributes to that term the "unu-

---

been confidential. Thus, whether or not recording sexual conduct is a violation of section 632, the recording of verbal communication indisputably is, and defendant was guilty of the charged violations under the latter theory, and the question of whether "communication" includes sexual conduct need not be decided. An appellate court will not ordinarily review a moot question....

Furthermore, I have found nothing in the record indicating that the defendant ever disputed the district attorney's argument or the trial court's ruling out of the jury's presence that sexual conduct is a form of communication, precisely because the district attorney was prosecuting on the alternative basis of the verbal communication.... In discussing the case, the trial court said to defense counsel, "Now you go up on appeal and they say you know what, the Judge was wrong. He should have never let the sex acts go to the jury as a confidential communication, it's clear they weren't. You're still dead in the water because the verbal conduct was. Do you follow me? ¶ [Defense Counsel]: Uh-huh." ... Indeed, the trial court never instructed that sexual conduct was communication, only that "A person may communicate with another by ... physical acts, gestures or any common system of symbols, signs or behavior, ... " (Id. at p. 266.) The record contains no objection to this instruction and indicates that defense counsel acquiesced in both the instruction and the ruling. Thus, any error was waived or invited and, therefore, at least arguably not preserved for appeal. While it is sometimes broadly stated that constitutional error may be raised for the first time on appeal ... that is not always the case.... Nevertheless, the issue of waiver of constitutional error is often bypassed, rightly or wrongly, to preclude a petition for writ of habeas corpus on the ground of ineffective assistance of counsel, which is typically used to circumvent a waiver....

sual meaning[ ]" of sexual conduct, a meaning which does not come "clearly within the import" of communication. Sexual acts are not the *communication* of thoughts and feelings; rather, they are *evidence* of feelings in the same way that a deadly assault is evidence, not communication, of malice.

To be distinguished from complex acts with multiple purposes in addition to communication, such as sexual conduct, are simple gestures and symbolic acts which have culturally determined meanings. Such acts as an affirmative nod and burning the flag are solely communicative in purpose in exactly the same sense as words or semaphore. The actor and observer are not so intent on the performance of these acts as on their meaning. The same cannot be said of more complex activities such as sexual conduct where multifarious purposes other than communication may be present exclusively, or concurrently and in varying degree, in any one instance, such as pleasure, procreation, and the satisfaction of a host of psychological, spiritual, and emotional needs and desires.

Thus, when one thinks of communication, one does not ordinarily or usually think of sexual conduct because sex has so many other meanings and communication has more obvious and concrete associations all associated with words, gestures, and symbols. Sexual conduct is not exclusively, nor even primarily or usually, communication in the sense that words, gestures, and symbolic acts are exclusively communication; therefore, the plain and ordinary meaning of communication cannot include sexual conduct, and the majority's construction to that effect is strained and assigns an "unusual" meaning to communication not "clearly with the import" of that term. Although recording sexual conduct might be considered "within the reason or mischief" and "of equal atrocity, or of kindred character" with the recording of a confidential communication, that is not sufficient to construe communication to include sexual acts. It is not the function of this court "to fill an asserted 'gap' in the law" by punishing the recording of private sexual conduct when the Legislature has not clearly done so....

In making this distinction between sex and communication, I recognize the unavoidable overlap of words and concepts at their margins which sometimes makes statutory construction an inexact process which is, perhaps, more of an art than a science. Indeed, I do not ignore that the oral communication, "I hate you," is evidence of a killer's malice just as is the assault, or that the sexual act does in a sense "communicate" affection. I do not mean that communication and evidence or communication and sex are mutually exclusive sets in a rigorous, mathematical sense. We figuratively say, "Acts speak louder than words."

However, an act communicates better than words, and sex is communication, only in the limited sense that sometimes the inferences to be drawn from acts are very clear, often because the actor was not intent upon restricting the inferences that could be drawn from his or her acts, whereas the actor can so easily lie with words. The point is that when a Legislature uses a word in a penal statute, unless the legislative history indicates otherwise, it is not speaking figuratively by poetic images, allegory, and figures of speech. Rather, the Legislature seeks to express the will of the people in direct, concrete, plain terms, not relying on peripheral meanings and innuendo when dealing with such a serious subject as the life and liberty of its citizens. Sexual conduct is not a direct, concrete, plain meaning of the term "communication"; we speak figuratively, poetically, romantically when we say that sexual intimacy communicates the thoughts and feelings of one for another.

In the context of this case, the legislative use of the plain and ordinary meaning of words means using the most general and unrestricted terms when it desires a broadly inclusive reading. The judiciary has recognized this legislative practice by the general rule of construction that the statutory construction most favorable to the defendant [generally the least inclusive] will be used when the statute is reasonably susceptible of two interpretations and legislative intent does not point to one of them. . . .

Thus, the majority is wrong in saying that the Legislature would have said "conversation" if they meant to preclude sexual conduct. If the Legislature had intended to reach the recording of private sexual conduct it would have used a term such as "confidential activity," an unmistakably broad and all inclusive term, not "confidential communication," as it did, which only includes sexual intimacy in an unusual, nonliteral, figurative sense. It cannot reasonably be held that the Legislature intended by the use of the term "communication" to lead us into the fog shrouded maze of the mind's associations connected with one of humanity's most fundamental, complex, and poorly understood drives.

Having decided that the language of the statute does not support the majority's construction, I turn to other evidence of legislative intent recognizing that "There are limits to this freedom to tamper with statutory language . . . [.] The primary source of the legislative intent and purpose is in the words used; if these are clear the court should not seek hidden motive or objects which do not appear on the face of the statute or from its legislative history.' . . . Contrary to the majority's holding, the above discussion justifies the holding that the term "communication" clearly does not embrace sexual conduct. We find no contrary indication in the legislative history which this court has examined consisting of the documents in the California State Archives concerning Assembly Bill No. 860 passed in 1967. . . .

Former sections 653i and 653j, repealed in 1967 by [Assembly Bill] 860, are the predecessors of section 632. . . . Section 653i, characterized by the Legislature as "relating to eavesdropping on confidential *communications*," prohibited the unconsented recording of *conversations* between a person in police custody and his or her attorney, religious advisor, or physician, indicating the terms were at the time considered equivalent.... Section 653j changed the wording to "communication," but, in view of the equivalency the Legislature accorded to the terms, this does not indicate any substantial increase in the breadth of the criminal prohibition, certainly not such an increase as would sweep along with it sexual conduct. More likely is the intent to include writings that were visually recorded.

The majority mentions the difference between the use of the term "communication" in section 632 and the use of "oral communication" in 18 U.S.C. §§ 2510-2511. However, there is nothing in the California legislative history that indicates the more limited language of the federal statute was considered in drafting section 632, and, more on point, there is no indication whatever that the distinction indicated a legislative intent to include sexual conduct as a kind of communication....

Section 630 sets forth the legislative intent in passing Assembly Bill No. 860, but cannot be read to support the majority's construction. That section makes clear that the purpose of the act was *not* to prevent all invasions of privacy, but only those invasions resulting from "the development of new devices and techniques for the purpose of eavesdropping upon private communications..." Thus, it makes clear that the Legislature was interested in protecting privacy by forbidding recording of private communications as a kind of "time-delayed" eavesdropping. The gravamen of recording private sexual conduct is not time-delayed eavesdropping, but time-delayed voyeurism, a wrong more directly related to section 647, subdivision (h), the "Peeping Tom" loitering subdivision. While voyeurism is clearly an invasion of privacy, section 630 nowhere indicates the Legislature's intention to protect privacy by punishing voyeurism. To construe Assembly Bill No. 860 as an antivoyeurism statute is the kind of judicial legislation condemned in *Keeler* [*v. Superior Court* 2 Cal. 3d 619, 632–33, 87 Cal. Rptr. 481, 470 P.2d 617 (1970)].

Furthermore, the legislative history of [Assembly Bill] No. 860 is replete with references to conversations, not nonverbal acts, as the equivalent of communications. The "Digest of Assembly Bill No. 860 (As Amended, June 5, 1967)" by then Assembly Speaker Jesse M. Unruh notes that "Under existing law, Penal Code section 653j, confidential *conversations* may be eavesdropped upon or recorded if only one party to the *conversation* gives his consent." (P. 3.) This at once shows the Assembly Speaker, and sole sponsor of Assembly Bill No. 860, equated the "communication" sections 653j and 632 with conversation, and shows the defect in section 653j that primarily motivated the adoption of section 632 that a participant could consent to the eavesdropping or recording of a communication without the consent of all participants.

The understanding of the term "communication" as referring to a conversation is also evidenced by a memorandum in the state archives file on Assem-

GRAVAMEN – the basic/significant part of a complaint/grievance.

bly Bill No. 860 to Speaker Unruh's legislative assistant from "Clyde Black-
mon, Consultant, Committee on Criminal Procedure." It states with reference
to section 653j, "The premise underlying the law is that recording a conversation or authorizing an outsider to eavesdrop is permissible . . . . " (P. 3.) How
the Legislature viewed the term "communication" in section 653j indicates
how the Legislature understood the same term in section 632 because the
"Bill Digest" prepared for the public hearing on April 25, 1967, before the Assembly Committee on Criminal Procedure states that section 632, subdivision
(c), "Defines the words 'confidential communication' and is adapted without
change from the existing section 653j(c)." (P. 2.)

Thus, the legislative history shows that the Legislature never considered the
issue of recording private activities as opposed to conversations, much less
sexual conduct, and was intent upon protecting privacy by preventing the recording of verbal communication. Without any support in the legislative history, the majority's unusual construction of communication to include sexual
conduct is without support and a violation of the separation of powers prohibition against judicial legislation as well as the due process requirement that
a defendant have fair notice that a statute applies to the act he or she
committed.

I now reach the third aid to proper construction of a statute, case law, and
find that as unsupportive of the majority's interpretation of the term "communication" as is the language and legislative history of section 632.

The majority quotes the California Supreme Court to the effect that almost
any act could be an attorney-client communication if it were intended as such.
. . . We first observe that the act specifically considered in that case was "a neu-
rological and psychiatric examination" requested by the client's attorneys. . . .
The Supreme Court held that the examination and its results came within the
attorney-client privilege, the doctor being "an intermediate agent for communication" . . . likening the examination to the examples listed in the full
quotation of the above passage taken from 8 Wigmore, Evidence, (3d ed.
1940): "The client, supposedly, may make a specimen of his handwriting for
the attorney's information, or may exhibit an identifying scar, or may show a
secret token. If any of these acts are done as part of a communication to the
attorney, and if further the communication is intended to be confidential . . . ,
the privilege comes into play.' . . . " . . .

I have no quarrel with the Supreme Court's holding, but find it inapplicable.
Conceivably an attorney might engage an expert to evaluate an injured plaintiff's sexual performance in the context of trying to prove injury, in which case
any sexual conduct evaluated would come within the privilege as part of a
communication to the attorney. However, in that context the sexual conduct
per se would not be the communication with the attorney any more than
would be any message in the words written as a sample of a client's handwrit-

ing. It is the characteristics of the act, not the act itself, that truly constitutes the communication to the lawyer, taking the place of the client's verbal description of the act or condition. Thus, the Supreme Court's holding that an act may be a communication for the purposes of the attorney-client privilege is not a holding that sexual conduct is communication for the purposes of section 632.

Furthermore, even if the rule in attorney-client privilege cases were applicable, a requirement of that rule was not the subject of any evidence or argument in the record I have seen. That requirement is proof that the sexual conduct was intended as a communication instead of merely a pleasurable experience.

The majority opinion cites *Granite Construction Co. v. Superior Court*, ... for the proposition that the construction of a statute so as to punish a particular act for the first time does not violate due process. I do not dissent for that reason; I dissent because there is no language, case, or statute, such as there was in *Granite Construction*, that gave fair notice of the extension of the term "communication" to sexual conduct....

The majority misconstrues *People v. Sobiek* ... to support its argument that "we are convinced defendant received fair warning. There can be little doubt defendant knew that in recording the sexual activity without the woman's consent, he was violating her right of privacy and that 'common social duty' would suggest a 'more circumspect conduct.' " ... While the court in *Sobiek* does quote a previous case to that effect, the court in the following paragraph narrowly construes the broad statement of law quoted and underlined by the majority: " 'common social duty' would have forewarned respondent that 'circumspect conduct' prohibited *robbing* his partners and also told him that he was *stealing* 'property of another.' " ...

Just as section 487, the section Sobiek violated, protects property by punishing the taking of property by theft but does not punish the taking of property by burglary, section 632 protects privacy by punishing the recording of confidential communications but does not punish the recording of private sexual conduct. While "common social duty' would have forewarned" Sobiek that he was committing theft by stealing his partners' property, "common social duty' would [*not*] have forewarned" Gibbons that he was recording a confidential communication by recording private sexual conduct. The forewarning must be of the offense punishable by the statute allegedly violated, not the violation of the broad societal interest that the statute protects.

I conclude that no case law supports the majority's construction of the term "communication" in section 632 to include sexual conduct. Since this construction also subverts the common, ordinary meaning of the term in favor of an unusual meaning finding no support in the legislative history, I find it to be judicial legislation enlarging the scope of section 632 without the fair notice to the defendant required by due process.

7

Law Library Survival

Legal Research

By now you have surely come to the conclusion that a legal question rarely has a clear cut and obvious answer. If only because of the critical role played by caselaw in the United States, "looking it up," or legal research, is essential in many if not most cases. In fact, the ability to identify legal issues and determine their probable resolution is at the heart of being a lawyer.

Doing legal research requires an understanding of both the mechanics of law material organization and the fundamentals of legal reasoning. Legal analysis skills are required for the lawyer (or law student) to be able to dissect a set of facts presented by a client's inquiry, to identify potential sources of law materials that may help the lawyer analyze the legal effect of those facts, to locate legal rules that govern the various aspects of the client's problem, and to focus the search in and application of those materials according to the organizational pattern of the governing rules and their relationships to the facts. Although it would be possible for you to learn the mechanics of law material organization as a beginning law student, learning the fundamentals of legal reasoning takes some time. This book, in part, is meant to introduce those fundamentals, but it will take some time and study before you have sufficient grounding in them to be ready for a serious run at learning legal research skills beyond those related solely to the mechanics of law material organization. As a result, we make no pretense of teaching you to do legal research in these materials; indeed, we think that too early an attempt at teaching legal research is likely to do more harm than good. Our goal is far more modest: this chapter is meant to provide you with the minimum library survival skills for a first semester law student.

The Law Library

If legal research is so essential to the lawyer it is no surprise that the law library is the heart of a law office or law school. If law is indeed a science, then the law library is the research lab. At the very least, it is the critical resource without which lawyers cannot practice. As the 21st Century dawns, law libraries are changing. Perhaps the most important change is the availability of enormous computer databases of statutes, cases, regulations, periodicals, treatises and the like. Only a telephone call away from a personal computer, these databases give even the solo practitioner access to the equivalent of some of the nation's leading law libraries. Law students customarily enjoy access to these same resources in their law school libraries and even from their own computers at home. As computer data becomes more available the need for books lessens. Books are not obsolete, by any means, however. Although computer assisted research may be readily available, it can prove less valuable than one might expect. Computer assisted legal research is cost prohibitive for many small law offices as well as for many clients. Further, traditional research methods yield valuable serendipitous effects not always available by computer. Many argue effectively that solid grounding in manual research skills is a prerequisite to learning effective computer assisted skills. Accordingly, computer assisted research and traditional, manual research should be regarded as two aspects of the same process. Whether research is electronic or manual, the central role played by law librarians remains unchanged.

Legal research is an art as well as a science. No matter how skilled an attorney, or law professor for that matter, the experienced advice of a law librarian can save time and point the way to unimagined materials. Good librarians take great pride in helping those in need of their skills and are an essential part of legal practice and education.

Although we cannot even attempt to teach you how to use a law library, we can emphasize the need for those of you who intend to become lawyers to master the skill of library usage. You should take your instruction in legal research most seriously. Your future and that of your clients will rest upon your research ability.

Library Survival; Citations

Whether you are a first semester law student or simply a person interested in the law, you will probably not need to perform legal research.[1] What you must be able to do, however, is to locate a few kinds of materials in the library when given a citation (or citation-like information) that refers to that material. If you are a law student, your need to locate such materials will primarily arise in one of two ways: you will be referred to additional materials by a text or by a teacher. Remember the Note material in chapter 5? As time permits, you will find it helpful to locate and examine sources referred to in the Note sections of your casebooks, particularly when you find that your study of the casebook

---

1. If you are, it will almost surely be in the context of a legal research course.

itself proves insufficient to your understanding of the concepts presented. In addition to locating Note materials, often your substantive law teachers will refer in class to outside resources. Again, you will often find it helpful to locate and examine these resources. There are also occasions when it may be helpful to locate and read the full opinion from a court rather than the edited version that is found in your casebook. In any case, you will be given either a full citation or citation-like information.

Law writing, like many other kinds of writing, requires that the writer refer to authority, the source used, that supports the writer's assertion. Unlike many other fields, law writing uses a "show me" system of citation to authority rather than a "trust me" system of citation to authority. In other words, a great deal of information about the authority is provided in a full law citation, and that citation must be provided to support each assertion made rather than providing a general bibliography of sources upon which the writer relied.[2]

Although other systems of citation form are making claims of superior lucidity, *A Uniform System of Citation*,[3] otherwise known simply as the "Bluebook," remains the overwhelmingly dominant system of law source citation form. In the *Bluebook*, among many other things, you will find lists of approved abbreviations for many law sources. You will study the *Bluebook* and its intricacies later in your law school career.

Given the citation or the information that would compose the citation, finding the source in the library is a fairly simple matter. Happily, that is all that most first semester law students are called upon to do. With the citation, all that is needed to find the reference is to know where the source is kept in the library. The three kinds of sources most commonly referred to either in Notes sections of casebooks or by teachers are case opinions, law review articles or other legal periodicals, and treatises or hornbooks. Below are citations to one each of the three kinds of sources with a model of the information that you should expect to find in a citation to that kind of source in proper form. Citation form, using the *Bluebook*, is complex. The rules differentiate between memoranda of law and books and articles,[4] between text and footnotes, and between material published with sophisticated equipment or typewriters. The illustrative citations that follow comply with the *Bluebook's* rules for periodical footnotes, the format you are most likely to encounter initially. In normal practice *italics* is represented by <u>underlining</u>.

---

2. For an example, see the sample memorandum of law at page 148.
3. Harvard Law Review Association (14th ed. 1986) [hereinafter the *Bluebook*].
4. Accordingly, the same citation will appear differently in different types of legal writing.

Court opinions:[5]

Johnson v. Cadillac Motor Co., 261 F. 878 (2d Cir. 1919).

Components:

Case Name: *Johnson v. Cadillac Motor Co.*
Volume: 261
Reporter:[6]   F.[7]
Page: 878
Court:[8]   2d Cir.[9]
Year: 1919

Law review article or periodical:[10]

James, Products Liability, 34 TEX. L. REV. 44 (1955).

Components:

Author: James
Title: *Products Liability*
Volume: 34
Periodical: TEX. L. REV.[11]
Page: 44
Year: 1955

Treatise or hornbook:[12]

3 F. HARPER, THE LAW OF TORTS, § 18.5 (2d ed. 1986)

Components:

Volume:[13]   3
Author: F. HARPER
Title: THE LAW OF TORTS
Section:[14]   §18.5

---

5. *See generally Bluebook* Rule 10, *supra* note.
6. Many cases are reported in more than one reporter. When this happens, there may be additional, parallel reporter citations required.
7. Standing for the Federal Reporter which reports the opinions of the United States Court of Appeals from the different circuits. "F.2d" would represent the Federal Reporter, second series.
8. If not apparent from the reporter name.
9. "2d Cir." stands for the second circuit.
10. *See generally Bluebook* Rule 16, *supra* note 3.
11. Texas Law Review.
12. *See generally Bluebook* Rule 15, *supra* note 3.
13. If a multi-volume set.
14. Or paragraph or page.

Edition:[15]   2d ed.

Year: 1986

Illustrative citations

The following pages contain citations to a number of sources of those three kinds that were either referred to in the Notes section of our simulated casebook, chapter 5, or that might well have been mentioned in class had you been studying the chapter 5 materials in Torts class. If you are a law student and time permits, you should, with the help of library staff, locate at least one source from each category.

Court Opinions:

Richmond and Danville Railroad v. Elliot, 149 U.S. 266 (1893).

Goullon v. Ford Motor Co., 44 F.2d 310 (6th Cir. 1930).

MacPherson v. Buick Motor Co., 217 N.Y. 382, 111 N.E. 1050 (1916).

Devlin v. Smith, 89 N.Y. 470 (1882).

In re Dakota Country Food Stores, 107 Bankr. 977 (D.S.D. 1989).

Law Review Articles or Periodicals:

Davis, *Re-examination of the Doctrine of MacPherson v. Buick and Its Application and Extension in the State of New York*, 24 FORDHAM L. REV. 204 (1955).

Bohlen, *The Basis of Affirmative Obligations in the Law of Torts*, 53 U. PA. L. REV. 237 (1905).

Note, *Manufacturers' Liability to Ultimate Consumers*, 37 MARQ. L. REV. 356 (1954).

Jeanblanc, *Manufacturers' Liability to Persons Other Than Their Immediate Vendees*, 24 VA. L. REV. 134 (1937).

Note, *Tort Liability to Third Parties Arising from Breach of Contract*, 14 MD. L. REV. 77 (1954).

Treatises or Hornbooks:

W. PROSSER, HANDBOOK OF THE LAW OF TORTS § 53 (5th ed. 1984).

D. NOEL, PRODUCTS LIABILITY IN A NUTSHELL 28-29 (1981).

M. SHAPO, THE LAW OF PRODUCTS LIABILITY ¶16.01(1) (1987).

5 S. SPEISER, THE AMERICAN LAW OF TORTS § 18:2 (1983 and Supp. 1989).

C. MORRIS, TORTS 143 (1980).

---

15. If other than the first edition.

8

Client Service

Introduction

More than anything else, lawyers serve clients. They do so in the context of many other duties and loyalties, but client service is the core of the lawyer's circle of activities. No discussion of law practice goes far without treating client service. Nor does a discussion of legal ethics go far without treatment of the implications of the client-lawyer relationship. Recognizing and considering this connection between lawyering activities and lawyer ethics will provide you with valuable insights into your work as a law student and later as lawyer.

Almost as important are the pragmatic and academic implications of client representation. You have now read a number of real cases. Note that those cases are entirely fact dependent. Change an important fact, and the results of the case and the law that will flow from it will likely change as well. Although appellate cases are procedure dependent as well and there are many other factors that will affect the way in which the case will be argued and resolved, facts are the most crucial. Where do those facts come from? Obviously, the facts must come from the mouth of the client and later from the fact gathering process. The simple failure to obtain a single crucial fact during the client interview could ultimately dictate the fate of the case. Candidly, it is not probable that this will occur if only because subsequent interviews and other fact gathering[1] will *probably* bring it to light. Yet, we can say only probably. Not only will the facts discovered from the client be of great importance, the client's desires and interests often will dictate the direction the case must go. In short, every one of the appellate cases you have and will read ultimately rest not just on client service and representation but also upon that magic moment when the lawyer first meets the client.

---

1. Such as pretrial civil discovery.

Interviewing Clients, the Beginning of Client Service

The process of interviewing a new client presents a fairly inclusive micro-cosmic view of the lawyer's ethical world. The process of interviewing a client potentially implicates a wide range of ethics topics that would be treated in a text on the subject, such as the duty of confidentiality, conflicts of interest, fees, fiduciary duties, pursuit of frivolous claims, solicitation, competence, representing unpopular clients, the lawyer's duty to provide public service, and zealous representation and its limits. But more importantly the interviewing process involves the lawyer in the process of answering the pervasive lawyer ethics question: "Who am I, and who do I want to be, as a lawyer?" The way in which the lawyer treats the client says much not merely about the lawyer's technical expertise but about the lawyer's self. As you read our description of the techniques of interviewing that follows, consider the ethical statement being made by the lawyer who follows the technique we describe.

The lawyer has two goals in the initial client interview: to create a positive relationship with the client and to gather information. A well-constructed interview will further both of these goals. To accomplish these goals, an interviewer should strive to make the client comfortable; if the client is comfortable, the lawyer's relationship with the client will likely be enhanced and the client will likely be more open with the lawyer.

The lawyer should strive to be patient, a skill that does not come naturally to all lawyers. People like to be listened to, and listening to a client helps further both the lawyer's goals in the interview process. Listening makes the client more comfortable and feel more important to the process of resolving the client's own problem. Listening also allows for more efficient fact gathering. That may seem counterintuitive. Many would approach the interviewing process with the assumption that the lawyer, who after all knows what questions to ask, should not allow a client to begin the interview with a long, sometimes rambling rendition of the facts that bring the client and lawyer together. Rather, intuition might say, the lawyer should have a list of questions for the domestic relations client, another list for the personal injury client and so on. Answers to the relevant list of questions would efficiently accomplish the fact gathering goal. Damage to the relationship-building goal aside, the intuitive approach to the interview is wrong. Clients do not come in cookie-cutter shapes and sizes. Problems that may at first seem to be of one type may mask even more serious problems of other types. Rarely does a client's problem fail to cut across subject matter lines. As such, giving the client an opportunity, and then being patient enough to let the client take advantage of the opportunity, to render the facts with a minimum of interruption from the lawyer will be more likely to lead to an accurate identification of the many facets of a client's reason for seeking the aid of a lawyer. Accurate identification of the client's interests is more efficient than quicker (but less accurate) methods of interviewing. These quicker methods might work well for a clerk at the department of motor vehicles, but are unsuited to the establishment of a relationship between client and lawyer.

Patience requires much more energy than you might think. Many lawyers who are excellent listeners find the interviewing process to be at least as exhausting as appearing in court. Restraining your natural inclination to inquire is hard work. The role of patience, augmented by good listening skills, finds its way into the general organizational pattern that a good initial interview follows.

A typical initial interview follows a pattern something like this:

(1) An icebreaking stage designed to relieve some of the initial tension that many clients feel;
(2) An overview-problem and goal identification stage;
(3) A directed, gap-filling stage;
(4) A response stage; and
(5) A closing.

At various points in the process, the lawyer will attempt to verify what has happened in the interview by reflecting and summarizing what the client has said.

Icebreaking

The icebreaking stage is what you might expect. A few moments of appropriate small talk serves the purpose well. At this stage, the attitude exhibited toward the client is more important than are the words that are spoken. Consider where and the way in which you greet the client, the arrangement of furniture, and your demeanor as being important parts of this stage of the interview: your goal is to allow the client to feel as comfortable with you as possible.

Overview

The overview-problem and goal identification stage is probably the most important and most easily misexecuted stage. Here, the interviewer seeks to elicit as much of the story of the client's problem as the client can deliver with a minimum of lawyer interruption. Using open-ended questions and using even them sparingly is the key. The lawyer should initially ask the client a starter question, such as, "How can I help you?" or "What brings you to my office?", then do nothing except listen and watch for as long as the client talks in response. When the client's rendition bogs down, the lawyer should be careful to use open rather than closed-ended questions to get the client to continue.

For example, a client might respond to the starter question by giving just a bit of the story, including the statement, "My neighbor won't let me use the alley that runs behind our houses." As tempting as it might be, the lawyer should resist the inclination to launch into a series of narrow questions such as: "What is your neighbor's name?" "What is your home address?" "What has your neighbor done to stop you?" or "Who owns the alley?" The answers to all of these questions might well be important, but when the lawyer begins asking narrow questions too early, a damaging message is delivered to the client. The client takes on the role of question-answerer rather than that of a partner in the process of resolving the problem that brought the client to the lawyer. When this change of role takes place, clients provide less information (they merely answer questions), clients feel less involved often producing an unhealthy relationship with the lawyer, and client needs often go undiscovered and therefore unserved. Rather than the narrow questions, the lawyer would more productively proceed with open-ended questioning, such as "Tell me more", or even better, with nonverbal ways of getting the client to simply continue the story, such as nodding, leaning forward or even silence.

The rare but notable exception to our suggestion of extreme patience in this interview stage occurs when a client demonstrates a willingness to carry on an extended monologue that obviously has no bearing on the client's problem. Even then, the perceptive lawyer can acquire considerable information about the client by allowing the rambling to proceed at least for a time.

During this early stage in the interview, the lawyer must determine what the client wants or hopes to achieve. The goals may range all the way from a business client's goal of setting up a lawful retirement program for employees to a personal injury client's goal of obtaining fair compensation to a criminal defendant's goal of staying out of prison. Whatever the goal might be, the lawyer needs to ensure that both lawyer and client have the same goal in mind *and* that the goal is one that the lawyer can ethically assist the client in seeking. In our alley-blocking case, the client may have responded to a goal identification question by saying, "I want the fence torn down," or "I think the fence itself is great; I want a key," or "I want that son-of-a-bitch neighbor dragged into court and kept there for as long as possible, and I want you to get the prosecutor interested in charging him with some criminal offense."

The issue of what sort of client-lawyer relationship should be developed must be considered at this stage: does one or the other "call all the shots" or can a more productive, ethically satisfying relationship between cooperative problem solvers be established? If the latter, the lawyer's role as a counselor and sometimes moral advisor is implicated by this stage of the interviewing process, and lawyer and client will work together to identify appropriate goals and analyze the means of achieving them.

Gap filling

Following a successful overview-problem and goal identification stage, the lawyer should carefully and systematically fill in the gaps. Often this can best be accomplished by taking the client back to the beginning point of the story's chronology, and walking through that chronology step by step. This would be an appropriate time for note taking to begin. Before this stage, all the lawyer's energy and concentration should be on listening and not note taking.

At each step of the chronology, questions about that part of the events should be directed to the client. For example:

Lawyer:	You've described the gate that your neighbor had built at the mouth of the alley. When did you first see it?
Client:	I watched my neighbor build the thing.
Lawyer:	Exactly when was that?
Client:	Saturday morning, July 11 of this year.
Lawyer:	Had anything happened prior to that Saturday that relates to your access to the alley?
Client:	No, this was the first I had any idea that my neighbor was up to something. We aren't close. We had no ill feelings that I know of, but we've never spoken to each other more than to comment on the weather.
Lawyer:	How long did you watch your neighbor work on the fence?
Client:	The whole time, probably two hours. I was flabbergasted.
Lawyer:	Where were you as you watched?
Client:	On my back porch.
Lawyer:	Did you and your neighbor have any conversation at that time?
Client:	None at all.
Lawyer:	Can you tell me everything you remember seeing for those two hours?
Client:	[Description of events]
Lawyer:	What first occurred after the neighbor completed the fence? Etc.

On occasions when a chronological pattern is unsuitable to the client's problem, a series of questions directed at a series of topics will usually present the preferred organizational pattern.

Response

Had you not already read the prior chapters, you might expect that responding to a client at this stage of the interview would be a straightforward matter: lawyers, by virtue of their specialized education, simply know and deliver the answers to clients' questions. Actually, as you no doubt now realize, it is more the exception than the rule for lawyers to know the answer to a client's question and give it at the initial interview. The law is broad and complex and every client's problem is different in at least some way from every other's. Further, the lawyer will almost always have to undertake a process of confirming the facts. As a result, in most cases, while a lawyer may make some fairly general remarks about the law that governs the client's legal problem, the obvious dangers to the client of venturing a guess militate against giving early, definitive answers. Ultimately, a lawyer will often answer a client's question at the initial interview by promising to have more information at a specific future time and by explaining the work that the lawyer will do to gather that information. Even when answers are found, as you will soon see, they are often qualified and not absolute. The law is less of a science of simple application of rule to problem data to reach certain results than you might presently think.

Closing

Finally, some appropriate closing is in order. The lawyer and client should both leave with a clear idea of the relationship between the two. This idea should include the parameters of the relationship,[2] the fee arrangement, and the division of responsibilities (for example, lawyer to do research and client to locate and deliver certain documents to the lawyer). There should be a clear indication of how contact will next be made.[3]

Once completed, the interview forms the lawyer's initial picture of the facts. A file will be opened with an appropriate summary of the facts and the client's interests, as well as an explanation of what the lawyer has undertaken to do for the client. Absent other early fact investigation activities, a lawyer will analyze the effects of the law's application to that set of facts and report the results of that analysis to both the file and the client.

An Example of Client Service

An interview transcript, an assignment from Partner to Associate, the Associate's response to that assignment by legal memorandum, and a letter to

---

2. Has the lawyer undertaken to represent the client through any conceivable course that pursuit of the client's goals might lead or is the representation limited to certain kinds of activities?

3. For example, lawyer to call or write to the client within two weeks and client to call with any new information in the interim.

the client relating the Associate's analysis follow. Consider these as a sample of client service generally and samples of interview technique and ethics, memorandum writing, and letter writing, in particular. As you read through the following materials, reflect on the court opinions that you read in chapter 5. Picture yourself again as the lawyer to whom the Thomases, or the kin of Hugh Devlin, or Donald MacPherson came. How would your early work for them have proceeded?

An interview with Pat Marshall

Lawyer:	Good afternoon Mr. Marshall. Did you have any trouble finding a parking space? Good. I assume that the receptionist told you that there is no charge for this initial interview. It's an opportunity for us to meet each other, to see if I can be of service to you, and to help both of us to decide if we can work together. How can I help you today?
Marshall:	Well, I need to get out of a lease.
Lawyer:	I see. Please tell me about it. [Lawyer listens attentively; does not take written notes.]
Marshall:	When I moved here a few weeks ago, I got an apartment at the Colonyshire Apartment complex. The apartment looked great when I looked it over, and I thought it would be fine. The problem is, my first night in the apartment, I found out that the place is infested with roaches. I can't stand them, and I need to get out of my lease.
Lawyer:	Could you tell me more about it?
Marshall:	I told the landlord—that's Great Chesapeake Realty—about the bugs, and they sent an exterminator out to spray the apartment the next day. It didn't do any good, though. The roaches were back the next night; in fact there were even more of them, if that's possible. On top of that, the bug spray made me really sick. I got a bad headache, and pretty severe nausea.
Lawyer:	So the bug spray wasn't effective, and it made you sick? [Nodding head in sympathy.]
Marshall:	Yes. When I got the headaches and nausea, I went to see my doctor, and she told me that it was because I was allergic to the insecticide. In fact, she said that I was allergic to basically all the common types of roach killers. She told me that I would probably have to be hospitalized if they spray my apartment again.

Lawyer:	That puts you in a real bind.
Marshall:	Well, I've been putting up with the bugs for the past two weeks, but it's really been getting to me. Then, a couple of days ago, a friend of mine invited me to share his apartment. It's closer to work, it costs less, and it has a pool, which Colonyshire doesn't. Oh, and it doesn't have any roaches.
Lawyer:	That sounds very nice.
Marshall:	Right. The problem is, I signed a one-year lease at Colonyshire, and I paid a $600 security deposit. I really can't afford to lose that money and I'm worried that if I leave I'll owe them 11 more months of rent. My lease says that if I move out early, I owe the $350/month rent payment for the rest of the year. If my math is right, that's $3850.
Lawyer:	I think I understand. Your apartment is overrun with roaches, there seems to be no effective pesticide that won't make you sick, and you've found another place that is better in many ways, but you can't afford to lose your security deposit or face liability for $3850.
Marshall:	Yeah, that's it.
Lawyer:	How would you like to see this resolved?
Marshall:	I have to move out. I can't stand the bugs or the bug spray. I'd like to get my $600 back and I can't pay $3850 rent for a place I'm no longer living in.
Lawyer:	O.K. Mr. Marshall, I'd like to go through what you've just told me again, and take down a few notes, to make sure that I've got all the facts straight. [Lawyer now gets out a pad of paper and takes brief, specific notes on information provided by Marshall.] Why don't you start at the beginning of your contact with Colonyshire? How did you find out about the apartment?
Marshall:	I drove by and saw a sign outside that said, "Apartment for rent."
Lawyer:	Then what happened?
Marshall:	Well, I stopped in the next afternoon, and was told about the cost and all, and it sounded just like what I wanted.
Lawyer:	What happened next?
Marshall:	I signed the lease.
Lawyer:	Did you bring it with you today?

Marshall:	No, I forgot to bring it with me, but I can get it to you.
Lawyer:	That would be fine; I'll need to see it. Tell me about your inspection of the apartment.
Marshall:	Well, I didn't really inspect the actual apartment. They showed me a model, and it looked good. They also pointed out the actual apartment, but I didn't go into it, because they were painting.
Lawyer:	Who were you dealing with?
Marshall:	Ms. Ida Colson, the sales manager for the complex.
Lawyer:	When did you move in?
Marshall:	On the 9th. That's also the day that I paid for the first month's rent, and the $600 security deposit.
Lawyer:	And when did you first notice the roaches?
Marshall:	That night. I got up and went into the kitchen after the news, at about 11:30. When I turned on the lights, it looked like a roach convention. It was awful. It gives me the shudders to think about it.
Lawyer:	What did you do next?
Marshall:	I called Ms. Colson the next morning, at 9:00. She had Zippo Exterminators in the apartment while I was at work, that day. When I got back to the apartment at 5:00 that afternoon, I got sick almost right away.
Lawyer:	And what about the roaches?
Marshall:	If anything, there were more of them that night. I think that they like the stuff.
Lawyer:	Who is the doctor you saw concerning your illness?
Marshall:	Dr. Jackie Otto. She has a clinic downtown.
Lawyer:	Did she give you any kind of letter or medical history sheet about your allergy to the roach spray?
Marshall:	Yes, she did. It's in my health file at home.
Lawyer:	Mr. Marshall, tell me again so that I'm sure I understand, what results you would like to see from this situation, what your goals are in this matter.
Marshall:	Well, I would like to be able to get out of my lease at Colonyshire so that I can move in with my friend. And I would like to get my $600 security deposit back. I really need that money. And I can't begin to pay $3850 rent for the rest of the year after I move out.

Lawyer:	Mr. Marshall, can you think of anything else?
Marshall:	Not really. Well, I met someone else at the apartment who had trouble with bugs and the complex really hassled him. Do you think that I can get my money back? Will I be liable for the $3850? Oh. And is this going to cost a lot of money? I've just moved here, and money is still a little bit tight.
Lawyer:	First, as to getting your deposit back, I'll have to do some research. I'd rather give you an answer that I'm reasonably sure of than one that's off the top of my head. Second, as to fees; as I mentioned at the beginning today, this initial interview is free. My fees for additional work would be $75 per hour, plus expenses incurred. I could not give you a definite statement as to how much time would be involved in this matter, but the initial research will not be more than two hours. It will take me somewhat more than two hours, but given your circumstances I'm willing to do this initial work for two hours' fee. Once I've finished the research, we can talk about what makes the most sense for you as a next step. I understand that your goal is to get out of your lease, avoid liability on the rest of the lease, and recover as much of your $600 as possible, so we don't want to eat up that money in legal fees. If it's agreeable to you, I'd be happy to take your case. You should feel comfortable with your attorney, whether it's me or someone else. If you would like to retain my services, I'll need you to sign the retainer agreement which my secretary explained to you in the reception area.
Marshall:	As long as we can keep the costs down, I'd like you to go ahead with my case.
Lawyer:	Good, I'd be happy to. I'll do the research and reach a tentative conclusion based on what I know now. As soon as I see the lease and the doctor's statement we should be able to meet again in a few days to discuss where we go from there.
Marshall:	Great. Thanks very much.

* * *

An assignment

Please presume that you are a junior associate in a small law firm. You have either interviewed Pat Marshall yourself or have been fully briefed as to the contents of that interview. A senior member of the firm requests that you research the "habitability" issue raised by Marshall's facts. Note that as is often the case, you are not being asked to resolve all of the issues raised by the client. Your research results are supplied because of the nature of this illustrative exercise.

Caution! Although you are welcome to complete each phase of this assignment and to compare it with the materials that follow, we primarily intend the following as a complete example of the results of a typical interview raising a limited legal problem.

Your assignment comes to you via memo:

MOLITERNO, LEVY & LEDERER

Date: July 23, 19xx

MEMORANDUM TO: Associate (You)

FROM: Partner

SUBJECT: Pat Marshall, warranty of habitability memorandum

Please prepare a memorandum setting forth your views as to whether your client can escape from the lease in question because of the conditions of the apartment, namely the roach infestation and resulting medical problems. In doing so, please consider the following:

1. Use only the case materials that are attached and the text of the Wythe Landlord-Tenant Act which provides that:

   > A landlord is obligated to furnish a lessee with premises which are fit for habitation. Should the landlord fail to comply with this requirement in a reasonable time, the lessee may inform the landlord in writing and vacate the premises if the noncompliance materially affects health or safety.

   Mr. Marshall is concerned both about his $600 deposit and about his potential lease liability of $3850. If he is entitled to rescind the lease, he should be entitled both to the return of his deposit and to be released from further rent obligations under the lease. Please do no additional research at this time. I have promised the client that we will bill no more than two hours for this initial work even though it may take you somewhat longer than that.

2. Remember to keep the memorandum brief; supply all necessary facts but no others; do explain the law's application to the facts with care.

After you complete your memorandum, draft a letter to Mr. Marshall that provides your analysis on this issue and your suggestions of alternative ways of treating his problem.

IN THE SUPREME COURT OF WYTHE

MIRA A. BETZ, Petitioner
v.
ALFRED Z. SMITH, Respondent

245 Wythe 143
[No. 1976-79]
Argued October 17, 1975. Decided January 24, 1976

Opinion of the Court

Justice Swartz delivered the opinion of the Court.

On September 19, 1973, pursuant to a leasehold interest granted her by Respondent, Alfred Z. Smith, Petitioner, Miss Mira A. Betz, took possession of a one bedroom apartment at 1231 Washington Street, Hamilton. The apartment was one of 25 such apartments in the building owned by Respondent at that location.

The trial court found as fact that immediately upon taking occupancy, Petitioner discovered major breaches in the walls, steam escaping from improperly heated hot water lines, and numerous exposed and frayed electrical lines. The court also found that these defects deprived Petitioner of the opportunity to use the leased premises in reasonable comfort. Petitioner gave immediate oral notice of these conditions to Respondent's rental agent who replied that Respondent had complied with his duty to make the apartment available to Respondent, and that its condition was not his responsibility. Subsequent written notice to Respondent yielded a similar result. Miss Betz then sued to have her lease declared void.

Both the trial and intermediate appellate courts expressed great sympathy for Petitioner's position but considered themselves bound by this Court's prior rulings.

We have considered a lease of land to a tenant as the equivalent of a land sale for the length of the lease. Accordingly the lessor has held no responsibility to the tenant for the condition of the leased premises. The doctrine of caveat emptor, "let the buyer beware" has been applicable. Although long hallowed, this result is unconscionable and is no longer tenable.

Caveat emptor assumes both equality of bargaining power and the capacity to inspect and adequately evaluate premises prior to entering into a residential lease. It is clear to all familiar with contemporary housing that these assumptions are rarely accurate. Given limited adequate housing, potential tenants are often ill equipped to bargain at arms length with landlords. Further, to the extent that such bargaining is possible, tenants are usually unable to ascertain actual or latent defects which might seriously threaten the habitability of the premises.

That a lessor owes a lessee something more than the mere right to "enjoy" otherwise uninhabitable premises is being increasingly recognized in other jurisdictions. We consider most persuasive the 1969 American Bar Foundation's Model Residential Landlord- Tenant Code and the 1972 Uniform Residential Landlord and Tenant Act (URLTA). Both of these model codes impose upon a landlord a duty to maintain premises in habitable condition. We recognize that the Wythe legislature has not as yet enacted either of these codes or any similar provisions. However, other states have not found such a statutory vacuum determinative. *See, e.g.* Green v. Superior Court, 10 Cal. 3d 616, 111 Cal. Rptr. 704, 517 P.2d 1168 (1974); Marini v. Ireland, 56 N.J. 130, 265 A.2d 526 (1970).

We find the logic of those opinions undeniable. Accordingly, we hold that a lease of residential premises carries with it an implied warranty of habitability. The scope of this implied warranty must await further development. However, at the very least we hold that to the extent that a landlord has actual notice of conditions in leased premises which render them unfit for safe human habitation, the landlord breaches this warranty and relieves the lessee of any requirement to comply with the lease. To the extent that our prior cases are inconsistent with this holding, *see, e.g.* Toure v. Giff, 177 Wythe 12 (1947), they are overruled. Inasmuch as the trial court failed to apply the appropriate legal test to the facts before it, this case must be returned to it for further action in conformity with this decision.

Reversed and remanded.

IN THE SUPREME COURT OF WYTHE

JOSEPH B. PATTERSON, Petitioner
v.
LUCINDA W. BISHOP, Respondent

252 Wythe 60
[No. 1982-282]
Argued September 10, 1982. Decided December 14, 1982

Opinion of the Court

Justice Ball delivered the opinion of the Court.

This case concerns facts the like of which have not been seen in this state in modern times. In February, 1979, Respondent, Lucinda W. Bishop and her three children, moved into Petitioner's two bedroom frame dwelling pursuant to a "standard" three year lease signed by Respondent. The trial court found that the house, although substandard and undesirable, was "adequate" at the time Ms. Bishop took occupancy. That condition did not continue indefinitely, however.

As found by the trial court, Ms. Bishop began to experience difficulties with various forms of vermin some three weeks after moving in. Although an unusual assortment of fauna seem to have poured through this major pest interchange, the worst was clearly the cockroaches. As extensively documented at trial, by May, 1979, Respondent suffered a cockroach invasion large enough to have constituted a biblical plague. They carpeted the walls, floors, refrigerator and stove and virtually inundated the bathroom. In addition to making the house very unhomelike, the trial court found that the roaches also posed a major health risk to Ms. Bishop's 10 month old baby whose mouth was found filled with roaches on at least two occasions.

Respondent notified Petitioner of these circumstances by letter four times. Petitioner failed to respond. Alleging a breach of Petitioner's implied warranty of habitability, Respondent subsequently moved out and sued Petitioner for damages caused by her untimely move. Petitioner alleged that Respondent had breached her lease and counterclaimed for damages caused by the need to find a replacement tenant.

Applying our decision in Betz v. Smith, 245 Wythe 143 (1976), the trial court held that the vermin in Respondent's home, whether resident or transitory, rendered it "unfit for safe human habitation," *id.* at 144, and gave judgment for Respondent, denying Petitioner's counterclaim. Petitioner appealed claiming that the trial court misapplied the law. The Court of Appeals denied Petitioner's claim, however. Petitioner subsequently appealed to this court pursuant to Wythe Ann. Code § 27-1363.

Petitioner alleges that an infestation of "bugs," however unpleasant cannot constitute the type of risk to safety required by Betz. Petitioner clearly misunderstands the import of Betz.

We did not lay out a comprehensive legal test in Betz expressly leaving the dimensions of the implied warranty of habitability to future development. Upon transfer of a leasehold interest a residential tenant is entitled to more than the right to occupy the leased premises. The tenant has a right to occupy the premises in reasonable safety and in reasonable health. Although we are not prepared at present to say that a leasehold interest includes some warranty of a minimum degree of comfort, it is apparent that one's psychological well being is often at least as important as one's physical health. Conditions which unreasonably imperil mental health constitute a violation of the implicit warranty of habitability.

The trial court found as a fact that Petitioner's house posed a major health risk to one or more of Respondent's family. We will not disturb a factual finding unless the court abused its discretion, and this petitioner has failed to show. We concede it is unclear whether the learned trial judge was concerned with physical or mental health or a mixture thereof. However, as noted supra, the type of health involved is unimportant. Accordingly, we hold that the trial court did not misapply the law.

Affirmed

IN THE SUPREME COURT OF WYTHE

MARC H. MUNY, Petitioner
v.
TIMOTHY A. UTHER, Respondent

274 Wythe 413
[No. 1986-101]
Argued March 15, 1986. Decided June 3, 1986.

Opinion of the Court

Justice Ball delivered the opinion of the Court.

Our modern age has brought with it innumerable changes most of which have been salutary. For every mistaken nagging computer bill, one can find a truly great advance. This progress sometimes comes at a cost, however.

Respondent is a thirty three year old executive. In February, 1984, he signed a three year lease for a four bedroom penthouse apartment in Trink Towers, Dukesville. Under the lease, Respondent was to pay Petitioner a monthly rental of $8,000.00. Approximately four months after taking occupancy, Petitioner began to experience tightness of throat, watering eyes, and chest pains. The condition worsened with time. After an extensive series of medical tests, Respondent was diagnosed as having an unusual allergy to the type of materials now customarily used in new dwelling construction. Completed in late 1983, Trink Towers is filled with such materials. Expert testimony at trial proved conclusively that Respondent's latent allergy was triggered by the "outgassing" of the newly constructed building. Once triggered, unfortunately, the allergy appears permanent.

As soon as the medical diagnosis was confirmed, Respondent sought to be released from his lease. Petitioner, the lessor, expressed sympathy for Respondent's condition but refused to release him from the lease, a lease which also prohibited subleasing. Respondent vacated his apartment, and Petitioner brought suit in the district court seeking to recover the value of the time remaining on the lease, approximately 29 months.

The trial court applied our prior cases in this area, Patterson v. Bishop. 252 Wythe 60 (1982); Betz v. Smith, 245 Wythe 143 (1976), and determined that through no fault of Respondent, Respondent had been deprived of his right to occupy his leased apartment in "reasonable health" and that accordingly Petitioner had breached the implied warranty of habitability. Judgment was given for Defendant Respondent.

Mr. Muny, Petitioner appealed to the Circuit Court of Appeals for the Second Circuit. That court sustained the decision of the trial court in a divided opinion. Dissenting, Judge Galloweigh persuasively argued that as neither party was "at fault" it was improper for the judicial system to interfere with a freely negotiated contract even though the consequences of that contract, the lease, proved to be unexpected.

Petitioner has appealed to this court under Wythe Ann. Code § 27-1363.

Petitioner alleges that the courts below misapplied the law. He argues that our prior cases assumed two features not present here: a condition injurious to the health of the average tenant, and a refusal of the lessor to correct a reparable problem.

In this case, Petitioner asserts, and the trial court found, Respondent's health problem is an extreme variation on what has come to be known as "new building syndrome." Although a number of people have mild versions of this syndrome, extraordinarily few have it to the degree that their health is significantly affected for the long term. Ordinarily, either factors giving rise to the syndrome moderate with time as the building ages or the condition itself is not so severe as to cause significant distress. Although the experts at trial could not agree on the number of people who could be expected to experience this version of the syndrome, they agreed that no more than one person out of two hundred thousand might be subject to it.

Petitioner further asserts, and the trial court found, that Trink Towers is properly constructed and in full compliance with all applicable building codes. To an average person; indeed, to virtually any person, Petitioner's building is the epitome of modern luxurious comfort.

The Wythe Landlord Tenant Act provides that:

> A landlord is obligated to furnish a lessee with premises which are fit for habitation. Should the landlord fail to comply with this requirement in a reasonable time, the lessee may inform the landlord in writing and vacate the premises if the non-compliance materially affects health or safety.

Like our prior decisions in this area, the Act fails to distinguish between premises which are "fit for habitation" for an average person and those which are "fit" for the specific occupant, and the legislative history sheds no light on the matter. It would be best if the legislature would clarify this conundrum. It is our duty, however, to resolve this pending case and to construe the Act, a statute which was enacted to codify our most recent holdings in the area.

We concede that this case is a difficult one and that reasonable men and women may differ as to the desired result. Given that we must resolve it, we think it proper to reexamine the public policy behind the Act.

The Wythe-Landlord Tenant Act was enacted to provide tenants with "safe, fit" housing and to require landlords "to maintain their leased premises in a condition that will foster the health, safety, and comfort of the citizens of this state." Senate Rep. 83- 8976 (October 11, 1983). We infer from this intent that if presented with this problem, the Legislature would focus on the actual tenant in a given situation and not an "average" tenant.

In effect, when Petitioner and Respondent entered into their lease agreement they did so with mutual mistake. Had either or both realized the effect that Trink Towers would have on the tenant, the lease would not have been executed. Although both acted in good faith and reasonably, neither knew the true circumstances that applied. Against this backdrop we must struggle with the unassailable fact that continued occupancy by Respondent would be seriously detrimental to his health.

We hold that both the implied warranty of habitability and the Landlord Tenant Act require a landlord to furnish a tenant with premises which are fit for the habitation of that tenant and if the landlord either refuses to do so or cannot reasonably do so, the lease shall be considered as void from the time either that the condition is discovered as uncorrectable or that the landlord refuses to or fails to take corrective action.

Accordingly, the judgment below is **affirmed.**

Separate Opinion

Justice Lehrman, dissenting, with the concurrence of Justice Celia.

It may be that the majority has reached a desirable result. Certainly, I would not quarrel with it should the legislature see fit to enact it into law. Unfortunately, the legislature has not done so as yet.

Petitioner acted reasonably and correctly throughout this unfortunate series of events. Nothing more could have been expected of him. His building is more than safe and comfortable; it is, as the majority notes, "the epitome of modern luxurious comfort."

In their review of the legislative history of the Wythe Landlord Tenant Act, the majority fails to note that the act was primarily passed to put an end to substandard housing maintained by uncaring, frequently, "slum lord," lessors. Nothing could be farther from the instant case.

Respondent entered into his lease intentionally and intelligently. No "mistake" was involved. Rather, Respondent ultimately discovered that because of unforeseen subsequent circumstances he had made a bad bargain. Respondent was not a deprived, ill educated, poor tenant forced to enter into this lease agreement. He is a modern businessman who must be charged with knowledge that nothing in life is certain except, perhaps, "death and taxes." We lack the authority to relieve him of the consequences of this bad bargain and should not do so. Consequently, I respectfully dissent.

An intraoffice memorandum of law

MOLITERNO, LEVY & LEDERER

Date: July 24, 19xx

MEMORANDUM TO: Celia Shoshonah

FROM: Associate (You)

SUBJECT: Pat Marshall, possible relief from lease obligations because of roach infestation and allergic reaction to exterminating spray.

QUESTION PRESENTED

Is a landlord's requirement to deliver a habitable, residential premises breached when the premises is infested with significant numbers of roaches and when the exterminator's spray causes a serious, idiosyncratic allergic reaction in the tenant?[4]

STATEMENT OF FACTS

Pat Marshall signed a one-year lease and recently moved into an apartment at the Colonyshire Apartment complex. Upon moving in, Mr. Marshall noticed that the apartment was seriously infested with roaches. In all other respects, the apartment is suitable. After Mr. Marshall notified the landlord about the roaches, the landlord sent an exterminator who sprayed.

Two difficulties ensued. First, the roaches reappeared the next night in even greater numbers. Second, Mr. Marshall became ill with headaches and nausea. Mr. Marshall's physician has diagnosed the illness as an allergic reaction to the spray; the illness is serious and may result in hospitalization if Mr. Marshall is exposed to the spray again. He has reluctantly lived with the roaches for the past two weeks.

Mr. Marshall would like to know whether the roaches and his reaction to the spray allow him to be relieved of his obligations under the lease.[5]

---

4. Notice in the Question Presented the same attention to precision as was needed in the issue section of the casebrief. Notice also the absence of references to the parties' names or dates. Such detail is undesirable in a Question Presented, except on those unusual occasions when that sort of fact has legal significance. Finally, notice the absence of any reference to which client the writer represents. An intraoffice memorandum should be objective in tone; under such circumstances, assuming that the parties have the same facts at their disposal, the memorandum written by one party's lawyer should look no different from that produced by the other's.

5. In the Statement of Facts the writer attempts to provide the story of this case *as it relates to the Question Presented and answered by this particular memorandum.* The need to focus on the task at hand to the exclusion of other concerns is an important skill of analysis. Here, that skill manifests itself in the choice of facts related in the Statement of Facts.

DISCUSSION

Landlords of residential property are required to deliver habitable premises. Wythe Landlord-Tenant Act (The Act); *Betz v. Smith*, 245 Wythe 143 (1976). A landlord fails to meet this requirement when he or she has actual notice of conditions rendering the premises unfit and fails to remedy them in a reasonable time. The Act; *Betz*. The conditions that trigger the failure must be such as to "materially affect health or safety." The Act. Whether the health affected is the tenant's physical or mental health makes no difference. *Patterson v. Bishop*, 252 Wythe 60 (1982). Whether the conditions are of a quality as to render the premises unfit is measured by examining the particular tenant involved and not a mythical, average tenant. *Muny v. Uther*, 274 Wythe 413 (1986). If the landlord fails to satisfy the obligation to deliver and maintain a habitable premises, the tenant is released from all obligations imposed by the lease. *Betz*, at 144. Procedurally, in order to benefit from the requirement, the tenant must inform the landlord in writing of any asserted failure by the landlord. The Act.[6]

Mr. Marshall's difficulties with his apartment are likely of a quality as to relieve Mr. Marshall of further lease obligations. His landlord has been or can easily be notified of the conditions in writing; the lease is obviously of a residence; and the effect on Mr. Marshall's health is "material" as the Wythe Landlord-Tenant Act requires. Only the last statement is controversial.[7]

An infestation of roaches, if serious enough, can be a condition materially affecting a tenant's health.[8] *Patterson*. In *Patterson*, the trial court's ruling that significant numbers of roaches in a tenant's home, "whether resident or transitory, rendered it 'unfit for human habitation' was not a misapplication of the law." *Patterson* at 60, 61, quoting from *Betz* at 144. Although the infestation in *Patterson* was "large enough to have constituted a biblical plague," Mr. Marshall's description of his own apartment's infestation indicates that great numbers of roaches have populated his home as well, even if not quite so many

---

6. Notice that the Discussion section begins with simple, straightforward statements of the legal rules that govern the analysis in this memorandum.

7. This paragraph takes the governing rule apart, separating each element of the rule from the others. In the process of disciplined application of a legal rule to a set of problem facts, you will find it necessary to treat each part of the rule and its application to the facts as a separate matter. This paragraph, after identifying the parts of the governing rule, narrows the scope of what follows to the application of the one part of the rule that is controversial.

8. Notice that the writer has now launched into a detailed analysis of what "material" means, and will apply that definition to the problem facts in the following paragraphs by drawing analogies and distinctions from prior decisions. Think back to your work in analyzing court opinions in chapter 5. This aspect of memorandum writing is much the same as the analogizing and distinguishing of prior opinions in the process of learning the law through case opinion analysis.

as confronted by the *Patterson* tenant. The Patterson court held that life with great numbers of roaches constitutes an "unreasonabl[e] . . . peril [to] mental health" sufficient to violate the landlord's duty to deliver a habitable premises. *Id*. at 61. The roaches in Mr. Marshall's apartment were sufficient in number to impress the landlord with a need to promptly enlist the exterminator's aid and are likely to be a sufficient health threat to satisfy the *Patterson* standard and the statutory materiality standard. The Act.

The conditions that faced Mr. Marshall were aggravated by the extermination effort. The effect of the exterminator's spray is plainly a material health effect; further exposure is likely to send Mr. Marshall to the hospital. Although the landlord was not at fault in sending the exterminator and was acting in good faith, such an argument is unavailing to the landlord. *Muny v. Uther*, 274 Wythe 413 (1986). Even the most desirable dwelling is unfit for habitation if one condition "materially affects health or safety" in an adverse way. *Id*. at 414, quoting from The Act.

Arguments of the *Muny* dissenters notwithstanding, Mr. Marshall's unique or at least uncommon reaction to the spray will not bar him from arguing that the reaction adversely affected his health in a material way.[9] *Muny*. The particular tenant and not an "average" tenant is the relevant reference when determining the condition's effect on health because the legislature in enacting The Act was motivated by an attempt to advance the "health, safety, and comfort of the citizens of this state." Senate Rep. 83-8976 (October 11, 1983), quoted in *Muny* at 414. Adopting an average tenant standard would undercut this goal to some extent. A fair counter-argument may be made that to the extent the legislature desired to have The Act effect a change in *landlord* behavior, no such effect will accrue from interpreting the Act to apply when the landlord is powerless to remedy a condition that affects a particular tenant in an adverse way. Because the legislature was concerned with providing "safe, fit" housing for the benefit of tenants and because such idiosyncratic effect cases are likely to be so rare, if asked the legislature would probably have opted to leave the loss in such cases with the landlord, who is better able to bear it in individual cases. *Id*. Just as the *Muny* tenant's idiosyncratic reaction to his otherwise very desirable apartment was held sufficient to excuse him from further lease obligations, Mr. Marshall's unusual allergic reaction to the exterminator's spray should excuse his obligations.

Any argument that Mr. Marshall has simply discovered that he made a bad bargain that he wants to escape should be rejected. Although such an argument was made by the *Muny* dissenters, it was effectively foreclosed by the *Betz* court when it ruled that the old doctrine of *caveat emptor* can no longer

---

9. Rather than ignore possible arguments that might militate against the writer's conclusion, the writer acknowledges them and explains why they should be rejected.

apply when conditions endanger a tenant's health. *Betz* at 143. The underpinnings of *caveat emptor* are simply no longer present in the context of residential housing leasehold transactions. *Id.*

CONCLUSION

Mr. Marshall's difficulties with the roaches and his allergic reaction to the exterminator's spray will likely serve to relieve him of his obligations under his lease. He should inform his landlord of the problems in writing and vacate the premises. Both the roaches and allergic reaction are conditions materially affecting Mr. Marshall's health. Although the landlord has taken all reasonable steps to remedy the roach problem, the allergic reaction is a condition beyond all parties' control and has resulted in a breach of the landlord's obligation to deliver a habitable, residential premises.[10]

A client letter

MOLITERNO, LEVY & LEDERER
The Blossom Building
Gerson, Wythe
Telephone 000 221-3792
Fax 000 221-3261

July 26, 19XX

Mr. Pat Marshall
Apartment 29R
Colonyshire Apartments
1783 Nina Drive
Gerson, Wythe

Re: Relief from lease obligations

Dear Mr. Marshall:

After our initial meeting on July 22, 19XX, I reviewed thoroughly the facts of your case, along with the copy of the lease that you provided. Preliminary research based upon this information indicates that you may well be entitled to release from your lease obligations.

I will restate the facts as I understand them to ensure that I have not misunderstood. If any of the following facts (which I have gathered only from my interview with you) appear to be inaccurate, please call me. If I have misunderstood the facts, then my legal analysis will likely be inaccurate. My understanding of the matter is that you entered into a one year lease with Colony-

---

10. Notice that the Conclusion contains no analysis, but rather is a summary of the reasoning that leads the writer to the conclusion reached. Often a conclusion will not be absolute; rather it will be qualified by words such as "A court will likely ... "

shire Apartments. Upon moving in you noticed serious roach infestation and notified the landlord of the condition. The landlord had the apartment sprayed by an exterminator, yet the roaches appeared in even greater numbers. Additionally, the spray caused you to suffer a severe allergic reaction that could result in your hospitalization if used again. As a result of these two problems, you want to be relieved of your lease obligations.

According to the Wythe Landlord-Tenant Act (Act), landlords are required to deliver habitable premises. This requirement is not met when, after having been notified of the problem rendering the premises unfit, the landlord fails to solve the problem within a reasonable time. If the landlord fails to satisfy this requirement, the Act provides that the tenant be released of all obligations under the lease.

A condition rendering the premises unfit is any condition that materially affects the mental or physical health or safety of a particular tenant. A roach infestation, if serious enough, can be a condition materially affecting a tenant's health. The fact that landlord felt compelled to enlist assistance from a professional exterminator indicates his or her awareness of the seriousness of the situation. Additionally, the conditions faced were aggravated by the exterminating spray, which quite clearly affected your health. Further exposure could send you to the hospital.

In short, your difficulties with the roaches and the spray will likely serve to relieve you of your lease obligations. Both have created conditions that materially affect your health. Although the landlord has taken all reasonable steps to remedy the situation, the allergic reaction is an occurrence beyond all parties' control and has resulted in a breach of the landlord's obligation to deliver a habitable, residential premises.

Please contact me as soon as you can to plan our next steps. The Act requires that the landlord be given written notice of your intent to vacate. If you still intend to vacate, we should provide this notice as soon as possible.

I look forward to hearing from you soon.

Sincerely yours,

9

Law School[†]

Thus far, we have primarily addressed law and law study and their relationship to law practice. Although we have surely touched on the topic, we have not as yet focused on the experience of law school itself. Yet, if you are considering law school or are now a new or relatively new law student, law school survival and success must certainly be uppermost in your mind. Let us, then, briefly examine law schools and the law school experience.

First, Legal Education's Goal, or, "Why *Isn't* There an Answer?"

The fundamental nature of legal education is usually misunderstood. Law schools neither "train" students to become practicing lawyers nor do they supply students with all the legal rules and information they will later need. Although law schools do accomplish part of each of these aims, the true function of a law school is different. Put simply but nonetheless accurately, the primary goal of a law school is to teach students to think. We realize that this is a sweeping statement, and one that seems insulting. Surely, after all those years of education and experience you can think. The truth is that many people do *not* learn how to analyze issues rigorously and logically.[1] To be fairer, we could rephrase our assertion. After all, virtually every new law student will hear at least once from a dean or professor that law school's purpose is to teach students how to "think like *lawyers*." When meant positively, this means only that students will learn how to carefully analyze all components of a problem and issue and to formulate possible solutions. When one "thinks *like* a law-

---

† The authors wish to acknowledge the kind assistance of Ms. Christine Raubaugh, Marshall-Wythe Class of 1992, and Mr. Scott Browning, Marshall-Wythe Class of 1993.
1. Those trained in logic or in science or mathematics are particularly likely to be exceptions.

yer," one sees every possible interpretation applicable to a given statement or situation and how a change in facts would affect the result.

We might argue that in the most fundamental sense a lawyer is a person who:[2]

1. Knows and accepts the ethical rules applicable to the profession;
2. Can analyze facts to determine whether and how they raise any legal issues;
3. Has the minimum knowledge of legal rules and the nature of law necessary to initiate useful legal research.
4. Can determine the current answer to a legal question via the ability to analyze legal issues, rules, and cases and mastery of the skill of legal research.

This functional definition has sweeping repercussions in law school. Although law school seeks to supply students with a **basic** set of legal rules, no school intends to supply the actual answers to a given client's problem, or even to a given legal situation. Such an attempt would be futile. As you now understand, law changes rapidly in the United States as a consequence of case law, legislative enactment, and regulatory rule making. Further, law depends on the jurisdiction one is in. In addition to the federal government, in the United States alone there are 50 states as well as territories and a number of specialized jurisdictions. Both substantive and procedural law vary by jurisdiction. Professor Lederer reports that one evidence student once commented that he expected to be taught the specific evidence rules for every state in the union. Can you imagine having to *learn* all that? What if it would be required in every course? What purpose would it serve?

Law school primarily teaches *process* and *method* so that new answers can be found at any time. It supplies tools valid for the rest of one's life, not rules that can be obsolete before graduation.[3] Legal education thus requires one to be able to analyze issues in unprecedented depth. Many of those legal issues and questions necessarily have no answers, either because they are new and have not yet been ruled upon, or because by their very nature there can be no clear cut answer.

We cannot emphasize this enough: **very often a legal question does not have an answer!** Instead, there may be many valid answers, and the key question will be the *method* by which the answer was derived. This is perhaps the most frustrating element of law school for many students. Everyone likes an answer

---

2. Setting aside the crucial element of bar admission.

3. Think about the Internal Revenue Code, for example. Although one must learn numerous basic tax rules, it is far more important to learn the concepts behind the Code and its structure. That way as Congress amends the Code, perhaps annually, one can adopt and adapt to the changes rather than having to relearn rules.

to a question; law students are no exception. Students want to know **the** answer. They want to know the "black letter rule" so that it can be written down, memorized, and recited on an examination. But, as we have already discussed, law school doesn't primarily teach such rules. Instead, it teaches method. Particularly as exams approach, this creates enormous uncertainty and frustration for students as there is no easy way for them to confirm that they have indeed mastered the material. Professor Moliterno has written that, while this uncertainty may have positive short-term effects on learning, it is ultimately harmful to learning unless it is combined with opportunities for students to experience success.[4]

The frustration may be sufficient to cause some people to drop out of school. In her article, *Remembering*,[5] Ruth Knight reflects the feelings so common to students who expect answers:

> I likened the lectures to learning to do modern math calculations in different bases — it made little sense when it was first explained. But I figured that at the end of the semester the professors would tell us what to study for the tests, and I would memorize whatever I had to.[6]

In the first year of law school in particular, professors are far more likely to be interested in *how* an examination question was analyzed and answered than in *what* the answer is.

The absence of clear answers is related to another potentially crippling aspect of law school life: the absence of feedback. With the probable exception of assignments in legal research and writing courses most schools have no institutional method for providing any evaluation of law student efforts other than final examinations. Accordingly, the typical law student is deprived of any official knowledge of how well he or she is doing until final examination grades arrive. It is little wonder that law students approach their first examinations with panic.

Most law schools go far beyond what would be necessary to comply with our minimalist functional definition. Acceptance of the basic goal of law school and its psychological effects is, however, often critical for individual survival as a law student.

Second, the Caveat

If you have not yet discovered it, let us be the first to introduce you to a crucial term in the lawyer's arsenal of jargon—the *caveat*. Just another way of

---

4. Moliterno, *The Secret of Success: The Small Section First Year Skills Offering and Its Relationship to Independent Thinking*, 55 Mo. L. Rev. 875, 877 (1990).

5. Knight, 40 J. Legal Educ. 97 (1990) [hereinafter *Remembering*]

6. *Id.* at 99.

saying "exception," no known lawyer or law student can deliver a statement of legal principle or rule without qualifying it with one or more known or possible exceptions. That's one of the reasons your friends, families, and clients will soon find conversing with you to be difficult and sometimes unrewarding.

Our primary caveat is simple: virtually nothing can be said about law schools that is absolutely true of all schools at all times. Each school and faculty is unique and generally proud of that status. Just as you can't be sure of the answer to a given legal question in any given jurisdiction without researching it, you can't be sure of requirements or practice at any given school without inquiry.

The Basic Structure
Accreditation

Law schools are either connected with a college or university or independent. An independent school which exists as a profit making entity is often termed a proprietary law school. Most but not all law schools are accredited by the American Bar Association (the ABA).[7] ABA accreditation requires compliance with ABA regulations. There is no other recognized accrediting agency for law schools in the United States. States may bar graduates of unaccredited schools from taking the bar examination, at least absent completion of some special requirement.[8] ABA accreditation should be distinguished from a school's membership in the Association of American Law Schools (AALS). The AALS is a professional association of law schools and a major player in legal education. It is not, however, an accrediting agency.

Although many law schools offer night or part time study, a large number do not. Absent a special joint degree program or summer school attendance, ordinarily full time law school consists of three years of study. The actual number of credit hours required for graduation varies by school.

Governance

Subject to any board of trustees or visitors, each law school is governed by its faculty acting collectively. The dean administers the school and has a fair degree of flexibility in the process. All critical decisions, however, are usually made by the faculty after faculty committee consideration.

Many law schools have some degree of student presence or participation in relevant committee activities.

Curriculum; requirements; specialization

Most schools require their students to take contracts, torts,[9] property, civil procedure, and some form of legal writing and research in their first year. A

---

7. Only California has a sizable number of unaccredited schools.
8. California requires students at unaccredited schools to take a preliminary examination (the "baby bar") during law school.
9. Loosely, what constitutes a wrong for which an injured party may seek relief from those responsible for the injury, and the type and measure of relief that may be obtained.

significant number of schools may also require constitutional law or criminal law in the first year. Otherwise, all bets are off as to curriculum predictability. Although some schools mandate as much as the first two years, many others provide either significant or nearly free choice after the first year. Indeed, some schools offer elective choices in the first year.

Quite often a school will also have some form of writing requirement, seminar requirement, or enrichment requirement.[10] A small number of law schools now require their students to provide a specified minimum number of hours of public service in satisfaction of the profession's obligation to the general public. These graduation requirements can be found in the school's catalog which ought to be read carefully as soon as possible. Schools may be unwilling to impose additional graduation requirements on a given class, e.g. the class of 1996, after that class has arrived.

Law students often apologize in their first week because they have not as yet picked their area of specialization. If you will forgive us, specialization at this stage is ridiculous. The curriculum of most schools prevents significant specialization until the second year at earliest. More importantly, a student's first goal should be to take those courses which will provide the knowledge and skills necessary to any competent lawyer and *then* consider areas of interest and possible specialization. Exposure to new areas of law quite often changes one's area of interest. We also note that in our experience five years after graduation few lawyers are working in the areas in which they planned to work when they graduated.

One thing is critical about curriculum choices: faculty and elective courses change! Although the mainstay courses will always be taught, specialized electives are likely to be dependent upon available faculty, and law school faculty vary as individuals retire or resign or, as is more likely, visit at another school for a semester or year or take a research leave. In addition, because of limited faculty, schools frequently offer some courses only every two or three years. Consequently, if you really want to take "Legal Implications of DNA Manipulation As Viewed from a Tort/Contract Perspective," grab the first opportunity to do so.

Curriculum guidance is of little value without knowledge of the specific options available and the identities of the faculty members teaching them so we won't even try. Specific guidance is available at every school via either formalized information or through individual faculty advice. We would warn you to be careful of what we believe to be a common factor in course selection— course scheduling. Understandably, many students (and faculty) would like long weekends, and many people would avoid like the plague early morning or late afternoon or evening courses. Consider carefully, however, whether short term advantage is worth the long term consequences of foregoing a more de-

---

10. *E.g.* a course in legal history or philosophy.

sirable course selection. Similarly, be careful of taking courses because the professor is said to be an easy grader. Such perceptions are often flawed. When true, there may be a price for the grade. In the long term, the best course is likely to be the one in which you worked hardest and learned the most.

We would add that every school has professors widely recognized as experts in their field, as great teachers, or both. You don't need our encouragement to take a course from such a professor. Sometimes, however, a great expert may not be an equally skilled teacher. "Taking" such a professor may involve more effort than courses taught by others, but may be far more valuable in the long term.

We are firm believers that students should acquire basic legal skills such as interviewing and negotiating as well as the more traditional legal research and writing and appellate practice. Accordingly, we encourage you to take enough courses to have a working knowledge of these mainstays of the lawyer's existence and practice. We urge this on you, however, not primarily because you ought to know it in order to practice but because it will enrich your legal education and allow you to put your more traditional courses in better context. When well done, these courses can also provide valuable learning of the ethics of lawyering not always available in a purely classroom oriented approach to the subject. Clinical courses in which students render legal assistance to real clients should also be considered. Not only are these courses particularly educational, they also provide real help to those in need.

Nearly every law student that we know has worried about passing the bar, getting a desirable job (however that is to be defined), and being successful. However, passing the bar is a short term goal that, when overstressed, can warp educational choices. Similarly, although skills education is important and enlightening, law school is not intended to teach, nor should it, the manifold details of law practice. As we have already discussed, "How to do it" is rarely the goal of law school. Instead, law school provides a strenuous educational experience intended not only to supply vast amounts of legal data, but more importantly the tools of legal analysis, research, and writing. Because law changes incredibly quickly in late 20th Century America, process and method are far more important than soon to be obsolete data. We recommend, therefore, taking those courses which will best prepare you for the 21st Century and not to concentrate on passing the bar. There are any number of "cram courses" that prepare graduates for the bar examination.[11]

Law school peers, grades, and competition

Law school is often an exhilarating yet humbling experience. Although the subject matter may cause such feelings, it is far more likely that the student

---

11. We trust that you will forgive us if we avoid the debate over the necessity for and nature of bar examinations.

body will be responsible. Given the large number of applications to law school, most law schools are competitive in their selection of students. Many are *very* competitive. As a consequence, large numbers of students have exemplary abilities and backgrounds. A first year class may be filled with individuals who dominated their college classes. As a result, a law student may suddenly discover that his or her fellow students equal or exceed his or her intellectual attainments.[12] While that leads to delightful and enriching conversation and debate, both in and out of the classroom, it also means for some people that they have academic competition for the first time. This can be a sobering experience, particularly for those who in the past have judged themselves and others purely on grades.

Experience has taught us that many law students will receive in law school the lowest grades they have ever earned. This may only be a B or C for some. Nonetheless, if the grade is unprecedented, it has significant psychological impact. We will address grades as such below, but you must realize that not only is law study sufficiently difficult and demanding to sometimes give rise to such grades, but that to some extent grades are relative. The very presence of talented peers of equal or superior ability may impel some to get lower grades. Although every student should make every proper effort to learn as much as possible in school and to achieve the highest grades, it is a serious mistake to value an individual by his or her grades. A person is a complex amalgam of personality, ethics, morality, intellect, wisdom, skills, and knowledge. Grades may reflect some portion of the underlying person, but it is only a small portion—at best. Because law students are so grade (and placement) oriented, it is hard to escape evaluating oneself by grades. For most people, however, happiness at school, if not downright survival, requires that grades be placed in their context and not given overimportance. Grades are tools and imperfect measuring devices. They are not ends in themselves, although a visitor to a law school might well think otherwise.

Competition for grades can sometimes create an atmosphere of cut throat competition. At some schools, students have been known to steal class notes, cut pages from books so that others can't use them, and generally break the basic rules of ethical conduct in an effort to obtain success. As should be clear by now, we think that such conduct is self-defeating on any basis. Even if temporarily successful, the lawyer that results is already a failure, one who is likely doomed to professional disaster later. More to the point, however, such behavior is damaging to the other members of the law school community.

Few law students need to be taught how to be competitive or assertive. What is often necessary is to take affirmative steps to decrease improper com-

---

12. Furthermore, each may loudly and confidently maintain that he or she is right when discussing case or policy positions.

petition. Subject to the rules of any given school, cooperation should be fostered. Responsible, cooperative, student work can be very fruitful. At some schools, though, students may have to make an affirmative effort to achieve this result. In a highly competitive school, one might look at this as if it were a disarmament problem. There may be pitfalls, but someone has to make the first move. At the same time, we would note that in a world in which Germany can be reunited and the cold war terminated, there must be hope in this area as well.

One other matter merits comment. Law students are almost always anxious and afraid. Beset by what they believe to be a unique lack of comprehension in some class, poor performance on an assignment, an unintelligible legal rule, fear of poor grades, flunking out, or not getting a job, anxiety reigns supreme. Yet, law students rarely concede these fears openly. Instead, they turn a confident face to everyone else. In effect there is a conspiracy of silence. Everyone is anxious and in need of support, yet each person believes that *only* he or she has such fears.

Working

Even in full time law schools many students work part time. Working in a local law office or for a professor can be both good experience and a helpful resumé item. Work is more often due to the understandable need for financial support. The American Bar Association limits the number of hours a full time law student may work, and an individual school may have its own rules. Notwithstanding these constraints, law students have been known to work highly demanding schedules. We can only warn of the obvious. Law study requires not only the amount of time needed to study and write, but also inherently assumes the exchange of ideas with other classmates. Excessive work makes this difficult if not impossible. It goes without saying that falling asleep in class due to exhaustion neither adds to one's knowledge nor wins friends and influences people.

Faced with major financial problems many students will feel trapped. In a limited sense the trap may be illusory. Given the need to work long hours and yet attend school, it may make more sense to take a leave of absence for a year in order to restore financial solvency than to try to work full time and study concurrently. Obviously, such a leave would postpone graduation and put one behind one's friends. Temporary delay in graduation, however, is likely to beat the psychological consequences of such a crushing overload, to say nothing of the probable poor grades that may result. Even if a student can balance both, is that balancing act worth the cost of a significant loss of legal education, a loss which may manifest itself during law practice when both the lawyer and client may pay for it?

Housing

No, we are not about to give you the secret of obtaining the perfect law school domicile. Of course there isn't one, and housing is a local matter. Consider your housing arrangements carefully, though. Professor Lederer was for many years a member of the Marshall-Wythe Academic Status Committee, the faculty committee charged with ruling on the petitions for readmission of students dismissed for academic deficiency. He reports that difficulties associated with housing arrangements were a significant factor in the academic problems experienced by some students. No one can readily forecast whether roommates will work out, whether in a dorm or an apartment, just as even a marital relationship may turn troubled. Rather than rushing into things, however, you can carefully consider what you're about to get yourself into. One particular situation merits comment. Sometimes members of college fraternities and sororities arrive at law school and arrange to stay at the local house with their brothers or sisters. Although we're sure this must be a good idea, somewhere, our limited experience suggests that this is likely to be a disaster. The social emphasis of most such groups is rarely compatible with the time demands of law study. Even if you can resist the parties and other social blandishments, noise and other factors are likely to complicate study.

Class

Everyone knows what a law school class is like. They've seen one in the *Paper Chase*, the movie or series, or some other Hollywood product. Like many media depictions, there is *some* truth in the *Paper Chase*, but the picture supplied is misleading.

Depending on the school, law classes often vary dramatically in size. First year course classes tend to be large, with perhaps as many as 150 to 200 students although efforts are often made to have one or more small sections. Upper class electives are smaller, and seminars may have 15 or fewer students. Class size varies by school and course. Instructional techniques vary as well.

The Socratic Method and Related Topics

The classic law school instructional technique is the socratic method. This approach can be described both as an extraordinarily useful instructional tool and as a tool for the infliction of psychic torment unparalleled elsewhere in education. As is often the case, which it is depends on the professor and his or her ability and intent.

In its purest form, the socratic method consists of posing a question, usually in the form of hypothetical facts, and asking a student to respond. The professor may shift to another student at any time to obtain a different view or to focus on a specific point and thus to develop a complete analysis. The technique is used so extensively not only because constant questioning requires the student to develop an analysis for himself or herself but also because when the question is asked *every* student mentally responds—every student compares his or her answer with that given by the student responding orally. In effect, the teacher has a socratic dialogue with every student in the class. Absent the opportunity for a one to one discussion between professor and student, the socratic method is the ideal tool to teach students to think and analyze.[13] Students will often leave a class, however, without any clear answer to the hypothetical question. As noted above, that is likely intentional as the goal is process and not answer.

Techniques associated with the socratic method vary. Some faculty may insist on the student standing to recite. Some will call on students either at random or via a secret selection process. Other professors will use seating charts and everyone will know well in advance who will be selected. Similarly, once chosen, some faculty will keep the student "on the grill" for as much as an entire class. Others will pass to another student quickly.

Students must learn to accept public recitation without stage fright or embarrassment.[14] After all, lawyers must often function within a public arena. Whether the socratic dialogue is used as a cutting sarcastic tool depends entirely on the professor. The technique itself is not inherently painful. Used by one professor, it can be a marvelously enlightening and even entertaining approach. In the hands of an academic sadist, it defies description.

The primary alternative to the socratic method is lecture. Although some courses, particularly upper level courses, may consist mostly of lecture, most classes have a mixture of lecture and the socratic method.

The case method uses judicial cases as the focus of both lecture and socratic dialogue. When the case method is used, normally a *case book* is assigned that consists mostly of judicial cases. Alternatives include texts or treatises that emphasize textual discussion rather than reprinted case portions and problem

---

13. The socratic method has its share of detractors, especially among students. Sharing her memories of the process, Ruth Knight has written:

> Finally what the orientation professors had said about a different kind of teaching began to soak in—it was not simply bad teaching—law professors did what they did on purpose. But for the method truly to work, it seemed to me that the focus of the learning should be on consistent and frequent examination of what each student personally brought forth after absorbing the reading. Classes with one teacher to seventy-five students could hardly do that effectively.

Remembering, supra note 5 at 100.

14. Student answers are sometimes funny either by intent or inadvertence. Students should learn early in the game that although it is fine to laugh *with* each other, it is poor form and counterproductive to laugh *at* each other. Class should be enjoyable, and both faculty and students should feel comfortable enough to give candid responses without unreasonable fear of public derision.

texts that set forth illustrative problems for class discussion. As a general rule, the case method is used extensively in first year classes while upper level courses are more likely to use a different approach. Courses that deal with codified laws, such as the Uniform Commercial Code, the Federal Rules of Evidence, or the Internal Revenue Code are likely to place major emphasis on the code and any implementing regulations.

What happens when a student is unprepared in class? Again the answer necessarily depends on the given professor and situation. In some cases, the student will be passed by and called upon later or on another day. There may or may not be a grade penalty. Other professors will not let the unprepared or recalcitrant student off the hook and will continue the discussion. This approach can be used often to develop a correct answer despite the lack of preparation. Indeed, it can sometimes be used as a kindly technique to minimize the student's embarrassment. At other times, it can be used to give the entire class a lasting object lesson.

Avoiding Being Called On

Unprepared or nervous law students often prefer not to be called upon by the professor. Numerous techniques exist to implement this attempt at academic escape and evasion. The most commonplace is to look downward intently at one's class notes while scribbling furiously. Another approach is to look upward in rapt concentration as if working through the most complex hypothetical variations. Still another method is to look totally confused. This is, however, the least likely to succeed.[15] The one approach most likely of success is reverse psychology. In other words, enthusiastically volunteer to answer. Wave your hand in the air exhibiting total self-confidence. This may work if the professor is trying to assist unsure students. It is particularly likely to work if you have established a prior track record of success. Of course, if the professor would like a correct answer, "you're dead."

The only problem with all of these techniques is that every professor was once a law student. We used them too.

Study and Class Preparation

Law school requires study. Every new student wants to know *how much study*? The answer depends, of course, on the individual and the course. Although some students, particularly those with science and engineering backgrounds, find law school similar to college, most find it far more demanding

---

15. Professor Lederer's mother wryly suggests hiding under the desk. This would surely be a unique and courageous approach. Unfortunately, such an act of desperation is likely to be seen by the professor. If not, the amazed stares of fellow students all gazing at the suddenly vacated seat is likely to be a dead giveaway.

in both time and attention. One of our students suggests that each class hour requires 25 pages of reading and thinks that a student should be able to complete 10 pages per hour. Reading speed depends on the type of material. Reading the Internal Revenue Code usually takes more time than reading legal history.

Make every effort to prepare for class. Reading assigned material before class makes class far more useful than it is without that background. It is very easy to fall behind in law school and difficult to catch up. Studying should be conducted on a scheduled basis. At the same time, it is essential to take some time off for other activities.

A study group is a group of students who meet together to review class work in a given course. Usually, a group should not have more than five people in it. A study group may be helpful *if* the students are compatible and no one attempts to use the group to avoid necessary effort. For example, preparation of a course outline is a desirable method of examination preparation. It is the personal preparation of the outline, however, that is truly useful rather than the final product. Dividing a course into components with each member of the study group taking one or more topics may produce a useful study aid but will usually do so at the expense of the knowledge and insight that would have been gained through personal preparation. Note that some study groups may fail if the group becomes a social entity or if personalties don't fit.

Many students will recommend study aids. Such aids often include commercially published case briefs[16] or course outlines. Please note that each professor structures his or her course in a unique fashion. Even if the aid is accurate, and some aren't, the aid may not be useful. The real problem is the use to which such an aid is put. If these materials truly are used as aids, rather than as substitutes for assigned reading or individual analysis, they may prove helpful.

Examinations

Although some professors will use quizzes and mid term examinations, most law school courses are evaluated solely by a single end of semester examination. Often the length of the examination in hours will equal the number of credit hours. A wide variety of examination types are possible including essay, objective, take homes, and forms completion.[17] Most first year examinations will be essay examinations as the emphasis in first year courses is issue identification and legal analysis. Examinations may be open or closed book.

Because single examinations are so important, the stress they cause can be incalculable. The wise law student takes careful notes during the semester and

---

16. See chapter 4, *supra.*
17. *E.g.* completing an IRS Form 1040 for a simulated client.

begins examination preparation well in advance of the examination, ideally, at least three weeks in advance.[18] We recommend preparation of a course synthesis. A synthesis is a master course outline prepared after review of the course text, classnotes including case briefs, and any other useful materials including applicable hornbooks (usually famous single volume treatises). The synthesis should distill the course into rules of law with any exceptions and major supporting authority. Cross-references to applicable text portions, cases, etc. can be quite helpful especially in open book examinations.

As to exam taking, the most important advice we can give in this area is first, **be calm,** and second, **Read the problem and answer it.** All too often, we have read examination answers in which the student obviously failed to notice one or more crucial facts or has even omitted an entire question or question section. Remember also to answer the question asked and not the question you would prefer to answer. The "shotgun" approach in which a student puts down everything he or she knows about the course subject is usually not very helpful.[19]

Grades

As we have already mentioned above, many people get their first low grades in law school. Grading philosophies vary by professor and school. Some professors will grade on a competency basis. In other words, everyone in the class can get an A if the requisite answers are given. Others will use a relative approach in which a grading curve dictates grade distribution. Indeed, some law schools have either mandatory or recommended grading curves. Where a curve is not required, many professors will use a combination method in which basic competency is adjusted by a curve. In most cases, therefore, grades are relative to some degree. In short, if you're convinced that an examination was impossible for nearly everyone, even if you're right — and few students are objective at this point — the odds are that you'll be "saved by the curve."

Halfway through the first exam my hands went numb; I forgot to breathe. I suffered nausea during my entire Christmas vacation, thinking I had flunked.

Well into second semester, grades were posted, and students crowded around them. I heard swear words that did not exist in the tiny Rocky Mountain religious community where I grew up or in the circles I had moved in since.

18. In fact, a student who keeps pace with the course and prepares for class diligently is preparing for the examination from the first day of the course.

19. We suggest that you review the sample examination and answer at the end of chapter 5.

I was amazed to see that I was nowhere near the bottom of the charts. In fact I ranked well enough that when other students mourned their grades, I let them believe that mine were worse.[20]

Given the importance of grades in law school, we can hardly suggest that you ignore them. We do think that it is imperative, *regardless of your grades*, that you not define yourself by your grades. Grades are only a partially successful evaluative tool. Indeed, a single grade may well be non-representative. Everyone has both good and bad days. However, consistent grades carry a message that ought to be read. All students should review examinations after grading. When you begin to see similar remarks made by different professors on your papers, it suggests strongly the presence of real problems, often problems in analysis.

There are people who do not test well. There is no excuse, however, for obtaining lower grades than can be earned based on your unique talents. Most faculty are willing if not eager to be of help. You need only ask.

Failure and Its Consequences

At some schools academic failure is infrequent. At others, large numbers of failures can be expected. The difference sometimes stems from admissions policies. Some schools have programs to assist individuals who are in academic difficulty, particularly when they have been placed on some sort of academic probation. Others leave it to the student to get such help as may be available.

Failure can take place for many reasons. It may be that family or personal tragedy made it impossible to study, and final examinations were deadly. It may also be that a student has significant problems that can—and ought to—be remedied. In such a case help ought to be sought to identify and rectify them. We note that it is not unknown for students in this position to discover that they are dyslexic or have other learning difficulties. Still others have been unable to cope with the stress of law school or examination taking or both. Particularly when such help is available on campus, students with difficulties may wish to use local psychological counseling services. We can assure you that law students are not uncommon visitors. At times, poor grades indicate internal conflict. Students sometimes are in law school because someone else, often their parents, want them there, and they would rather be elsewhere. This type of conflict needs resolution.

Should a student "flunk out" of law school, most schools have a faculty committee charged with reviewing applications for readmission. Although the standards and procedures vary by school, it is likely that a petitioning student

---

20. *Remembering, supra* note 5 at 100.

will have to explain why he or she had academic difficulty and why it is not likely to recur.

Significant academic difficulty has been experienced at one time or another by many fine law students and lawyers. An isolated problem is certainly not grounds for panic. Yet, a long term substantial problem may be indicative of graver difficulty. It may be that career goals should be re-examined. Every profession and occupation requires certain skills and abilities. The practice of law is no different. Just as some people cannot be draftsmen or engineers because they lack the ability to see or draw objects in three dimensions, some people lack the specific traits necessary to be a lawyer. *If* that is the case, an alternative to law must be found. It is always unfortunate when a person must change his or her aspirations yet such a change is neither necessarily bad nor an admission of defeat. As has often been pointed out, the nation needs qualified people in thousands of other callings. Lawyers help make society work, but lawyers do not discover new basic scientific truths, produce our food, design and manufacture new products, supply medical care, etc. An inability to become a lawyer is not failure. It is simply a reorientation to other and potentially more important options.

A student considering whether to leave law school should seek whatever counseling is available at that school. At the least, the situation should be discussed with a friendly professor. Stress, frustration, and unreasonable personal standards and goals frequently cause distressed students to improperly evaluate their academic abilities and future.

Law Reviews, Moot Court, and Other Activities

In other scholarly professions, professional articles are published in journals that are managed by recognized members of that profession. Law reviews are the great exceptions. The reviews are student managed and edited journals which publish virtually all of the nation's legal scholarship outside book form. Customarily, each issue of a review will contain articles by professors, judges, and lawyers as well as pieces by student members of the review. Third year executive board members select the articles to be published and supervise the review while second year members do much of the actual editing work under third year supervision. Membership on a law review is greatly valued both because it is so competitive and because at its best it supplies an extraordinary advanced course in legal writing and research. In fairness, we might also add that at its worst, work on a review can be incredibly time consuming and deadly boring.

Each law review has its own method of selection. Usually, students are selected at the end of their first year on the basis of grades, writing ability, or a combination of each. A law school usually has one review. Some schools have a number of different journals. Usually when this is the case, one will be a general journal and the others more specialized.

The simple truth is that law review membership is an important resumé item. Even if one sets snob appeal aside, review membership is some evidence of analytical, research, and writing ability. Failure to obtain review membership, or an intentional decision to reject it, does not, however, consign the individual to the utter depths of placement failure. Law review membership is only *one* factor that is considered by employers during the placement process. It must be said, however, that to some employers it is *the* factor or at least a prerequisite to further consideration of the applicant.

Similarly, membership on a school's competitive moot court teams may also be quite useful. Moot court team participation is again often a guarantee of research and writing abilities as well as, in this case, competence in oral advocacy. Participation in the National Moot Court Competition or the ABA Competition appears to be particularly prestigious.

There are, of course, far more activities in law school than just law review and moot court. Many of those activities are equally educational. Some are more enjoyable, and some more useful to the individual and society. Many schools will have one or more activities in which students can assist real clients. Given our profession's commitment to public service, these are of particular importance.

Personal Life and Family

Notwithstanding the importance of study and assignment completion in law school, there can be too much study and work. Every student is entitled to a personal life. There is more to existence than the law. Viewed strictly in terms of efficiency, everyone has a break even point at which the law of diminishing returns sets in. Sleeping, novel reading, going to the movies, hugging your spouse, or talking with friends may make you far more productive later than digging in for just one more case. Taking a weekend off and getting out of town can also be useful if not essential.

The stress of law school life is hard to overstate as are its possible consequences. Spouses, significant others, and children soon grow tired of, "Gee, I'm sorry, but I've just got to study a bit more." Law school life is rough on marriages, and small children can hardly be expected to fully understand the implications of a short notice paper assignment. If law school is worth such effort, is your family worth less? Supportive family members and friends need and deserve your time and effort as well.

Placement and Its Effects

Let's face it, for most law students the need and desire for part time, summer, and permanent employment is not just a legitimate and proper student goal, it may be an overwhelming one. Placement, however, can have enormous effects on a student's study.

Because of the variety of law schools and placement programs it is impossible to discuss the various placement options available at and through law schools. It may suffice to say that some schools give little or no assistance in seeking employment while others run programs[21] that would make an industrial conglomerate proud. Each extreme has its benefits and limitations. What is clear, however, is that student job seeking often becomes such an obsession that it preempts everything else. During the "interview season" students will miss class, forego studying, and if given a call back interview at an employer's office will flee the school for however long may be necessary. Placement can thus have significant direct detrimental impact on study, law school performance, and grades.

Recognizing the importance of employment, we can only suggest that the search must be commensurate with the law student's present and future responsibilities, including the responsibility to later competently practice law.

Placement's Other Effects

What is not often immediately obvious to law students is that their expectations of the employment market often color not just their course selections but sometimes their entire self-definition as a person and as a lawyer.

The general public's view of law and lawyers is usually shaped by the television show of the moment,[22] Hollywood's most recent efforts,[23] and any personal contact with lawyers. Law students are usually more knowledgeable but not necessarily much more so if they have already worked in the legal area in some capacity. Both law student and lay people alike assume, for example, that litigation is a mainstay of legal practice. In fact, few lawyers try many cases although pretrial litigation leading to settlement is more common. There are numerous lawyers who have never tried a case or represented a client on appeal despite what television or movies may suggest. In fact, most lawyers render advice, draft documents, and negotiate. The classic adversarial battle is comparatively infrequent. Similarly, despite media suggestions to the contrary, most lawyers have no significant contact with criminal cases, leaving defense work to public defenders or a relatively small number of private attorneys.

Although most lawyers are in solo practice or in small firms, the tendency for many first year law students is to look at large firms as the norm. Students

---

21. Many law schools have placement offices that assist students in obtaining interviews on or off campus and give useful advice in obtaining employment. Procedures for obtaining interviews vary by school.

22. *E.g. Perry Mason, The Defenders, LA Law, Law and Order.*

23. *E.g. The Verdict, Presumed Innocent.*

may classify potential legal employment as highly prosperous law firms, secure but not highly remunerative government work, or poverty level non-governmental public service.[24] Non-firm work, particularly non-large firm work, may be viewed as caused by either idealism or lack of ability. This is, of course, nonsense.

Upon reflection, it is immediately apparent that there are numerous types of law and law practice. Civil law, defined for the moment as non-criminal practice, includes everything from corporate law to intellectual property (patent and copyright) to environmental law to the law of air and space, to name just a few. Although tort law, particularly personal injury work, may be commonplace for many lawyers, there are many others whose practice seldom touches it.

Legal practice includes mammoth law firms of a 1000 or more lawyers, medium and small firms, corporate law departments, city attorneys, prosecutors and defense counsel, and sole practitioners. Although most lawyers work full time, an increasing number work part time, particularly during child care periods. Compensation ranges from poverty levels to a level of return that almost defies belief.

Why spend your time in such a review? The tendency in many law schools is to assume that the only *proper* legal job is to work in a law firm, preferably one of some size. This stems not only from hopes of large future incomes, but also because many law faculty are graduates of large firms, and because the cases used in case books tend to suggest classical civil practice as found in law firms. Often, a school unintentionally sends a message that large firm practice is the right goal, and that anything else is well, a bit unusual.

Large firm practice, when it can be obtained, can indeed be immensely rewarding financially. There are, however, costs. The workload at such a firm can be extraordinary, arguably inhuman on occasion. Few associates become partners, and although the work can be exciting, often it is boring and subject to multiple levels of supervision. Small firm work or other types of legal practice can be equally or more rewarding albeit usually with a smaller financial return. Alternative legal employment may provide exciting opportunities to serve the public.

The point is simply that there is a place in the legal universe for everyone. There is no reason for a law student to decide in the first semester that he or she must withdraw from school because he or she will never get a big firm job or can't live with such a position. As students progress in their education and become more knowledgeable they ought to discover ever more options, whether expressed as types of law or types of practice. It is true that peer pres-

---

24. And, of course, law teaching.

sure may create a school goal, and a public acknowledgement of different goals may draw sympathetic smiles. Since when is that important?

Every law student should seek to define his or her own personal career goals and then attempt to achieve them. There is virtually no limit to the available possibilities.

Summer positions

Although most law students wish to obtain a summer legal position at the close of their first year, the number of such positions is diminishing, and it is likely that many first year students will be unable to obtain one. Besides non-legal employment (or just taking the summer off to recover) students might wish to participate in one of the many summer law school programs abroad. These programs customarily permit a student to earn transferable credits while living in and enjoying a foreign nation.[25]

A Closing Note

For many people, law school is a new, exciting, and anxiety producing experience. The instructional techniques are often novel and demanding. Because of the primary law school goal, development of analytical skills, much that a professor does in the first year may not seem to make sense. In our experience, normally there is a reason for everything a faculty member does, a reason that will become apparent only later during law school or, occasionally, after graduation.[26] Successful survival as a new law student requires not only intellect and hard work, but also patience, common sense, and a good sense of humor.

---

25. A commercial plug: William and Mary is the home of the nation's oldest program. The School has programs in Exeter, England (with a week in London) and Madrid, Spain.

26. This is not to deny that some teachers may not measure up to professional standards. All of us are human—and fallible.

10

The Interrelationship Between Law School and Law Practice

There is something unique, misleading, and almost subversive about the teacher-student relationship. The educational model, at least for law school, is the classical socratic dialogue: teacher and student sitting together on the log learning from each other. In such a relationship the teacher is merely first among equals; teaching is motivated not only by the desire to impart thinking skills and knowledge *to* the student but also by the need to learn *from* the student.

Perhaps because of recollections of elementary school, it often seems that most law students expect to come to class, be *taught*, study, and regurgitate the proper analysis and data on final examinations. Faculty are often elevated to superhuman status, and the relationship between student and faculty is usually a distant one characterized by reluctance on the part of the student to disturb the illustrious woman or man who periodically delivers wisdom in the classroom. Obviously, few faculty measure up to such an unreasonable standard, and as they regularly fall from grace, students become disenchanted. This is unfortunate, but of minor comparative importance. The real problem is elsewhere.

As a group, law students are extraordinarily bright and able.[1] Not a few come from years of responsible employment often characterized by supervisory responsibilities. These adults come to law school, sit down in class, and become "students," passive individuals[2] who all too often mentally seem to

---

1. A number of commentators have questioned the value to American society of so many talented women and men foregoing other critical occupations for law.

2. Some years ago, one colleague reported an experiment he had conducted in a first year law class. Troubled by the passivity of his students, during one lecture class he spoke little but "gobblygook" with appropriate legal jargon for twenty minutes. The students bent to their notes writing down every word. Finally, totally exasperated, he confessed that he had been speaking nonsense and asked why no one had thought to at least question him, if not to challenge the material. True education cannot be passive.

behave as if they were undergraduate or even younger students. Three years later, these students are lawyers who are charged with zealously representing their clients in an environment in which ethics, creativity, attention to detail and rule, intelligence, and responsibility are critical. Further, they must often function with little or no supervision, either of their work or their ethics. Is graduation or the bar examination a rite of passage which marvelously converts students to attorneys and counselors at law?

Clearly, we overstate the case. Unfortunately, we don't think that we overstate it very much for many people. The point that we are making is deceptively simple: law students do not suddenly become lawyers at some magical point; rather, they spend all of their time in law school *becoming*.

Law is a learned profession. As we have already discussed in Chapter One, at a minimum a profession is characterized by monopoly status, a commitment to public service, and self-regulation. We *serve the public* through our clients, and we serve ethically. We firmly believe that the key—the single most important element—to successful legal practice is professional ethics. We fully concede that professional ethics, those rules with which lawyers must comply to be viewed as upstanding attorneys by other members of the bar, are more limited than general ethics. Notwithstanding this, an ethical lawyer nearly always is a successful one. An unethical lawyer is a trap for the unwary, whether client, lawyer, or judge, who almost always brings the profession as well as herself or himself into disrepute.[3] Highly significant among the rules of professional ethics is the duty to *zealously represent the client*.

The duty of zealous representation is often misunderstood. It does not mean "pulling out all the stops," and doing anything that is necessary to achieve the client's desired result.[4] Instead, it requires that the lawyer do his or her utmost for the client within the law and ethical rules. Phrased differently, the duty of zealous representation requires the **competent** representation of the client. The lawyer who is unprepared, unskilled, unethical, or unwilling is not competent and does not zealously represent the client. Within the terms of the attorney-client agreement, the client must receive nothing less than the benefit of the attorney's full abilities and dedication, subject only to the limitations of law and ethics. **Competence** is not a minimal goal. Rather, it is the ultimate goal that every lawyer must seek continually. It is all inclusive.

Competence is difficult to achieve and maintain, particularly in a world in which the practice of law seems ever more business oriented and defined. Lawyers do not supply the client with the abilities and ethics paid for, and no more.

---

3. And who likely fails at the practice of law, sometimes all too many years later.
4. Often the lawyer's duty is to educate the client as to the consequences of the client's preferred result and to demonstrate that alternative options may be preferable. Some client wishes are, of course, unlawful or unethical, and these the lawyer is forbidden to seek.

Absent unusual circumstances, once the lawyer "takes the case," the client deserves the lawyer's full attention and abilities. Even a client's inability to pay will ordinarily not relieve a lawyer's of the duty to serve. The attorney-client relationship is a special one that evades easy definition and that resists every effort to transmute it to a dollars and cents transaction notwithstanding the common obsession, and need, of lawyers to worry about billable hours.

But what of the law student? Students do not suddenly become lawyers except by operation of law. Admission to the bar is a great and memorable moment[5] but it alone does not prepare a new lawyer to practice law. Some lawyers will spend their first few months in what amounts to an apprentice status "learning the ropes" from other, more experienced, lawyers. Useful? Certainly, but this too does not create a lawyer. The process of becoming a lawyer is exactly that, a *process*.

Conceding that a person's character and abilities begin to develop at birth, the process of becoming a lawyer truly begins with the first day of law school. Virtually every school makes a point of telling students that they are being taught to think like lawyers. At the very least this means that students must learn the skill of careful legal analysis, after which they will be incapable of seeing any problem in a simplistic one sided fashion.[6] As this is at the heart of being a lawyer, most students are well on their way after the first few weeks of law school. There is, however, far more than this to being a lawyer. What students sometimes ignore is that their law school experience will likely shape the type of lawyers they will become.

Like lawyers, law students too must *zealously represent the client*. However, during law school the student is the client. He or she is, in proxy, all the future clients to be represented and helped. The knowledge, skills, belief, and ethical responsibilities learned and assumed during school make the student the lawyer. Less than competent service as student is likely to yield a less than competent attorney.

Competence as a law student is nearly as demanding as competence as a lawyer. It demands that the student take personal responsibility for his or her legal education. It is not enough to say, "the professor didn't cover it;" if you need to learn it, *learn it* even if you research it yourself.[7] If the professor seems to be in error, question the statement. Faculty members are human and fallible too.

It goes without saying that one can hardly lie, cheat, and steal in law school and then suddenly become an ethical attorney. As Professor Moliterno is fond

---

5. Similar to and only slightly greater than the moment of total mental collapse and relief that follows leaving the bar exam.

6. Giving rise, of course, to the general public contradictory distaste for, and absolute dependence on, lawyers.

7. One of the goals of law school is, of course, to learn how to do exactly this. Law practice requires it continuously.

of saying, "There are no ethics police in law school." Although some law schools have honor codes and some do not, no school devotes its resources to trying to ferret out those students who lie to their peers and faculty, who cheat, or who steal books or pages from the law library. As in any other type of school, it is possible to cheat in law school and perhaps evade discovery. As lawyers and law students, however, we must police ourselves. That is a commitment made by every member of the profession, and, at least pragmatically, it is a commitment made too by every law student.

Absent such a commitment, at least some evaluate whether to break a rule based upon an analysis of the likelihood of getting caught. Once such a commitment has been made by *you*, however, the likelihood of getting caught becomes 100% by definition—because you catch yourself. *Your* standards have been violated by *your own actions*. You cannot escape self-detection. Your life as a lawyer, if indeed you continue to have one in spite of such conduct, will be empty and unrewarding. This commitment includes the obligation to report ethical violations by your colleagues. This commitment to self-enforcement makes us special as lawyers and students.

It is also easy for students to cheat *themselves* and their future clients by inadequate study, shoddy work, or inadequate attention. Like law practice, the study of law is not just time intensive, it can be all consuming. There is never enough time to do it all. Yet, no student could, or should, devote every waking moment to the law any more than any practitioner should. Part of both study and practice is learning when to quit; when to relax, read a novel, see a movie or play, or hit the tennis court or track.[8] But these must be intentional decisions rather than customary sloth. Learning how to decide when further effort is counterproductive should begin in law school.

The habits and behavioral assumptions formed in law school often persist afterwards for years, if not for life. All too often those habits are formed unthinkingly. Those of you who are and plan to be law students have one basic decision to make—what type of lawyer will you be. If you are to be truly a competent attorney, one who can look in the mirror every morning with pride rather than self-disdain, you must take charge of your own legal education. Each school supplies truly enormous resources. It is, however, your responsibility to marshall and take advantage of them. Do not sit passively for three years. Learn as much as you can from as many sources as possible. Get as much from the faculty as you can. If an answer seems facile or simplistic, and it is not apparent that a more comprehensive answer will be forthcoming at a more appropriate time, however respectfully press for such an answer. De-

---

8. As lawyers are fond of saying, this is merely an illustrative list. One of Professor Lederer's associates is a rock climber, for example. While others prefer not to emulate her, they all have their escapes.

velop your mind; but also develop your skills so that you will be able to use your knowledge and powers of analysis and so that you will better understand the way theory becomes practice and practice may corrupt theory. Perhaps most important, perfect your knowledge of and sense of ethics. A sloppy law student, a late law student, is likely to be a sloppy or late lawyer. Law students may complain of excessive work or unreasonable deadline, but the realities of legal practice "cut no one any slack." The disbarred lawyer, the lawyer sued successfully for malpractice, the lawyer held up to the ridicule of his or her peers will usually find the roots in law school.

Few questions are individually as important as the sober question, "What type of lawyer—what type of person—do you plan to be?" We cannot adequately answer that for you, for each person must respond individually. We can say with confidence that that question must be answered every day for the rest of your life for each person's resolve will be tested continually. Few of us will pass our lives without examination, and few will fail to be tempted and on some occasion perhaps diverted from our resolve. Yet, as we answer that question daily and, as is sometimes necessary, minute by minute, so shall we shape our lives and through them our clients and the nation. You must answer that question, as we must.

Those of you who will be or are law students will perhaps make the most important answer of your legal careers on the day that you attend your first day of classes and decide, wittingly, we trust, the type of student and lawyer you plan to be.

There are times in every lawyer's life when he or she despairs of the legal profession. We do not pretend that the profession is trouble-free. Indeed, in the late twentieth century it may have more difficulties than ever before. It may be that we stand at a cross-roads. Shall it be the legal *profession* dedicated to service or shall it be something else, something far less?

The answer to this question shall be provided by you, both individually, and collectively. Welcome to the legal profession, colleague!

Appendix

If you are reading and studying the cases in chapter 5 without benefit of a classroom discussion of them, you may wonder what we think are the key points in the cases. On the next several pages are, for each case, two things: first, a well written student prepared casebrief of each opinion (using different styles); and second, our comments on the cases themselves. If you will be discussing the cases in class, do not read this appendix until the classroom experience is concluded. Reading this appendix too early will rob you of both your own opportunity to form analytical practices and your opportunity to learn about the law school classroom experience itself.

Seixas v. Woods

Supreme Court of New York
2 Caines 48, 2 Am. Dec. 215 (1804)

FACTS

Plaintiff bought some wood from Defendant under the belief that the wood was an expensive type called brazilletto. Defendant had prepared advertisements and a bill of parcels listing the wood as brazilletto. When Plaintiff took possession of the wood he discovered that it was actually a much cheaper quality wood called peachum wood. Plaintiff offered to return the peachum wood in exchange for his purchase money, but Defendant refused this offer. Defendant did not know that the wood was peachum rather than brazilletto. Plaintiff brought suit to recover his purchase price for the mislabeled wood.

PROCEDURAL HISTORY

Plaintiff won a verdict at the trial. Defendant brought this appeal to the appellate court.

ISSUE

Whether a seller of mislabeled goods who gives no warranty as to the goods and acts without deceit is liable for a defect in those goods.

HOLDING

No. In the absence of a warranty or of deceit on the part of the seller, the purchaser buys at his own risk.

JUDGMENT (or DISPOSITION)

Judgment of the trial court for Plaintiff is reversed.

REASONING

The common law tradition provides that a good faith seller who does not warrant the quality of the goods he sells is not liable for a latent defect in such goods. In the present case, the Defendant's description of the wood as brazil-letto did not amount to a warranty, and Plaintiff did not contend that the Defendant had acted fraudulantly, so the Plaintiff had to bear the cost of the defect in the goods.

The purchaser has the duty to use his own faculties of observation and judgment in deciding to purchase the goods, and the vendor must disclose any known defects which would not become apparent to a vigilant purchaser. The purchaser has the opportunity to provide against his own lack of vigilance by requiring that the vendor expressly warrant the quality of the goods. A description of goods by a vendor will not amount to a warranty unless there is evidence that the vendor intended to make a warranty rather than to express his opinion of the quality of the goods.

Judge Kent notes that he prefers the civil law position which implies a warranty where no express warranty appears, but he acknowledges that the contrary common law tradition is settled regarding this point of law.

"Professor's Notes"

Seixas v. Woods sets up this line of cases by introducing the common law's treatment of the buyer-seller relationship. As you might expect, merchants need some expectation that the law will treat their contracts with consistency. Otherwise, no business-person would feel comfortable going forward with a deal, and commerce would grind to a halt. The common law treatment of the buyer-seller relationship is one that contemplates that parties to transactions will take care of themselves; it contemplates that buyers need no protection against bad deals. Only when buyers are intentionally misled by sellers or when sellers make special promises (warranties, for which buyers presumably pay) will the law step in to protect a disappointed buyer.

The relationship contemplates that buyers will inspect goods or accept the risk of being disappointed by goods that do not conform to the contract. Sellers are duty bound to refrain from deceiving buyers, to comply with warranties made, and to disclose known defects that buyers could not perceive upon reasonable inspection. If a seller does these things, he or she can transact business without fear of liability to disappointed buyers. This expectation that buyers will be diligent, we will see later, is the foundation of the rule limiting a seller's liability to those in privity, that is, those with whom the seller has a contractual relationship.

When Judge Kent sets out to apply law to the facts of the case at hand, he uses a prior case. From this prior case, Judge Kent restates the governing legal rule: absent fraud or warranty, sellers are not liable to disappointed buyers. Kent uses the prior case to apply that rule to the problem facts as well. He says that the prior case is "in point and decisive." Kent means that at all points of legal significance, the facts of the prior case are analogous to the facts of the Seixas case, and the prior case was decided by a court whose decisions are mandatory authority and binding on the court deciding *Seixas*: "in point and decisive." When a court makes law, as did the court deciding the prior case, it does so by virtue of its power to resolve disputes. When a court resolves a dispute, it leaves a trail for future courts facing similar cases to follow. This trail is marked by the policies that underlie the rule itself. A significant clue to what these policies are may be found by careful examination of the facts of the prior cases. The facts of legal significance in a given case are those that are implicated by the policies supporting the rule. When a judge finds that all facts of a prior case are analogous to those of the present case, it is a good bet that the rule should be applied in the present case to reach the same result as was reached in the prior case. That seems to be what occurred in *Seixas*, Judge Kent ruling that the established rule of law applied to the current facts by analogies drawn from the facts of the prior case.

The *Seixas* case also provides another opportunity to see the effect of our system of precedent. Judge Kent confesses that he prefers the rule of the civil law (see chapter 3 for more on the civil law system itself) system to that of the common law. But he recognizes that the common law system requires that he follow precedent rather than depart from it because of his personal preference for another rule. We might call unprincipled a judge who finds a thin reed to support a departure from precedent to accommodate his or her personal view of the case being decided. Judge Kent did not do this; rather, he acknowledged that he would prefer the civil law rule were he free to follow his own view, but decides the case as he feels bound to do in accordance with the precedent. A tension develops in such a system between two conflicting, positive values for a legal system to have: predictability and flexibility. While the law develops slowly because of the system of precedent, some room is left for flexibility because of the system's primary interpretive reliance on the rationale underlying a given rule rather than on a rigid application of the fixed language of an unchangeable rule.

A final point from Seixas is worth comment. Kent says that this is "a clear case for the defendant." But Chief Judge Lewis is "contra." If one judge can regard a case as clear and another judge disagree with the result in the case, there must be considerable room for independent thinking in legal analysis; this, it turns out, is quite true.

Thomas v. Winchester

6 N.Y. 397 (1852)
Text page 3

FACTS

1. Defendant Winchester was a manufacturer and seller of various vegetable extracts. Defendant Gilbert was Winchester's employee. Two of the extracts they carried were extract of dandelion, a mild medicine, and extract of belladonna, a poison.
2. They sold a jar of the extract of belladonna labeled as extract of dandelion to a third-party druggist. The druggist later sold the jar to another druggist, both druggists believing that the jar contained extract of dandelion as so labeled.
3. Plaintiff Samuel Thomas bought the substance for his sick wife upon the prescription of her physician. Mrs. Thomas became extremely ill as a result of ingesting the extract of belladonna.
4. The Thomases sued Gilbert and Winchester in a negligence action for the injuries sustained by Mrs. Thomas.
5. The defendants argued that this action could not be maintained because, as remote sellers of the extract, they owed no duty of care to the Thomases. They maintained that their duty of care was owed only to their purchaser, the first druggist, and that if anyone was liable to the Thomases, it was the druggist from whom they bought the poisonous extract because of the contractual relationship between buyer and seller.

PROCEDURAL HISTORY

At trial, the court directed a verdict for defendant Gilbert on the grounds that he was acting as an agent of defendant Winchester. The jury returned a verdict against Winchester. Winchester's motion for a new trial was denied by an intermediate court and he now appeals to the highest state court.

ISSUE

Whether a manufacturer of poisonous drugs has a duty of care to a consumer who buys from an intervening seller despite a lack of privity between the manufacturer and the consumer.

HOLDING

Yes. The manufacturer of poisonous drugs has a duty of care despite a lack of privity with a purchaser who buys through an intervening seller.

JUDGMENT (or DISPOSITION)

Judgment of the trial court for the plaintiff affirmed.

REASONING

To be liable in a negligence action, the defendant must have breached a duty of care which he owed to the plaintiff. Thus before a defendant can breach a duty, such a duty must actually exist. The duty of a manufacturer/seller of poisonous drugs owed to a purchaser who buys through an intervening seller arises not from any contract of sale but from the original seller's conduct of putting a foreseeably dangerous item into the stream of commerce. It is foreseeable that the consumer, not an intervening vendor, will be the party to suffer injury from the negligent mislabeling of a dangerous substance and thus it is the consumer who needs to be protected by imposing a duty of care on the manufacturer.

The defendant relied on *Winterbottom v. Wright* which set out the rule that there must be privity between the plaintiff and the defendant in order for a duty to exist and therefore for liability to attach. However, the court distinguished *Winterbottom* and created a special rule for cases such as this in which the defendant manufactures and/or sells substances that have a high potential for imminent danger. The court supports this decision by looking to the criminal law and pointing out the severe criminal sanctions imposed on sellers of dangerous substances who are found guilty of culpable negligence.

The court declines to decide if the intervening druggists had a duty to inspect the extract before selling it to a purchaser; however, the court does hold that the defendants cannot defend on these grounds. Even if the intervening vendors had such a duty, that does not wipe out the duty of the original seller. In any event, the jury found that the intervening druggists had not acted negligently in failing to inspect the extract before reselling it.

The concurrence agreed that the defendant Winchester did have a duty to the Thomases because selling poison without a label stating that it is poison is a criminal violation.

"Professor's Notes"

Thomas v. Winchester brings us face-to-face with the problem of an injured person trying to obtain a judgment against a negligent but distant maker and seller. Because the Thomases had no contractual relationship with the maker of the mislabelled poison, it is urged, the negligent maker has no liability.

The court rejects this argument. While acknowledging the rule that strangers to a sales contract cannot ordinarily recover damages from the seller for the seller's negligence, the court creates an exception. The court's language would support two different interpretations of this exception:

1. it might be said that the exception applies when the product is itself inherently dangerous, calculated to do harm to mankind; or
2. it might be said that the exception applies when circumstances make harm to people situated like the injured party in the case the likely result of negligence of the seller-maker.

Under the first interpretation, the factual focus would be on the item that caused the harm in its non-defective state (here, poison). Under the second interpretation, the focus would be on the item if defective and, more importantly, from the perspective of the defendant the ability to foresee harm to people like plaintiff from negligence of the defendant.

On its way to creating this exception, the court refers to a number of facts that may be reasons supporting the creation of the exception. It refers to the nature of defendant's business: that he had every expectation that interim buyers would not inspect or use the drugs, but rather would resell them to users. It referred to the possibility of criminal liability that could arise from the negligent labelling of a drug. Indeed, Judge Gardiner concurred in the judgment for plaintiffs on this ground alone. And the court referred in several different ways to the character of the item that caused the harm. As we will see, later courts struggle with attempts to discern which of these facts is the key to an understanding of the reason for the *Thomas* exception. It may be that they are all keys, or, in effect combine with each other to tell the story. In any event, as we shall see, often the full import of a decision is not realized until later courts use the rule of the decision to resolve new problems. As we go forward, we will see what later courts think is the core value of the *Thomas* decision. Whatever it is, we can be sure that the *Thomas* court has found the rationale underlying the limitation-of-liability-to-those-in-privity rule to be inapplicable to the resolution of the dispute framed by the *Thomas* facts. In other words, the usual buyer-seller relationship has not adequately accounted for the distribution of risk in this new circumstance. How will later courts view the *Thomas* exception?

Loop v. Litchfield

Court of Appeals of New York
42 N.Y. 351 (1870)

FACTS

In 1861, Defendant Litchfield manufactured a balance wheel to be used with a circular saw. The balance wheel had a hole in its rim which Litchfield filled with lead riveted into place. Litchfield then finished the surface of the wheel making it appear to be a sound wheel. Collister bought the wheel with knowledge of the defect. In 1864, Collister leased to Plaintiff Loop a frame for a circular wood saw which contained the defective balance wheel. Collister did not notify Loop of the hole in the rim of the balance wheel. In 1866, the balance wheel burst while Loop was using the wood saw. A fragment of the wheel hit Loop and inflicted a mortal wound. Loop's widow and next of kin brought this suit for negligence.

PROCEDURAL HISTORY

The trial court returned a verdict for the Plaintiff. The intermediate appeals court reversed and ordered a new trial. The Plaintiff appealed the appellate court's decision.

ISSUE

Whether a manufacturer of a defective balance wheel owes a duty of care to a third party not in privity with the manufacturer, when the manufacturer disclosed the defect in the product to the purchaser and the wheel was used safely for five years before causing the harm.

HOLDING

No. The manufacturer of a product which cannot be considered a "dangerous instrument" does not owe a duty of care to users of that product who are not in privity with the manufacturer.

JUDGMENT (or DISPOSITION)

Judgment of the appellate court for Defendant is affirmed.

REASONING

Loop, the Appellant, argues that the balance wheel was a dangerous instrument, and therefore the rule of *Thomas v. Winchester* imposes liability on the Appellee, Litchfield. Judge Hunt rejects the assertion that the balance wheel is a dangerous instrument. Dangerous instruments are those which are designed and calculated to inflict injury, such as poison or gunpowder. Any object may, through misuse, inflict injury, but this is not a sufficient justification for calling such an object a dangerous instrument. Furthermore, the jury's verdict for Loop did not establish that the balance wheel was a dangerous instrument, because the jury was not asked to decide that question.

Judge Hunt further distinguishes *Thomas v. Winchester* by noting that in the case of a mislabeled poison, injury is more foreseeable because every use of the mislabeled product will cause injury. In the present case, Collister used the defective balance wheel for several years without injury. The injury caused by the bursting of the wheel was not the natural and expected result of the manufacture and sale of the wheel.

"Professor's Notes"

It might fairly be said that the *Loop* case adds nothing to the law, but merely resolves a dispute between parties according to the existing rules of law. Certainly, no dramatic effect such as that wrought by *Thomas* is to be found in the wake of the *Loop* case. The court combines the privity rule and the *Thomas* exception to rule that heirs of Mr. Loop may not recover for the negligence of Mr. Litchfield. Mr. Litchfield was indeed negligent and his negligence caused Mr. Loop's death: the jury so found the facts. But the privity rule limits the liability for negligence to those in privity of contract unless the *Thomas* exception applies.

In ruling that the *Thomas* exception does not apply, the court refers to several of the facts that we previously said may be the keys to understanding the reasoning behind the *Thomas* exception. The court talks of the absence of the potential for criminal liability in the present case; it talks of the nature of the original transaction between Litchfield and his immediate buyer as being different from the putting out to commerce of the poison in *Thomas*. But arguably, at least, the court's focus is on the nature of the item that caused the injury, the iron wheel. Here the court focuses on the natural state of the item rather than its defective nature: it compares poison to gunpowder, torpedoes, spring guns, and loaded rifles, all "dangerous instruments, articles in their nature calculated to do injury to mankind. . . ." Naturally, given this characterization, the court distinguishes an iron wheel from these other items. By focusing on the natural state rather than the defective state of the items, the court has committed to the first of the two possible interpretations we said earlier might be given to the *Thomas* exception. By so doing, the court distracts attention from the defendant's ability to foresee harm and refocuses that attention on a narrow examination of the nature of the item that caused the harm. This seems a mistake unless the examination of the item is designed to shed light on the ability of the defendant to foresee the kinds of harm that his negligence might produce to people like the plaintiff. But if defendant's ability to foresee is the real focus of the *Loop* court's inquiry, it would be a more accurate inquiry if it were focused on the defective nature of the item involved rather than its natural state, for it is the defendant's ability to foresee the results of his possible negligence that we should be interested in evaluating.

Although it may be accurate to say that the *Loop* decision adds nothing because it merely applies a given rule rather than modifies a rule, it might just as accurately be said that there is at least an incremental addition to the law by the *Loop* decision. This may be said because every decision supplies the law with a new example of a set of facts that illustrate the meaning of the applicable legal standards. Here for example, if nothing else we can learn that five years of safe use may support a finding that any danger was not imminent; that the *gravity* of the harm (Jeremiah is dead, after all) will not alone produce a finding that the item that caused the harm was dangerous; and that at least one court regards the meaning of the *Thomas* exception as being confined to things of danger. Each of these small lessons amounts to an addition to the law governing such cases.

Losee v. Clute

Commission of Appeals of New York
51 N.Y. 494 (1873)

FACTS

Defendant Clute manufactured a steam boiler and sold this product to the Saratoga Paper Company. The boiler was improperly constructed of poor quality material, but Saratoga Paper Company inspected and accepted it. Clute knew that the boiler would be used in a residential area and that if it exploded it would be likely to cause injury to people and adjacent property, but after the paper company's acceptance of the boiler, Clute had nothing more to do with the boiler. Three months after the sale the boiler exploded injuring the Plaintiff's neighboring property. Losee, the Plaintiff, sued Clute for negligence in manufacturing the boiler.

PROCEDURAL HISTORY

Losee's complaint against Clute was dismissed at the trial court, and the intermediate appeals court affirmed this dismissal. Losee appeals from the appellate court's judgment.

ISSUE

Whether a manufacturer of a defective steam boiler owes a duty of care to a party not in privity, when the purchaser of the steam boiler inspected and accepted the product.

HOLDING

No. A manufacturer of a steam boiler owes no duty of care to a party not in privity, when the purchaser of the steam boiler has inspected and accepted the product.

JUDGMENT (or DISPOSITION)

Judgment of the appeals court is affirmed and the action is dismissed.

REASONING

The court relied on *Albany v. Cunliff* which held that an architect or builder is not responsible for injuries occurring after he has completed his work. In the present case, Clute completed his work when Saratoga Paper Company inspected and accepted the steam boiler; Clute's responsibility ended with Saratoga Paper Company's acceptance of the product. The court noted that the holding of *Loop v. Litchfield* precludes application of the holding of *Thomas v. Winchester* in the present case.

"Professor's Notes"

The *Losee* court applies the *Thomas* exception via the *Loop* decision with barely a hint of its reasoning. It provides a mere shorthand form of legal analysis that can be quite frustrating to lawyer, law student, and law professor alike. We can only surmise from the court's brief reference to *Loop* and *Thomas* that the court has adopted the *Loop* court's approach to the application of *Thomas*, and has determined that the present case facts (particularly those relating to the nature of the item that caused the harm) are analogous to those in *Loop* and distinct from those in *Thomas*. In other words, a boiler is more like an iron wheel than poison, at least with respect to the perspective on the fact that the legal rule makes relevant.

In *Losee*, we revisit the nature of the buyer-seller relationship and see its effect on the seller's liability to strangers to the transaction once again. The *Losee* court tells us that one reason the plaintiff cannot recover for the negligence of the boilermaker is that the buyer fully inspected the boiler at the time of its acceptance. This fact would seem to have little to do with an examination of the item that caused the harm as we seem to be directed to do by the focus of the *Loop* case. Perhaps there is more to an understanding of the *Thomas* case than has been articulated by the courts so far.

Notice here, as in all the cases, the effect on the appellate court of the procedural history of the case. Here, the trial court had dismissed the plaintiff's complaint. By doing so, the court did not give the case to the jury to decide the fact issues; by doing so, the court in effect said, "even if the jury believed everything you said, Mr. Plaintiff, and even if the jury drew all reasonable inferences from the evidence in your favor, the law would not afford you any relief." In other words, the law would say, "even if everything you say is true, Mr. Plaintiff, so what?" A more straightforward example may serve to illustrate. Let's say that I sue Mr. Defendant for calling me a sore loser following a hotly contested game of one-on-one basketball. It would not matter that I could prove my allegations because even if what I say is true, the law will say to me, "So what?" The law simply doesn't afford me any sort of relief for having been called a sore loser. A trial judge would be justified in such a case to dismiss my complaint. (In my example, unlike the *Losee* case, the judge would not likely even have allowed the matter to come to a trial, but the affect on later proceedings is much the same.) Rather than bother a jury at all, or any further if the case has entered trial, the judge will simply say that even if what the plaintiff says is true, the law entitles plaintiff to nothing. In *Losee*, by dismissing Losee's complaint, the trial judge was saying that the *Thomas* rule would not apply, and therefore even if Losee could show that Clute was negligent, the law would entitle Losee to nothing. Because of this procedural history, there have been no jury findings made when the case goes to the appellate court. (As we saw earlier, when the jury has found the facts, those found facts are the facts to which the appellate court applies the law.) When no jury findings have been made, the appellate court must apply the law to some fixed set of facts. Because the appellate court is reviewing the trial court's decision, it is sensible for the appellate court to look at the facts in much the same way that the trial court had to in making its decision. Here that means looking at the facts in the light most favorable to the plaintiff. In other words, if what the plaintiff said was true, was the trial court correct in saying that the law would entitle plaintiff to nothing? If the appellate court concludes that the trial court erred, the case will be sent back (*remanded*) to the trial court to conduct a trial and send the matter to a jury for determination consistent with the appellate court's legal rulings.

Devlin v. Smith

Court of Appeals of New York
89 N.Y. 470 (1882)

FACTS

Plaintiff's deceased, Devlin, was killed when the scaffolding on which he was standing broke causing him to fall ninety feet to the ground. Defendant Smith, Devlin's employer, had contracted with Defendant Stevenson to build scaffolding to enable Devlin to clean and paint the dome of a court-house. Stevenson knew the scaffolding from which Devlin fell was improperly constructed, but Smith, who did not inspect the scaffolding, did not know of the defect.

PROCEDURAL HISTORY

Devlin's complaint was dismissed by the trial court. The appeals court affirmed this dismissal. Devlin appeals from the appellate court's judgment.

ISSUE

Whether an architect of a structure that if defective is "imminently dangerous" owes a duty of care to a user of the structure who is not in privity with the architect.

HOLDING

Yes. An architect does owe a duty of care to a third party when a defect in the architect's structure renders the structure imminently dangerous and when serious injury is likely to result from use of the structure.

JUDGMENT (or DISPOSITION)

Judgment of the appeals court is affirmed as to Defendant Smith but reversed as to Defendant Stevenson. A new trial is ordered to determine whether Stevenson was negligent in constructing the scaffolding and therefore caused Devlin's death.

REASONING

There are two classes of cases regarding a manufacturer's liability to a third party. If a defect in a product will naturally and necessarily cause serious injury to a third party, the manufacturer owes a duty of care to the third party. If such a defect will not naturally and necessarily cause such injury, the manufacturer owes a duty of care only to the purchaser as defined by their contract.

The circumstances of the present case are similar to those giving rise to liability in *Thomas v. Winchester*. An improperly constructed scaffold, ninety feet in height, will, by its nature, cause serious injury to a user of the scaffold, just as improperly labeled poison will, by its nature, cause serious injury to its user.

Judge Rapallo notes that in *Coughtry v. The Globe Woolen Co.*, a recent New York case, the court imposed liability on the builder of a scaffold for the death of a workman. This holding was based in part on a characterization of an improperly constructed scaffold as a "dangerous trap, imperiling the life of any person who might go upon it."

The court distinguished *Loop v. Litchfield* and *Losee v. Clute* on the ground that serious injury was not the natural consequence of using defective products in those cases.

"Professor's Notes"

Analogies and distinctions are important components of legal analysis; comparing the facts of prior cases with those of present problems gives us insights into the appropriate resolution of cases under study. To know how to make these comparisons with facts from a particular prior case, we must determine what was significant about the facts from the prior case. From the *Thomas* case on, we have wondered whether the important attribute of the item that caused the harm was its natural state or its defective state. The differences in focus are apparent: are we to compare poison with an iron wheel or mislabelled poison with a defective iron wheel that, when used, will spin rapidly in close proximity to the user? We found mixed signals in the courts' reference to danger caused by defects and their comparisons of poison to things like torpedoes and gunpowder. The *Devlin* Court was faced with a similar problem and had three different possible choices of focus on the item causing the harm. The court might have talked of a scaffold in its non-defective state, an item designed not to endanger life but to protect it. It might have talked of rope and wood, the parts of the scaffold, certainly not dangerous things. Or it might have, and did, talk of a defective scaffold, a thing that was most sure to cause harm to workers, not parties to the contract.

The choice of one over the others as the fact perspective of significance is not a random one. Rather, the reasons and policies that underlie the applicable rule of law ought to guide the court in its perspective selection. Here we return to the reasons for the *Thomas* court's departure from the general rule requiring privity of contract and indeed to the reasons supporting the privity rule itself. It appears that the privity rule is designed to encourage the sort of relationship in commerce between buyers and sellers that we saw in *Seixas*. Buyers inspect and sellers warn only of known hidden defects. Commerce goes forward smoothly, each party taking risk and being compensated for it in the price of the thing traded. But when defects are hidden, the buyer is not the person harmed, and the circumstances dictate that the seller would contemplate the danger not to the buyer but to others, the general legal rule fails to properly allocate risk and responsibility, and the relationship between buyer and seller fails to produce fair trading and safety. Sellers will be less motivated toward care when they sell things with hidden defects that will harm those other than the buyer if they will have no liability to those harmed third parties. Hidden defects will go undisclosed and undiscovered by both buyer and seller, and the thing will pass into the hands of the unsuspecting user. How far should the *Thomas* rule extend? As far as its rationale will allow. Here, probably as far as a maker of things can foresee harm to people like the plaintiff resulting from the maker's carelessness. Seen this way, a fact perspective that focuses on the inherent nature of the item has only limited appeal; while it may be that makers of inherently dangerous things can expect harm to come of them more often than makers of other things, without knowing more we could not say that the harm was more likely to befall others than buyer. But looking instead at the nature of the thing *when defective* gives us much greater insight into when the maker could reasonably have foreseen harm to people other than buyer. Now we can answer questions about the kind of harm a particular defect might cause, when it might be discovered, and by whom it is likely to be used when the defect manifests itself. Answers to these questions in a particular case will be far more enlightening in the examination of whether the normal relationship between buyer and seller could have been expected to prevent or at least account for the placement of culpability for this harm.

Happily, the *Devlin* court talks of *defective* scaffolds meant by the maker to support those other than the buyer, at their great peril if made poorly. Although the court uses some language that might indicate otherwise, it does not seem to care about the inherent nature of well made scaffolds except as that nature illustrates what will happen when one is made poorly. Because it takes this approach, some would quite reasonably say that *Devlin* and not *MacPherson* is the case that made the greatest impact on the law of the series of cases. And this is a reasonable assertion because the *MacPherson* court later tells us that *Devlin* marked the course.

MacPherson v. Buick Motor Co.

Court of Appeals of New York
217 N.Y. 382, 111 N.E. 1050 (1916)

FACTS

Defendant, Buick Motor Co., manufactured a car and sold it to a retail dealer who sold it to Plaintiff, MacPherson. MacPherson was injured when the car collapsed because of a defective wheel. Buick Motor Co. did not manufacture the wheel, but it could have detected the defect through a reasonable inspection of the wheel. MacPherson sued Buick Motor Co. for negligence.

PROCEDURAL HISTORY

The trial court entered a verdict for the Plaintiff. The intermediate appeals court affirmed this verdict, and the Defendant appealed from the appellate court's judgment.

ISSUE

Whether a manufacturer of a product that if negligently made is a "thing of danger" owes a duty of care to foreseeable users with whom it is not in privity.

HOLDING

Yes. A manufacturer of a "thing of danger," that is, a product which by nature is "reasonably certain to place life and limb in peril when negligently made" does owe a duty of care to foreseeable users of the product who will use the product without further inspection.

JUDGMENT (or DISPOSITION)

Judgment of the appeals court in favor of the Plaintiff is affirmed.

REASONING

The court holds that in order to impose liability on the manufacturer, the nature of the product must give warning that it will probably cause injury if it is defectively manufactured. An automobile that is designed to travel at fifty miles an hour does warn its manufacturer of likely injury that would result from a defect in its wheel.

Furthermore, in order for liability to accrue, the manufacturer must know that others would use the product. Buick Motor Co. knew that parties not in privity with its contract with the retail dealer would use the car because the car was designed to hold three passengers and because Buick knew that its purchaser was in the business of selling cars to third parties.

Justice Cardozo extracts a basic principle from a series of English cases which is that one who invites others to use a product is bound to use reasonable care. Whether the invitation is addressed to a specific or an indeterminate group of people does not affect its applicability. In the present case, Buick Motor Co. invited the retail dealer's customers to use their cars, and therefore Buick Motor Co. owed those customers a duty of care.

Buick Motor Co. was not absolved of a duty to inspect the wheels because it bought them from a reputable manufacturer. Because Buick was a manufacturer of cars, not merely a vendor of cars, it was responsible for the component parts of the finished product.

DISSENTING OPINION

Chief Justice Bartlett filed a dissenting opinion. He noted that Buick Motor Co. has bought 80,000 wheels from the manufacturer who supplied the wheel in question in this case. He added that no other defects have been found in those wheels, implying that Buick's reliance on the wheel manufacturer's tests of the wheels was reasonable.

Chief Justice Bartlett believes that applicable caselaw does not support the extension of manufacturer's liability resulting from the holding in this case. He notes that this court should either leave it to the legislature to change the law regarding manufacturer's negligence to third parties, or it should overrule those previous cases denying such liability.

Bartlett also worries that extending liability for negligence beyond the contract's parties will clog the courts with all manner of claims against manufacturers.

"Professor's Notes"

Even if it is true that the *Devlin* court charted the course by using the proper focus for its analogy drawing, much remained to be done in the *MacPherson* case. We are all the better for this work having been done by a quite famous judge, later Justice of the United States Supreme Court, Benjamin Cardozo. Cardozo's influence on the law was not only the result of his intellectual ability, but also his clarity of expression. Even if the *Devlin* court told the tale, it took Cardozo's clarity of thought and communication to convert the tale into doctrine that has dramatically affected the future of commerce and consumerism. The *MacPherson* case is often regarded as the starting place of modern products liability law.

Cardozo expresses the *Thomas* rule as if it had always been the rule through whatever decisions had struggled to apply it in the interim. Although some doubt is expressed as to the correctness of some of the interim decisions, Cardozo makes an effort to harmonize all of the decisions with the foreseeability-based articulation of the rule: Clute could have been expected to foresee less likelihood of harm to Losee because of his expectation that the paper company would be conducting tests; Litchfield could hardly have been expected to foresee harm to people like Loop because he disclosed the defect to his buyer and sold it to him for his own use. Perhaps foreseeability was always the rule but no one knew it. If so, you ought to say, it wasn't a very effective rule because if it was not understood it did not operate to govern behavior. Someone knew though, even if only through extraordinary perception and legal judgment, because the Thomas' lawyer, way back then argued to the court that the standard for determining the reach of a maker's liability ought to be measured by the maker's ability to foresee harm to people like the plaintiff. (See the passage in the Note section following the *MacPherson* case in chapter 5.) If only the *Thomas* court had used the Thomas's lawyer's language in writing the opinion, the law might have been clearer from that point on instead of this point on.

Another choice of fact perspective question appears in the *MacPherson* case. Cardozo says that the car was designed to go fifty miles per hour. Dissenting Chief Judge Bartlett tells us that the car was only travelling at eight miles per hour when the wheel collapsed. Which is the proper fact for analytical purposes? Perhaps both are correct for different reasons. The rule of the case is that when harm is to be *foreseen*, a duty is owed. Harm is foreseen or not at the time the item is sold or placed in commerce. Thus, for purposes of determining the harm to be foreseen, the design speed is the proper focus of analysis. For other purposes, (none of which we think were in the mind of Judge Bartlett necessarily), the eight mile per hour figure might be more relevant. For example, to prove that a defect in the wheel rather than some extraneous force caused it to collapse, it would be relevant to show that the car was not being driven at a high speed, but at a mere eight miles per hour. If the car were being driven at fifty miles per hour over a bumpy road at the time of the collapse, we might infer that a carelessly struck chuck-hole rather than a defect caused the collapse. That the car was designed to go fifty miles per hour would be of little value to proving that defect, not chuck-hole caused the collapse. Knowing the present purpose of analysis will illuminate the choice of fact perspective in such cases.

Cardozo tells us what we must always remember in doing common law analysis: a rule, with its standards and tests in its "underlying principles," is the law. When we interpret and apply a legal rule, whether to prepare for a law school class, write an exam answer or a legal writing project, or advise a client, the policies and principles that moved the court to create the rule are the law to a far greater degree than the language of the rule itself. Certainly, we expect that a court will choose language of a rule that will account for those underlying principles, but when hard cases arise as they always do, the underlying principles are the force that guides our choice between competing, plausible alternative interpretations of the rule. This, in the final analysis, is the central point of studying this line of cases.